150 best
Indian, Asian, Caribbean and more
Diabetes recipes

SOBIA KHAN, MSc, RD

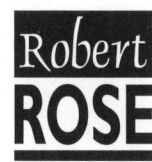
Robert
ROSE

150 Best Indian, Asian, Caribbean and More Diabetes Recipes
Text copyright © 2014 The George Brown College of Applied Arts and Technology and Sobia Khan
Photographs copyright © 2014 Robert Rose Inc.
Cover and text design copyright © 2014 Robert Rose Inc.

For complete cataloguing information, see page 249.

Disclaimer
The recipes in this book have been carefully tested by our kitchen and our tasters. To the best of our knowledge, they are safe and nutritious for ordinary use and users. For those people with food or other allergies, or who have special food requirements or health issues, please read the suggested contents of each recipe carefully and determine whether or not they may create a problem for you. All recipes are used at the risk of the consumer.

We cannot be responsible for any hazards, loss or damage that may occur as a result of any recipe use.

For those with special needs, allergies, requirements or health problems, in the event of any doubt, please contact your medical adviser prior to the use of any recipe.

Design and production: Daniella Zanchetta/PageWave Graphics Inc.
Editor: Sue Sumeraj
Recipe editor: Jennifer MacKenzie
Proofreaders: Sheila Wawanash (recipes) and Kelly Jones (introductory text)
Indexer: Gillian Watts
Food photographer: Colin Erricson
Associate food photographer: Matt Johannsson
Food stylists: Kathryn Robertson and Michael Elliott
Prop stylist: Charlene Erricson

Other photographs:
SOUTH ASIAN photo group: Asian vegetable market © lmjp; Pushkar street scene © ferrantraite; Colorful spices © ra-photos; Naan © kjohansen; Lentil scoops © MamaMiaPL; Kaffir limes © idizimage; Coconut © enviromantic; CHINESE photo group: Bamboo shoots © Bihaibo; Silk Chinese lanterns © winhorse; Chinese 5-spice mix © lenazap; Bok choy © Elenathewise; Long beans © williv; Ginger © iwka; Enoki mushrooms © koosen; HISPANIC photo group: Jalapeño peppers © DNY59; Church with orange tree © ngreening; Saffron threads © olgakr; Black olives © FernandoAH; Nopali cactus © Musat; Avocados © AgisilaouSpyrouPhotography; Yellow and purple corn © traveler1116; CARIBBEAN photo group: Plantains © Maybaybutter; Pier and ocean © Jeff Biglan; Scotch bonnet peppers © Flander; Ginger © Elenathewise; Okra © Geoarts; Coconuts © Taylor Hinton; Shrimp with chile and lime © robynmac

Cover image: Sichuan Beef Stir-Fry *(Si Chuan Jiang Bao Niu Rou)* (page 124)

The publisher gratefully acknowledges the financial support of our publishing program by the Government of Canada through the Canada Book Fund.

Published by Robert Rose Inc.
120 Eglinton Avenue East, Suite 800,
Toronto, Ontario, Canada M4P 1E2
Tel: (416) 322-6552 Fax: (416) 322-6936
www.robertrose.ca

Printed and bound in USA

1 2 3 4 5 6 7 8 9 CW 22 21 20 19 18 17 16 15 14

Contents

Preface 4
Acknowledgments. 5

Diabetes and Prediabetes 7
Diabetes in Multicultural Communities 7
Traditional Recipes Made Healthier 8
Turning Traditional Recipes into Meals 13
The Multicultural Pantry. 15

South Asian Cuisine: Recipes from Bangladesh,
    India, Pakistan and Sri Lanka 24
Chinese Cuisine: Sichuan, Hakka and
    Cantonese Recipes. 94
Hispanic Cuisine: Recipes from Latin America
    and Spain 148
Caribbean Cuisine: Recipes from Antigua,
    Barbados, Guyana, Jamaica and Trinidad 201

Appendix 1: Homemade Stocks 245
Appendix 2: About the Nutrition Information. 247
Index 250

Preface

For as long as I can remember, I have enjoyed eating foods from cuisines around the world. I am of South Asian descent, was born in Canada, grew up in the Middle East and have traveled to many countries, both as a child and as an adult, so I have experienced a variety of diverse foods and cultures throughout my life. I've always said one of the main reasons I became a registered dietitian, and ultimately began teaching nutrition and culture to future chefs, was my love of sampling and eating diverse foods!

I grew up eating mainly South Asian cuisine at home, so when my father was diagnosed with type 2 diabetes, I saw him struggle with how to fit our traditional foods into a healthy diet for diabetes. When I started to work in Toronto with various multicultural communities, especially those with diabetes and heart disease, I could relate. I, too, was finding it a challenge to suggest diabetes-friendly recipes and provide advice to clients who wanted to eat traditional multicultural foods at home and yet follow healthy eating guidelines. I wanted to preserve the unique traditional recipes that my grandmother and mother had passed on to me, and learn about other traditional recipes and cultures from around the world. I also wanted to find a way to make all those traditional recipes suitable for people with diabetes.

A few years ago, I set out to do just that, along with my students at the Centre for Hospitality and Culinary Arts at George Brown College in Toronto. I used my personal recipes, and we collected recipes from chefs, home cooks, friends and family members who were members of traditional communities that are at high risk of diabetes. We learned everything we could about their cultural traditions and ingredients, and then proceeded to make the recipes diabetes-friendly.

The result is this cookbook, which I am delighted to share with you and your family. Whether you grew up cooking and eating traditional foods or just want to be adventurous and try different dishes from around the world, if you or someone you love has diabetes, this cookbook is for you. The recipes are healthy, delicious, as authentic as possible and, most important, made with a lot of passion and care. Enjoy!

Sobia Khan

Acknowledgments

Working with multicultural communities is a passion of mine, and I dedicated myself to creating these recipes with a lot of passion. It was my honor to develop multicultural recipes that would help people enjoy their traditional cultural cooking but also prevent or manage diabetes. I had my own father, and his struggles with diabetes, in mind when putting this cookbook together. Thanks, Dad (Nasim Khan), for sharing your thoughts and opinions and for taste-testing many of the recipes.

This book was certainly not created alone. It took a huge team of people from various cultural communities; my own family, especially my mother (Nargis Khan), her friends, my friends and their family members; various community health centers in the Greater Toronto Area; and the George Brown College (GBC) community of chefs, nutrition experts and students. Together, we have created recipes that not only taste great but are true to the culinary traditions of our great multicultural communities in North America.

I would like to thank the team at Robert Rose Inc. for working tirelessly for long hours to make this book happen, especially Bob Dees, for his faith and patience, and Sue Sumeraj and Jennifer MacKenzie, dedicated editors with keen eyes for detail. I learned a lot from all of you. Thanks also to Sharon Zeiler and Joanne Lewis from the Canadian Diabetes Association (CDA) for their advice throughout the recipe development and nutritional analysis process.

I want to call out for special thanks the following people, whose time, dedication, enthusiasm and countless hours grocery shopping, taste-testing and providing expertise was truly appreciated!

Geremy Capone

Geremy is a culinary graduate of GBC who does recipe research and development to meet the needs of specific patient populations. He is currently the Specialized Wellness Chef at ELLICSR: Health, Wellness & Cancer Survivorship Centre, developing content and delivering cooking classes to live and virtual audiences.

Avery Chin

Avery is a successful entrepreneur and cook who has over 17 years' experience as an owner of a West Indian market and Jamaican restaurant. Avery was recently diagnosed with type 2 diabetes and feels passionate about cooking healthier Jamaican food. His recipes and inspirations come from his childhood memories of growing up in Kingston, Jamaica.

Mali Fernandez

Chef Mali is of Spanish descent and was raised in Mexico. Her passion lies in both Mexican and Spanish cuisine. She recently opened a Mexican restaurant in Toronto called Xola. For Chef Mali, "food is the expression of passing on the essence in one's culture to others."

Andrea Gourgy

Andrea is a chef and a culinary graduate of GBC. She has worked with several prominent organizations, including the Canadian Diabetes Association, the American Heart Association and Toronto's University Health Network. She is currently the food editor at *Clean Eating* magazine.

Jiaqi Li

Jiaqi is a clinical food service manager with a strong culinary background in Asian cuisine. She is a culinary graduate of GBC and is passionate about creating healthy recipes within the Chinese community, as her father has diabetes.

Adriana Salvia

Adriana is a chef and culinary graduate of GBC. She has worked professionally as a television producer, live events manager and cooking instructor for kids and youth. She also founded passeddown.com, a website that was dedicated to preserving food memories.

Amy Symington

Amy is a nutrition professor and culinary graduate from GBC, a vegetarian chef at ameliaeats.com and the Nutrition and Kitchen program coordinator at Gilda's Club Greater Toronto. She enjoys developing recipes for various publications, including the Toronto Vegetarian Association and *Clean Eating* magazine.

Hemant Tellur

Chef Hemant has developed many recipes for South Asian food products. He currently owns and runs a ready-to-eat-food company called Eat-In Foods, Inc. with his partner, Minal Tallur, a food scientist.

George Brown chefs, nutrition experts and students

Faiqua Ali, RD
Deepti Batra
Sharon Booy
Winnie Chiu
Moira Cockburn
Chef Ian Grady
Chloe Jung
Chili Leung
Sharon Li
Utkarsh Limbachiya
Ken Ly
Minako Mori
Irene Ngo
Julie Rochefort, MHSc, RD
Malini Roy
Chef James Smith
Bre Urquhart, RD
Anthony Vargas
Janapiraba Vinayagamoorthy
Dorothy Vo
Chris Yang

Community chefs

Marcia Carby
Preety Dhir
Muharram Hameed
Nargis Khan
Sherene Mohammad
Mini Samuel
Siva Swaminathan
Puja Uppal

Organizations and community health centers (CHCs)

EatRight Ontario (recipes included from Diverse Foods and Flavours, a resource developed collaboratively by EatRight Ontario, GBC and CDA)
Canadian Diabetes Association
Black Creek CHC
The Four Villages CHC
LAMP CHC
Parkdale CHC
Rexdale CHC
Riverdale CHC
The Anne Johnston Health Station

Diabetes and Prediabetes

Diabetes develops when the body cannot make enough of the hormone insulin and/or cannot properly use the insulin being made by the pancreas. After you eat, certain foods are broken down by the body into sugar, or glucose. Insulin helps move glucose from the blood to the cells of the body. If insulin is not present or is not functioning properly, then glucose builds up in the blood, leading to higher than normal blood glucose levels. The inability to use insulin properly is called insulin resistance. There are three main types of diabetes: type 1 diabetes, gestational diabetes and type 2 diabetes.

In type 1 diabetes, which is primarily caused by genetic factors, certain cells of the pancreas are destroyed by the body's own immune system. As a result, the pancreas makes no or very little insulin, causing blood glucose levels to rise. Gestational diabetes occurs when a woman's blood glucose is higher than normal during pregnancy. Type 2 diabetes is the most common type of diabetes and is most related to lifestyle choices, particularly diet. In type 2 diabetes, the pancreas does not produce enough insulin to meet the body's needs or the insulin does not get used properly by the body.

Because type 2 diabetes develops over a long period, many people are diagnosed with prediabetes first. In prediabetes, blood glucose levels are higher than normal, but not high enough for the person to be considered to have diabetes. Someone with prediabetes is still at higher risk of complications such as heart disease. Not everyone with prediabetes will develop diabetes, but some studies show there is a risk of developing diabetes within 10 years. The good news is, if you have prediabetes, you can delay or prevent getting diabetes by making lifestyle changes, such as making healthier food choices and increasing your level of physical activity.

Diabetes in Multicultural Communities

In North America, we are lucky to live in culturally rich communities. However, some of these communities have been identified as having a higher risk of developing type 2 diabetes or heart disease than the rest of the North American population. Some of these include the South Asian, Chinese, Pacific Islander, Hispanic, African-American, Native American/Aboriginal and Caribbean communities. Experts are not sure why, when people move to North America from these regions, their health becomes worse. A theory called the healthy immigrant effect states that most people demonstrate good health when they first arrive in a new country such as the United States or Canada. After some time, however, their health worsens, perhaps due to changes in their diet, their level of physical activity, the accessibility of medical services or the amount of stress they experience. These environmental factors, combined with pre-existing genetic factors, can lead to a higher risk of diabetes.

One common lifestyle change could well be a switch from the traditional diet of their home country to a more North American diet that is higher in fat, sugar and salt. Genetic factors also lead these communities to develop prediabetes or type 2 diabetes at higher rates than other populations, and at a younger age. They also have poorer management of their blood glucose levels and higher rates of complications, such as heart disease, at a younger age than the general North American population. If you feel you or a family member is at high risk of diabetes, it's best to go see your health-care provider and get your blood glucose levels tested.

Traditional Recipes Made Healthier

Lifestyle changes, including healthy eating and physical activity, are an important part of managing or preventing diabetes. Healthy eating helps you control your blood glucose levels and avoid further complications, such as heart disease. Maintaining a healthy weight enables you to better manage type 2 diabetes and, if you have prediabetes, reduces the risk of developing diabetes. If you are overweight or obese, losing just 5% to 10% of your current body weight can improve your blood glucose levels.

This book features healthy recipes from some of the fastest-growing multicultural communities in North America who are also at high risk for diabetes. Many people ask me whether their traditional cultural foods are the cause of their diabetes. Unlikely. Fast foods, little physical activity and high stress levels are far more likely contributors to chronic diseases such as diabetes and heart disease. *However*, once you have diabetes, it is important to make some changes to the way you prepare and eat your traditional foods, such as enjoying smaller portion sizes and cooking with less oil, soy sauce and other high-fat, high-sugar and high-sodium ingredients.

Cooking and eating your own foods at home, using fresh ingredients, will always be a healthier choice than going out to a restaurant, ordering takeout or purchasing prepared meals. If you enjoy your own culture's or any other culture's traditional foods, you should be able to continue to eat those foods, with some modifications. That is why I have created great-tasting, healthy recipes for you, with the necessary changes already thought through and incorporated, so all you have to do is prepare them and savor the authentic flavors!

But there are sure to be times when you want to modify your own recipes and experiment with your own meal combinations, so here you'll find some key information on the main nutrients that have an impact on diabetes management, along with some tips on what to look for and adjust when cooking your favorite recipes and planning meals at home.

Carbohydrates and Added Sugar

Carbohydrates include fruits, vegetables, grains, starches (such as potatoes, sweet potatoes, yams and taro), legumes (beans, lentils and peas), milk products, milk alternatives and foods with added sugar, such as regular soft drinks and desserts. Carbohydrate-containing foods break down into glucose in the blood and raise our blood glucose levels. You need a certain amount of carbohydrates in your diet to fuel your brain and give you energy, but you need to choose these carbohydrates wisely when you have diabetes. The key lies in adding more fruits, vegetables, legumes and whole grains to your diet and reducing the amount of added sugar you consume.

When I was growing up, eating South Asian foods at home or with family friends, we would eat a plate full of biryani or rice pulao, often with flatbread for sopping up every last bit of curry. We'd end the meal with a traditional dessert or sweet drink. Indeed, many cultures eat a lot more grains than fruit and vegetables as part of the main meal. When you are managing diabetes, you can still enjoy your favorite traditional carbohydrate-heavy meals, but it becomes necessary to cut back the portion sizes, choose higher-fiber alternatives for all or some of the ingredients and add more vegetables and legumes, as I have done with the recipes and meals in this book.

Fruits and vegetables, whether fresh, frozen or canned, should contribute to the most servings each day and should be eaten at every meal. (The meal suggestions included with many of the recipes in this book all incorporate servings of vegetables and fruits.) In addition, grain products, preferably made with whole grains such as oats, whole-grain flour, barley, rye, millet, quinoa, whole-grain pasta, wild rice, red, black or brown rice, should be a part of every meal. I have tried to strike a balance by incorporating more whole grains into traditional cultural recipes without taking away from the authenticity of the dishes.

Foods with added sugar should not be eaten at every meal or even every day. Rather, they should be enjoyed as an occasional treat. This book includes a few examples of traditional sweetened drinks, to show you how you can incorporate these into a healthy diet. The traditional homemade desserts from the cultures discussed in this book tend to be deep-fried and/or have lots of added fat and sugar (which is what makes them taste so good). As a result, they are a source of unnecessary extra calories and carbohydrates and are low in fiber. If you crave something sweet to follow your meals, stick with fruit.

Fiber

Although fiber is a type of carbohydrate, it actually lowers blood glucose and low-density lipoprotein (LDL or "bad") blood cholesterol and provides a feeling of fullness that can help manage weight. The American Diabetes Association recommends that adults with diabetes eat between 25 and 30 g of fiber per day; the Canadian Diabetes Association recommends between 25 and 50 g. Most traditional cuisines are full of great dishes that provide a lot of fiber, such as whole grains, vegetables, legumes and nuts.

There are two main types of fiber: soluble and insoluble. Soluble fiber is especially important in lowering blood glucose after eating, and lowering LDL blood cholesterol. Many of the ingredients in traditional cuisines are high in soluble fiber, including beans, lentils, barley, eggplant, okra, avocado and soybeans.

Simply adding a little more fiber to your traditional recipes and daily meals, as I've done with the recipes and meals in this book, can make a huge difference in your ability to manage your blood glucose, and will help reduce your risk of heart disease. Here are some easy ways to increase the fiber in your meals:

- Incorporate whole wheat or lentil-based flours into your empanadas or rotis.
- Switch to brown or red rice instead of white rice.
- Use barley instead of rice in your grain-based dishes.
- Replace rice noodles with buckwheat noodles.
- Add more vegetables and legumes to stews and curries.
- If you need to add more fat to a meal, dry-roast some nuts or seeds and add them on top of a dish or eat them on the side.
- Complete a great meal by enjoying a fresh fruit for dessert.

Fats

Fats are another important part of our daily diet. The key is to watch the amount of fat you eat and choose healthier fats that help to manage or prevent diabetes, weight gain and heart disease. There are different types of fats: the good (monounsaturated and polyunsaturated fats), the bad (saturated fats) and the ugly (trans fats). Choose mainly good, healthy fats, reduce bad, unhealthy fats and, as much as possible, eliminate the ugly, very unhealthy fats.

Monounsaturated fats are found in everyday cooking oils, such as olive oil, safflower oil and canola oil, as well as olives, avocados and peanuts. When choosing oils for everyday cooking and especially for the recipes in this book, it is important to select vegetable oils that will remain stable at higher temperatures and will not oxidize or break down easily.

Polyunsaturated fats include soybeans and soy products, soft margarines, nuts, seeds, sesame oil, fish and fish oil. One type of polyunsaturated fat that is of particular importance is omega-3 fatty acids, which come mainly from fatty fish, such as mackerel, salmon, tuna and sardines; nuts, such as walnuts; tofu; and seeds, such as flax seeds and hemp seeds. Omega-3 fatty acids are good for the heart, and health authorities recommend including fatty fish in your diet at least twice a week. Avoid frying it, or you risk negating its health benefits.

Saturated fats include fatty cuts of meats, meat with skin on, organ meats, sausages, shortening, palm oil, coconut and coconut products, butter, ghee, lard and high-fat dairy products, such as cream, full-fat yogurt, whole milk and cheese. Traditional dishes sometimes use a lot of saturated fat, and it's fine to incorporate some into your meals, but try to reduce it or replace it with healthier unsaturated fats as much as possible.

Trans fats raise LDL cholesterol and lower high-density lipoprotein (HDL or "good") blood cholesterol and should be avoided as much as possible. They are found in hydrogenated margarines and some commercially prepared foods, such as baked goods (pastries, pies, doughnuts), deep-fried foods (french fries, pakoras, samosas, empanadas) and fast foods. The Nutrition Facts table on foods lists trans fat content, so if you purchase packaged foods, read labels to make sure you are getting a minimal amount of trans fats each day.

Choosing healthier fats is a great shift in eating habits, but keep in mind that any type of fat has the same number of calories and should be added sparingly to your dishes. The overall fat content of the recipes in this book is reduced to meet guidelines for people living with diabetes or prediabetes. The recipes use very little oil, even though traditionally many of the dishes use a lot more. It is important to measure the oil you use, rather than just eyeballing it. Here are some other easy ways to reduce fat in traditional recipes:

- Bake or grill foods such as samosas, kebabs, fish or empanadas rather than deep-frying them.
- Replace ghee or pork fat with a vegetable oil.
- Reduce the amount of fresh coconut used in a recipe, and use light coconut milk in place of regular coconut milk.
- Choose nonfat (skim) or low-fat (1%) dairy products and lower-fat cheeses.
- Use smaller quantities of high-fat cheeses, such as queso fresco and full-fat paneer.
- Choose skinless meats and cuts of meats with a lower saturated fat content.
- Reduce the amount of organ meats you add to your dishes or omit them altogether.
- Decrease the overall amount of meat in a dish and replace it with vegetables or legumes.
- Reduce the amount of sausage, such as chorizo or Chinese sausage, used in a recipe.
- Use less oil dressing (*tarka*) on top of South Asian dishes.
- Replace oil with apple juice in marinades where possible.

Protein

In North America, we love to eat protein, especially from animal sources — and lots of it! Many of us feel a meal is not complete without it. Protein can be helpful in managing weight, as protein foods are filling and help you eat less. Unfortunately, many of us are choosing fried meats, red meats, processed meats and high-fat cheeses — all of which are high in saturated fat and dietary cholesterol — over healthy protein sources such as fish, legumes, nuts and seeds, soybeans and soy products. In the recipes in this book, the servings of protein from meat sources (especially red meats or organ meats) are small and there are many options for healthier protein sources. The meal suggestions that accompany many of the recipes will help you ensure that you are eating the right amount and type of protein. If you are adapting your own recipes, be sure to follow the USDA's MyPlate guidelines or Eating Well with Canada's Food Guide and consult a registered dietitian to ensure your daily meal plan incorporates the right amount of protein for you.

Sodium

The North American population is consuming way too much sodium — about 3400 mg per day, much higher than the upper limit goal of 2300 mg. High sodium intake increases the risk of high blood pressure, and people with diabetes are at even greater risk. A holistic approach to reducing dietary sodium focuses on eating fresh, unprocessed foods such as vegetables, fruit, low-fat dairy products, whole grains, poultry, fish and nuts, and including smaller amounts of red meats and sweets.

Reducing sodium can be a challenge — even for the experts! But the easiest way to make a big impact on your sodium consumption is to cook foods at home, from scratch. This means making your own butter chicken, spinach paneer, wonton soup, dumplings, salsa, chimichurri, jerk marinade or mango chutney, rather than buying ready-to-eat versions.

The great thing about cooking traditional cuisines is that flavor is often added with herbs and spices, fresh garlic, ginger, chile peppers, citrus juice and vinegar rather than salt. On the other hand, traditional recipes often incorporate a wide variety of ready-made sauces, condiments, spice blends and other ingredients that are very high in sodium. Here are some common culprits to watch out for:

- Asian bean pastes
- browning sauce
- canned vegetables and legumes
- cassareep
- cheese
- Chinese cooking wine
- Chinese sausages
- cured Spanish chorizo
- curry powders or spice blends
- fish sauce
- garlic or ginger paste
- green seasoning
- hoisin sauce
- instant recipe mixes (e.g., for rasam, idlis or dosas)
- jerk seasoning
- masala pastes or powders (e.g., korma, vindaloo, butter chicken)
- oyster sauce
- pickled products (e.g., vegetable preserves, chutneys)
- soy sauce
- tamarind block or paste
- tomato sauce or sofrito

The recipes in this book use reduced amounts of many of these ingredients; others are made from scratch. When purchasing ready-made ingredients, always read the Nutrition Facts table and choose brands with the least amount of sodium. When the use of high-sodium ingredients is unavoidable, use them sparingly and infrequently.

The amount of sodium in each recipe in this book is much lower than in traditional versions of the same recipe. I recommend you leave the salt shaker off the table to avoid adding more salt. Each recipe was carefully developed to maximize flavor while keeping the sodium content in check. Even so, the sodium in certain recipes is still on the high side. To help you recognize these recipes, I have added an asterisk (*) next to any sodium value higher than 500 mg. For recipes that include ready-to-use reduced-sodium vegetable or chicken broth as an ingredient, you can reduce the sodium further by using homemade broth (see pages 245 and 246) or no-salt-added broths, if available.

If the overall sodium content of the meal you're planning is high, look for ways to replace some of the higher-sodium recipes with unsalted, unprocessed foods, such as a mixed green salad, steamed vegetables or long-grain brown rice. This book features great chutneys and sauces that can be eaten alongside your meal, but limit your portions, as these additions can also add to the overall sodium content. Whenever you do eat a dish or a meal that is high in sodium, balance it out by making lower-sodium choices throughout the rest of the day.

Turning Traditional Recipes into Meals

Regular meals are important for people with diabetes, as they prevent the low and high blood glucose levels that can result from waiting too long between meals, then overeating when mealtime finally arrives. The best meal pattern has proved to be three meals a day, spaced 4 to 6 hours apart. Each meal should include representation from all the food groups, as defined by the USDA's MyPlate guidelines and Eating Well with Canada's Food Guide: vegetables, fruits, grains, meat and alternatives (protein) and milk and alternatives (dairy). An exception can be made for milk and alternatives (dairy), of which you only need 2 to 3 servings per day. If you don't have a serving of dairy at every meal, that's fine, as long as you have the right number of servings over the course of the day.

At each meal, you also need to make sure you get the right balance of nutrients — especially carbohydrates, proteins and fats — without overeating. Many of us are not used to eating this way, particularly if we eat traditional meals at home. If you are of South Asian descent, you may be accustomed to eating a large helping of rice and a few pieces of roti with a side of either a vegetable or a meat curry. If your family is from the Caribbean, you may have been brought up eating meat-heavy dishes served with large portions of potato dishes or rice and very small portions of vegetables (if any) on the side. So how is to possible to eat more balanced meals while staying true to your culture's traditional cuisine (with some healthy modifications, of course)?

The keys are portion control and meal planning. You can keep eating all your favorite foods, but you likely need to eat smaller portions of them. You may need to combine them with other foods in ways that are not quite traditional, but that are much healthier ways to eat now that you have diabetes or prediabetes. There's nothing wrong with forming new, healthier traditions for your own family! This way of eating is also a great way to add variety to your diet.

One tool that may help you understand how to divide your meals into balanced portions is the Plate Method. Here's how it works: picture your plate as a circle divided into four quarters. For each meal, fill two-quarters (or half) the plate with vegetables, one-quarter with a meat or meat alternative and one-quarter with a grain or starch. Add a serving of fruit and a serving of a milk product or a milk alternative on the side, and you have a complete meal!

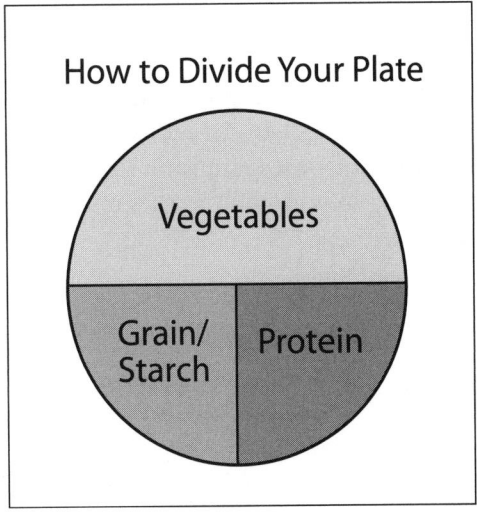

How to Divide Your Plate

Vegetables

Grain/Starch

Protein

Now, the Plate Method is easy enough to follow when the foods you have prepared are simple and distinct unto themselves: a grilled chicken breast (your meat), brown rice (your grain) and steamed broccoli and carrots (your vegetables), for example. But recipes are often for mixed dishes that include a combination of meat and vegetables, or vegetables and grains, or all three. How do you decide how to divide your plate with a mixed dish?

In truth, doing so involves a bit of guesswork and some common sense. If your mixed dish includes equal parts meat and grains, it can cover half your plate while vegetables cover the other half. If your dish includes meat, grains and vegetables but is a bit light on the vegetables, it might cover three-quarters of your plate and you might serve another vegetable dish on the side.

To take some of the burden of guesswork off you, many of the recipes in this book feature a "Make It a Meal" box. It tells you what other recipes and foods you could pair that recipe with to create a complete, balanced meal. The meals can be eaten for either lunch or dinner, and you can add other meals of your choosing to create a daily menu plan. These boxes are merely meant to serve as guidelines to help you plan meals and your daily menu plan; you can substitute in similar recipes and foods that better suit your mood and taste, and for variety. Of course, if you're experimenting with a cuisine that's unfamiliar to you, these boxes are also a great way to figure out what should be served with what!

Don't feel that you are limited to the recipes in this book. Sure, your meal could be made up entirely of recipes from the book. But you could also make just one or two recipes and complete the meal with your own salad, steamed vegetables or cooked basmati rice. I've included some milk-based drinks, such as masala chai and mango lassi, or you can just have a glass of milk or your favorite milk alternative on the side. Or switch it up for a meal and have a traditional non-dairy drink. For meals where no beverage is suggested, choose water or another carbohydrate-free beverage.

Two other tools that will help you plan diabetes-friendly meals are included with every recipe: a nutrient analysis, including calories, total fat, saturated fat, cholesterol, sodium, total carbohydrate, fiber and protein; and the Canadian Diabetes Association's Food Choice values, for those who follow that system.

The suggested meals are meant for smaller appetites (1200 to 1600 calories per day) for lunch or dinner. Each meal provides approximately the following Food Choices:

Carbohydrate: **4 Choices**
Meat & Alternatives: **2 to 3 Choices**
Fat: **1 to 3 Choices**

If you have higher caloric needs or a larger appetite, or need more meal planning advice, speak with a registered dietitian.

The Multicultural Pantry

This cookbook includes a variety of traditional dishes from many countries and cultural groups. If you have not tried a particular cuisine before, some of the ingredients may seem unfamiliar and intimidating. So I have created a list of ingredients to stock your pantry with before you begin cooking.

These ingredients are versatile and can be used in other dishes from cultures around the world. Because they are pantry items, mainly dried herbs, spices and sauces, they will keep for up to a year. Once you get going, you are certain to find endless uses for these ingredients!

South Asian Cuisine

Asafetida (*Hing*)

Asafetida comes from the sap of the plant *Ferula assa-foetida*. The sap is dried and crushed to produce a fine yellow-white powder. It has a very strong, pungent smell, like pickled eggs, but when cooked, it develops more of a roasted garlic aroma. Because of its powerful smell and taste, asafetida should be used in very small amounts.

Caraway Seeds (*Shahi Jeera*)

Caraway seeds are sometimes called wild cumin, and may therefore be confused with cumin seeds, but they are not the same spice. Caraway seeds are brown, crescent-shaped, striped seeds from the caraway plant, a member of the parsley family. They have a mild, earthy aroma and a flavor similar to anise or fennel seeds.

Cardamom (*Elaichi*)

Cardamom is the dried fruit of a plant from the ginger family. It is available as dried pods, whole seeds or ground seeds. The pods can be green, black or bleached white. Each type of cardamom pod has a different flavor profile, and all are highly aromatic. Be sure to buy unsplit pods, because the flavor and intense aroma diminish when the pods are split. However, just before cooking the pods, split them open to enhance the flavor of the dish. All types of cardamom can be found at South Asian grocery stores.

Carom Seeds (*Ajwain*)

A close relative to parsley, carom seeds look similar to cumin and caraway seeds and have a flavor similar to that of thyme. They are pale khaki in color and are highly fragrant. Carom is commonly used in vegetable dishes, flatbreads, savory pastries and lentil curries. The seeds may be difficult to find at local supermarkets, but they are available at South Asian and Middle Eastern grocery stores. Carom seeds have a lot of oil (thymol), which can go rancid, so it is best to buy them in seed form and grind them as needed.

Cassia Cinnamon (*Dalchini*)

Cassia cinnamon, also known as Chinese cinnamon, has a rough, gray-brown outer surface and a smoother red-brown inner surface. During the drying process, cassia bark rolls in from both sides toward the center, so it looks like a scroll. When ground, it has a bittersweet aroma and flavor and is used to make spice blends such as garam masala. Cassia is the type of cinnamon that is readily available in North America, but if you buy it from a South Asian grocery store, it may be labeled as *dalchini*, the Hindi word for cinnamon. Most South Asian dishes call for pieces of cinnamon stick. If you plan to use ground cassia cinnamon in other recipes, it is best to buy it ground, as grinding the bark at home can be a difficult chore.

Chaat Masala

Chaat masala is a blend of spices used mainly in Indian and Pakistani salads, snacks and fast foods. Its distinctive spicy, sour and tangy flavor comes from black salt, which is usually combined with mango powder (*amchoor*) and ground spices including ginger, cumin, black peppercorns, coriander, carom, fennel, asafetida and chile peppers. Chaat masala can have 425 mg or more sodium per 1 tsp (5 mL), depending on the brand, so use it sparingly. Several brands are available at South Asian grocery stores and even some local supermarkets.

Cilantro Leaves and Coriander Seeds (*Sabut Dhania*)

Cilantro leaves and coriander seeds are parts of the coriander plant, which belongs to the parsley family. There is a considerable flavor difference between the fresh herb and the seeds: the leaves are more citrusy, while the seeds are more nutty. In South Asian cuisine, cilantro leaves are used primarily in chutneys and as a garnish for cooked dishes. Coriander seeds, on the other hand, are a pantry must, as they are used whole and ground in many dishes. It is best not to purchase large quantities of ground coriander, as the fragrance and flavor disappear quickly after grinding. Instead, buy coriander seeds and grind your own powder as needed.

Cumin Seeds (*Jeera*)

Cumin is the seed of a flowering plant in the parsley family. The seeds are light brownish yellow, with a distinctive sharp, astringent and sometimes bitter flavor. In South Asian cuisine, they are often combined with coriander seeds to form the mixture *dhana-jeera*. Cumin seeds are available either whole or ground and come in many varieties, including a dark variety from Kashmir called black cumin (*kala jeera*). As with other spices, it is best to buy the seeds whole and then grind them as needed.

Curry Leaves (*Kari Patta*)

Also known as sweet neem leaves, curry leaves do not taste like curry, as their name suggests. Rather, they have a smoky flavor. They get their name because of their common use in South Asian curries. Curry trees are native to southern India and Sri Lanka, so the leaves are used more often in dishes from those regions than in recipes from northern India and Pakistan. Curry leaves add a unique, citrusy, savory aroma that is mildly bitter. Both fresh and dried curry leaves are used in South Asian dishes, and both are sold at South Asian grocery stores. Always choose curry leaves that are bright in color and free of brown spots. To bring out their full flavor, cook fresh or dried curry leaves in oil before adding them to your recipe.

Curry Powders and Other Spice Blends

Curry powders and other spice blends are not a traditional part of South Asian cuisine, but thanks to the cuisine's popularity, a demand has arisen for spice blends that make the job of cooking great South Asian dishes easy. Traditional cooks still insist on creating their own spice mixtures from scratch. But these days, when time constraints often make that option impractical, a ready-made spice blend is a great alternative to have on hand.

Certainly spice blends have come a long way. They now have fewer additives and less sodium, and use better-quality spices. A huge variety of spice blends from different regions of South Asia is available, making it easy to try many different dishes. But that very plenitude can also make shopping for a spice blend a bit confusing. In this book, I have indicated which region each dish is from, so it will be easier for you to find the right curry powder or spice blend. If you're still not sure what to buy once you're at the South Asian grocery store, ask a clerk for help; they usually have a wealth of information and can help you narrow down the perfect choice for a particular dish.

Fennel Seeds (*Saunf*)

The seeds of the perennial herb fennel have a distinctive sweet licorice flavor similar to anise. They are available either whole or ground, and may be brown, green or yellow-green. For South Asian cooking, bright green (Lucknow) fennel seeds are the best choice, for their intense aroma. The seeds are often toasted or tempered in oil before they are added to a recipe. Fennel seeds are readily available in local grocery stores or in South Asian stores.

Fenugreek (*Methi*)

Fenugreek is used in many forms in South Asian cuisine: its seeds, whole or ground, are used as a spice; its leaves, dried or fresh, are used as an herb in dishes such as mustard leaf curry (*sarson ka saag*) and spinach paneer curry (*palak paneer*). *Kasuri methi* — the best-quality dried fenugreek leaves — comes from the Kasur region of Pakistan and is very fragrant. The flavor of fenugreek seeds is strong, so toasting them or cooking them in oil first is common in South Asian cooking. Be careful, though, as toasting or tempering them for too long will only make them more bitter.

Garam Masala

Garam means "hot" and *masala* means "spice mixture," so, as you'd expect, garam masala is a spice blend with some heat to it. The spice mixture varies but usually includes ground black cardamom, coriander, cumin, cinnamon, star anise, cloves and black pepper. Garam masala is commonly used to add flavor and color early in the dish or as a garnish on top when the dish is complete. I prefer to make my own garam masala rather than purchase a store-bought blend, as homemade blends have a more intense flavor. Plus, some brands have added salt, and they may not provide a Nutrition Facts table if imported from South Asia. The recipe on page 57 is easy to make and comes to you courtesy of my mom, so you know it's authentic.

Kashmiri Chile Peppers (*Kashmiri Mirch*)

These chile peppers, grown mainly in northern India, are bright red and sweet, with a very mild heat. They are available dried, either whole or ground, and their bright color makes them easy to pick out in a market full of dried chiles. They are used to add rich color to dishes such as tandooris and Goan vindaloos. If heat is also desired in the dish, it needs to come from a different source, such as ground dried red chile peppers (*lal mirch*). Kashmiri chiles will last for months if stored in a dry place in an airtight container.

Mango Powder (*Amchoor*)

Mango powder is made from green mangos that are sun-dried, then ground into a powder and mixed with turmeric for a nice yellow color. It has a fruity and tangy flavor, and is primarily used in South Asian chutneys, soups, curries and lentil dishes. It is best to buy pre-ground mango powder, as grinding dried mango slices at home may be difficult. Store mango powder in a cool, dark, dry place.

Mustard Seeds (*Rai* or *Sarson*)

Mustard seeds are small round seeds from a variety of mustard plants. There are three main varieties: white or yellow, brown and black. On their own, as whole seeds or ground, they have no flavor or aroma, but when cooked in oil or crushed and mixed with liquid, they add a distinctive pungent, nutty and bitter flavor to dishes. Yellow/white mustard seeds are used more in North America and Europe, particularly to make mustard condiments. Both black and brown mustard seeds are indigenous to India, but brown mustard seeds are more widely used in South Asian dishes. All types can be found in South Asian grocery stores. It is best to buy whole brown or black mustard seeds and grind them as needed.

Nigella Seeds (*Kalonji*)

Nigella seeds are small black seeds from the flowering *Nigella sativa* plant, which is grown mostly in India. Although they are also known as black onion seeds or black cumin seeds, nigella seeds are not related to either onions or cumin. They are also easily confused with black sesame seeds, so make sure to check the label on your spice jar before adding them to your recipe! Nigella seeds have an aroma that is reminiscent of oregano, and a nutty and peppery flavor.

Tamarind (*Imli*)

Tamarind is a fruit grown in tropical climates such as South Asia and Africa. It is available in South Asian, Middle Eastern and Asian grocery stores in a "block" that needs to be reconstituted with water. Check the label and choose a brand with no added salt or sugar. Once reconstituted, the moist, sticky brown paste is used as a souring agent in many dishes. Tamarind is high in carbohydrate, so be cautious about how much you add to dishes.

Turmeric (*Haldi*)

Turmeric is a plant in the ginger family, and its root looks similar to gingerroot. In some regions of Southeast Asia, turmeric leaves are used to wrap and cook food, but turmeric root is more commonly used, usually as a ground powder, which is bright yellow and has a slightly spicy and bitter flavor. Be careful when handling the root or powder, as the bright yellow color stains everything it touches. Buy small quantities of ground turmeric and store it in an airtight container in a cool, dry, dark place, to preserve its color and flavor.

Chinese Cuisine

Anise Seeds

The anise plant is native to the Mediterranean, North Africa and Southwest Asia, and its seeds are used primarily in the cuisines of these regions. But anise seeds (or aniseed) are also used occasionally in Chinese cooking. The seeds are pale brown and have a mild flavor similar to licorice.

Annatto Seeds

Annatto seeds, also known as achiote seeds, are brick red and have a mild peppery, earthy flavor. The small triangular seeds are available whole or ground and are used as both a spice and a natural coloring agent, as they impart a rich yellow-orange color. Saffron or turmeric can be substituted for annatto. In Chinese cooking, annatto is used to add color to preserved meats or meat dishes.

Cassia Cinnamon

See page 16. In Chinese cuisine, cassia cinnamon is used to add a robust flavor to braised meat dishes and is a component of Chinese five-spice powder.

Chile Bean Paste

Chile bean paste, or chile soybean paste, is a specialty from the province of Sichuan. It has a different flavor and a thicker consistency than chile paste or chile sauce. Chile bean paste is a hot and sour red-brown sauce made with fermented broad beans and/or soybeans, chiles, sugar and vinegar. Always measure chile bean paste precisely, as it is high in sodium — I have seen brands with 350 mg in just 1 tbsp (15 mL), so choose your brand wisely!

Chinese Cooking Wine

Chinese cooking wine is a very important part of Chinese cuisine. It is made by fermenting rice or other grains soaked in water. It is usually fermented for 10 years or more and is used for both cooking and drinking. The best-quality wine is Shaoxing, named after the district where it is made. Wangzhihe is a very old and popular brand made by fermenting glutinous rice and millet. Chinese cooking wines have a higher alcohol content than grape wines, and have added sugar. In North America, they also have a lot of salt, which is added so they can be sold in Asian grocery stores rather than in liquor stores. (Note: in some regions, you may be able to find Chinese cooking wines without added salt in liquor stores; in others, they are banned from sale completely.) Dry white wine or dry sherry can be used as a substitute; this will reduce the sodium content of the dish, but may alter the flavor.

Chinese Five-Spice Powder

Five-spice powder is used extensively in Chinese cuisine. It usually includes ground fennel, cloves, cinnamon, star anise and Sichuan peppercorns, although brands vary. Look for a brand with no added salt. The spice gives a licorice flavor to dishes, and is most often used with pork, duck or poultry. If you don't have five-spice powder on hand, you can make your own with equal amounts of the five ground spices.

Fish Sauce

Fish sauce is a thin, brown, strong-tasting liquid that is often used in place of salt as a seasoning and is also used as a dipping sauce. It is made by fermenting small whole fish in brine and then collecting the liquid. It has a pungent smell and a very salty flavor. Upon cooking, the fishiness is greatly reduced and a layer of flavor is added to the cooked dish. Chinese brands may label it as "fish gravy." Fish sauce can have 1270 mg or more sodium per tbsp (15 mL), so be conservative when adding it.

Hoisin Sauce

Hoisin sauce is widely used in Chinese cooking. *Hoisin* means "seafood sauce" in Cantonese, but despite its name, hoisin sauce does not contain any fish or seafood. Instead, it is more of a thick barbecue sauce. The main components of hoisin sauce are fermented beans, sugar, salt, red chiles and garlic. A good hoisin sauce should have a fragrant aroma and a sweet, spicy and salty flavor. Hoisin sauce has a lot of added sugar and salt — 2 tbsp (30 mL) can have 25 g of carbohydrate and over 1000 mg of sodium — so use it sparingly.

Oyster Sauce

Oyster sauce is a thick, brown, soy-based sauce flavored with oyster juice, salt, sugar and sometimes caramel. It has a versatile and pleasant flavor and is added to both bland and strongly flavored dishes. It is important to buy good-quality oyster sauce, as less expensive brands may not have much oyster flavor and may just taste salty. One tablespoon (15 mL) of oyster sauce contains nearly 1000 mg of sodium, and there are no reduced-sodium varieties available, so use it sparingly. Vegetarian brands that use mushrooms instead of oysters are also available.

Sambal

Sambals are an array of extremely hot chile sauces. Be careful how much you use, as they can have a lot of sodium. In this book, sambal is suggested in a couple of recipes as a way to add more heat.

Sichuan Peppercorns

Sichuan peppercorns are not actually part of the pepper family, but are the husks of the red-brown berries of Chinese prickly ash trees. The inner seeds are discarded and the husks are used whole or ground into a powder. They are often used in spicy dishes. Pan-frying whole peppercorns brings out their aroma and flavor. For the best flavor, buy whole peppercorns and grind them as needed.

Soybean Paste

Soybean paste is a seasoning made of cooked soybeans, malt and salt. It is similar to Japanese miso paste, but the Chinese variety is oilier and saltier and has a stronger soy flavor. It is dark brown and has a smooth consistency similar to peanut butter. Be careful how much you add to recipes, as some brands have a lot of sodium (650 mg or more per 1 tbsp/15 mL).

Soy Sauce

Chinese soy sauces are made mainly of fermented soybeans, wheat flour, water and salt. There are several types of Chinese soy sauce, but the ones used in this book are regular soy sauce and dark soy sauce. Regular soy sauce (just called "soy sauce" in the recipes) is used in many common dishes such as stir-fries and soups. Reduced-sodium options are readily available and should be used. Dark soy sauce is aged longer than regular soy sauce, is thicker and darker and may have caramel added. It is used to add color to some dishes and as a dipping sauce. It can also have more sodium — as much as 1200 mg per tbsp (15 mL) — and there are no reduced-sodium varieties available. However, it is an integral part of certain dishes, creating the color they are known for, so use it where it is called for, but use it *very sparingly*.

Star Anise

A star anise pod is the star-shaped fruit of an evergreen tree native to Asia. The points of the star contain amber seeds. In Chinese cuisine, whole star anise pods are used mainly to add a licorice-like flavor to slow-braised meat dishes such as chicken, pork or duck. Both the seeds and the husk are used to make the ground spice.

Toasted Sesame Oil

Toasted sesame oil (also called dark sesame oil or Asian sesame oil) is used extensively for flavoring in Chinese cuisine. It is made from sesame seeds that have been toasted to bring out their flavor; hence, it is darker in color than regular sesame oil. Heating intensifies the aroma of toasted sesame oil, but it should not be heated for too long, as it burns easily. Therefore, it is usually added at the end of a recipe.

To get the best quality of toasted sesame oil, you may need to go to an Asian grocery store, although the same brands are sometimes sold in well-stocked supermarkets. Sesame oil is best stored in a dark, cool, dry place, or in the refrigerator, as heat and light adversely affect its aroma. It is more volatile than other oils and goes rancid more quickly, so purchase a small bottle if you do not do a lot of Asian cooking.

Hispanic Cuisine

Ancho Chile Pepper

The deep red ancho chile is the dried version of the mild green poblano chile pepper, and it's the most commonly used chile in Mexico. An ancho chile is large — 4 to 5 inches (10 to 12.5 cm) long and about 3 inches (7.5 cm) wide — which explains its name (*ancho* means "wide"). It has a sweet, smoky, rich flavor, similar to that of a bell pepper, and is often used to make sauces. Before use, the seeds are shaken out and the flesh of the pepper is torn and puréed to remove any bitter taste. It has a heat rating of 1,500 to 2,500 Scoville units.

Canela Cinnamon

Canela cinnamon is also called Ceylon cinnamon, true cinnamon or soft-stick cinnamon, and is quite different from cassia cinnamon (see page 16). Canela cinnamon is more delicate, mellower and less spicy, and its bark is softer, lighter in color and easier to grind. It is commonly used in desserts and sweet drinks, such as *horchata* or Mexican hot chocolate.

Chipotle Chile Pepper

Chipotles are smoked dried jalapeño chile peppers and are fairly hot, with a smoky aroma and flavor. They are long and tapered, with dark red-brown, wrinkled skin. On average, they are about $2\frac{1}{4}$ inches (5.5 cm) long and less than $\frac{3}{4}$ inch (2 cm) wide. Chipotle chiles are used primarily in Mexican cuisine. They have a heat rating of 15,000 to 30,000 Scoville units. Morita chipotles are smoked for a short time over a wood fire after being sun-dried. They are lighter in color than other chipotles and retain a fruitier taste.

Epazote

Epazote is also known as Mexican tea, goosefoot or American wormseed. It is a strong-smelling herb that looks similar to mint, though with longer pointed, serrated leaves. The fragrance of epazote is difficult to describe; some say it smells like gasoline or anise or fennel or even mint. But everyone agrees that both the aroma and flavor are strong, so it is important to use only a small amount and to use whole sprigs so they can be easily removed before serving. Because of its strong flavor, epazote should not be used in combination with other herbs. It can be used either fresh or dried. If epazote is not available, it can be omitted from the dish.

Pasilla Chile Pepper

The pasilla chile is the dried form of the chilaca chile pepper, and is 6 to 8 inches (15 to 20 cm) long and about 1 inch (2.5 cm) wide. It has a dark, wrinkled appearance and a fruity, licorice-like flavor. In Mexico, pasillas are often used in combination with guajillo and mulato chiles and are used in mole sauce. They have a heat rating of 1,500 to 2,500 Scoville units.

Sherry Vinegar

Sherry vinegar should not be mistaken for cooking sherry. It is a specialty wine vinegar produced in Cádiz, Spain. Just like good sherry, good-quality sherry vinegar is aged in oak barrels for a long time (6 months to over 30 years). It has a mild, sweet, rich flavor and is used a lot in Spanish cuisine. It can be found in gourmet stores and well-stocked supermarkets, but cider vinegar usually makes an acceptable substitute. Red wine vinegar has a stronger flavor and is not as sweet, so if it's all you have on hand, substitute a smaller amount.

Spanish Paprika

Paprika is a powdered spice that comes in a range of bright red colors. It is made from the fruit of the paprika plant, called the pimento, which is in the same family as the chile pepper and resembles a small bell pepper. There are many different grades and varieties of paprika, so it can get very confusing! The most popular paprikas come from Hungary and Spain. Spanish paprikas are the best complement for authentic Spanish dishes. For the recipes in the Hispanic Cuisine chapter, I used *pimentón de La Vera*, a type of smoked Spanish paprika made in the La Vera region of Spain. Sweet smoked Spanish paprika (*pimentón dulce*) has a sweet and smoky aroma and an intense red color. Hot smoked Spanish paprika (*pimentón picante*) has a hot and smoky aroma. If you are not able to purchase these paprikas at a Spanish or Latin American store, they are easily purchased online.

Spanish Saffron

Saffron is the golden stigma of a purple flower in the crocus family. The stigmas are hand-picked and then dried, and are used to flavor and give a golden yellow color to many dishes, such as paella and *fideuá*. Saffron has a strong, sweet smell and a pungent flavor, so very little is needed — which is lucky, since it is very expensive! Spanish saffron is considered very high-quality. Choose saffron threads rather than powdered saffron, as with powdered you cannot be sure whether the saffron is good-quality or a cheap imitation, and powdered saffron can have added salt. Store saffron in an airtight container, away from the light, but not in the refrigerator or freezer.

Caribbean Cuisine

Allspice

Allspice is the dried unripe fruit of an evergreen tree and is also known as Jamaican pepper or myrtle pepper. When dried, allspice berries are dark brown and look similar to peppercorns. Allspice has the flavor of a combination of cinnamon, cloves and nutmeg. You can find allspice, in whole berries or ground, at your local grocery store. For the best aroma and flavor, buy whole berries and grind as needed.

Browning Sauce

Browning sauce, a blend of caramel coloring and spices, is commonly used in Caribbean cuisine to add flavor and dark, rich color to sauces, stews and soups. It is available in well-stocked supermarkets. Use it sparingly, or your dish can turn very dark. Different browning sauces can have significantly different amounts of sodium. I have seen brands as high as 160 mg per tsp (5 mL) and as low as 15 mg per tbsp (15 mL)! Make sure to read the labels and compare brands. And be precise in measuring browning sauce, so as not to increase the overall sodium content of the dish.

Caribbean Curry Powders

There are as many different types of Caribbean curry powders as there are countries in the Caribbean. Common ingredients include turmeric, coriander, cumin, fenugreek, black peppercorns, garlic, cloves, star anise and allspice. The whole spices are dry-roasted and ground into a powder. Allspice is the ingredient that makes Caribbean curry powders different from other curry powders, such as those used for South Asian cooking (although South Asian curry powders are sometimes used in certain Caribbean dishes). It is important to note that some Caribbean curry powders include chile peppers for added heat.

Any variety of Caribbean curry powder will work in the recipes in the Caribbean Cuisine chapter, but to be truly authentic, buy a curry powder from the country where the recipe originated. Always read the label to make sure there is no salt added and to check if the ingredients include chile peppers. You may be able to find Caribbean curry powders at your local supermarket. If not, look for them at Caribbean grocery stores or even South Asian markets. You can also create your own curry powder by grinding your own fresh spices.

Cassareep

Cassareep is a sauce made from the juice of the cassava root (also known as manioc or yuca). The juice is cooked until it reduces and caramelizes into a dark, thick black liquid with a consistency similar to molasses. This sweet sauce is used to add flavor and dark color to dishes such as Guyanese pepperpot. Most cassareep in North America is imported, usually from Guyana. Be sure to read the label, as different brands have varying amounts of salt and sugar. (And if you find one without a Nutrition Facts table, avoid it.) The brands I have seen have as little as 96 g of carbohydrate and 36 mg of sodium per 1 cup (250 mL), which isn't bad — but be careful how much you use: some recipes call for 1 cup or more!

South Asian Cuisine

Recipes from Bangladesh, India, Pakistan and Sri Lanka

Soups, Salads and Snacks

Spicy South Indian Soup
(Rasam). 26

Split Yellow Pigeon Pea Soup
(Sambar) 28

Punjabi Lachha Salad. 30

Tomato Mint Salad
(Kachumber) 31

Whole Wheat and Besan
Flatbread (Besan Roti) 32

Chickpea and Potato Snack
(Aloo Cholay) 33

South Indian Dosas 34

Potato and Pea Samosas. 36

South Indian Dhokla. 38

Pakistani Oven-Baked
Shami Kebabs 40

Fish Amritsari. 42

Homemade Low-Fat Paneer 44

Vegetarian Dishes

Sri Lankan Eggplant Curry
(Baigan) 45

Sri Lankan Bitter Melon Curry
(Karawila). 46

Okra and Tomato Curry
(Bhindi) 48

Zucchini Curry (Turaii) 49

Bengali Yellow Lentil Curry
(Cholar Dal) 50

Red Lentil Curry (Masoor Dal). . . . 52

Kidney Bean Curry (Rajma). 53

Spinach and Tofu Curry
(Palak Tofu) 54

Vegetable and Cheese Curry
(Paneer Bhurji) 56

Pakistani Potatoes and
Cauliflower (Aloo Gobi) 58

Sri Lankan Red Rice Congee. . . . 59

Pakistani Spicy Vegetable
Rice *(Tahari)*. 60

Chickpea Rice *(Chana Chawal)*. . . . 62

Savory South Indian Semolina
Cakes *(Rava Idlis)* 64

Meat, Poultry, Fish and Seafood Dishes

Easy Pakistani Veal Stew
(Karahi Ghosht). 66

Pakistani Lamb Stew
(Mutton Korma) 68

Goan Pork Vindaloo 70

Goan Pork with Liver *(Sorpotel)*. . . . 72

Butter Chicken
(Makhani Murgh) 74

Pakistani Chicken Stew
(Murgh Korma). 76

Pakistani Chicken Pilaf
(Murgh Pulao) 78

Goan Fish Curry
(Machhi Curry) 80

Bengali Fish Curry *(Doi Maach)* 82

South Indian Coconut Shrimp
Curry *(Jhinga Malai Curry)*. 83

Goan Shrimp Vindaloo 84

Sauces, Condiments and Beverages

Cucumber Yogurt *(Keera Raita)*. . . . 86

Mixed Vegetable Yogurt
(Sabzi Raita) 87

Cilantro Mint Chutney
(Hara Dhania Chutney). 88

Coconut Chutney
(Nariyal Chutney) 89

Pakistani Sweet Tamarind
Chutney *(Imali Chutney)*. 90

Tamarind Purée *(Imali)* 91

Mango Yogurt Smoothie
(Aam Lassi) 92

Masala Tea
(Masala Chai) 93

Spicy South Indian Soup *(Rasam)*

Makes 7 servings

This thin, tangy and spicy soup can be eaten on its own as a first course, or alongside sambar (page 28), with dosas (page 34) or idlis (page 64). I got this recipe from Hemant Tallur, a chef from India, and it turns out great every time!

Soaking time: **30 minutes**
Preparation time: **20 minutes**
Cooking time: **2 hours**

- **Blender, food processor or immersion blender**

1 cup	dried split yellow pigeon peas (*toor dal*), rinsed	250 mL
	Water	
4	medium tomatoes, diced	4
8	dried red chile peppers, divided	8
1/8 tsp	ground turmeric	0.5 mL
1 tbsp	vegetable oil	15 mL
1 tsp	mustard seeds	5 mL
2 tbsp	finely minced garlic	30 mL
1 tbsp	dried curry leaves	15 mL
2 tsp	cumin seeds	10 mL
1 tsp	ground coriander	5 mL
1/2 tsp	black peppercorns, crushed	2 mL
1/8 tsp	asafetida (see page 15)	0.5 mL
1/2	medium red onion, minced	1/2
2 tbsp	Tart Tamarind Paste (see box, page 71)	30 mL
1/2 tsp	salt	2 mL
2 tbsp	chopped fresh cilantro	30 mL

1. Place pigeon peas in a bowl with enough water to cover; let soak for 30 minutes.

2. Drain soaking water from peas and transfer peas to a medium saucepan. Add 3 cups (750 mL) fresh water and bring to a boil over high heat. Reduce heat and simmer for about 1 hour or until tender.

3. Add tomatoes, 4 red chiles and turmeric; cover and bring to a boil over high heat. Reduce heat to low and simmer for about 30 minutes or until peas are very tender. Discard chiles.

4. Transfer pea mixture to blender (or use immersion blender in pot) and purée until smooth (see tip, opposite).

5. In a deep pot, heat oil over medium heat. Add mustard seeds and cook, stirring, for about 2 minutes or until seeds pop. Add the remaining red chiles, garlic, curry leaves, cumin, coriander, peppercorns and asafetida; cook, stirring, for 2 minutes. Add onion, reduce heat to low and cook, stirring, for about 5 minutes or until softened and golden.

Nutrition info per serving	
Calories	145
Fat, total	3 g
Fat, saturated	0.3 g
Cholesterol	0 mg
Sodium	185 mg
Carbohydrate	25 g
Fiber	6 g
Protein	7 g

Food Choices

1	Carbohydrate
1	Meat & Alternatives
1/2	Fat

Make It a Meal

1 serving Spicy South Indian Soup

1 serving Split Yellow Pigeon Pea Soup (page 28)

2 South Indian Dosas (page 34)

1 oz (30 g) Homemade Low-Fat Paneer (page 44)

1 serving Coconut Chutney (page 89)

6. Stir in pea purée and 3½ cups (875 mL) water; bring to a boil over high heat. Reduce heat and simmer, stirring often, for 5 minutes.

7. Stir in tamarind paste and salt; increase heat to high and cook for 1 minute. Skim off any froth that forms on top. Discard chiles. Stir in cilantro and serve immediately.

Tips

In this recipe, the rasam spice blend is made from scratch to control the amount of salt added to the dish. If you purchase a store-bought rasam masala powder (which would replace the spices added in step 5), make sure to compare labels, as some brands contain a lot of sodium.

When blending hot liquids in an upright blender, fill the blender no more than half full, leave the center hole in the lid open and cover the hole with a towel. Hold down the towel and the lid while the blender is running, allowing steam to be released.

Toor Dal

In South Asian cuisine, the word *dal* (or *dhal*) refers to dried beans, peas and lentils. Dal may or may not contain the outer husk and can be split or whole. It is usually used in vegetarian dishes. *Toor dal*, *toovar dal* or *arhar dal* — dried split yellow pigeon peas — is one of the most popular dals in India. It is used in the popular soups rasam and sambar, and in a variety of other dishes, such as breads, curries and even desserts. You can find *toor dal* in any South Asian grocery store. Oil is added to some brands to preserve shelf life; it is best to purchase *toor dal* without added oil, as it will have less fat and will not foam as much when cooked.

Split Yellow Pigeon Pea Soup
(Sambar)

Here's another tangy and spicy South Indian soup, which is traditionally served alongside rasam (page 26), with dosas (page 34) and coconut chutney (page 89). This combination is my favorite meal at traditional South Indian restaurants, and now you can make an even healthier version at home!

Nutrition info per serving	
Calories	171
Fat, total	3 g
Fat, saturated	0.0 g
Cholesterol	0 mg
Sodium	429 mg
Carbohydrate	30 g
Fiber	7 g
Protein	7 g

Food Choices	
1	Carbohydrate
1/2	Meat & Alternatives
1/2	Fat

Preparation time: **20 minutes**
Cooking time: **2 hours**

Pea Mixture

3/4 cup	dried split yellow pigeon peas (*toor dal*), rinsed	175 mL
1 tsp	ground turmeric	5 mL
1 tsp	salt	5 mL
7 cups	water	1.75 L
1 cup	small cauliflower florets	250 mL
1 cup	chopped zucchini	250 mL
1/4 cup	Tamarind Purée (page 91)	60 mL

Tomato Mixture

1 tbsp	vegetable oil	15 mL
1 tsp	brown mustard seeds	5 mL
15	dried curry leaves	15
1 cup	minced onion	250 mL
1/2 tsp	chili powder	2 mL
1/2 tsp	ground coriander	2 mL
1/4 tsp	ground fenugreek	1 mL
3	small green chile peppers, seeded and minced	3
1/2 cup	no-salt-added canned diced tomatoes, with juice	125 mL
2 tsp	minced garlic	10 mL
1 cup	water (approx.)	250 mL

1. *Pea Mixture:* In a medium pot, combine peas, turmeric, salt and water. Bring to a boil over high heat. Reduce heat to low, cover and simmer for 60 minutes. Whisk to break up pigeon peas.

2. Stir in cauliflower, zucchini and tamarind purée; cover and simmer for 30 minutes or until peas are very tender.

3. *Tomato Mixture:* Meanwhile, in a medium skillet, heat oil over medium heat. Add mustard seeds and cook, stirring, for about 2 minutes or until seeds pop. Add curry leaves, onion, chili powder, coriander and fenugreek; cook, stirring until onion is translucent.

4. Stir in chile peppers, tomatoes and garlic; cook, breaking up tomatoes with a spoon, until tomatoes are crushed and mixture is thickened.

5. Add the tomato mixture to the pea mixture and simmer, uncovered, stirring occasionally, for 10 minutes. Stir in up to 1 cup (250 mL) water to achieve the desired consistency; simmer for 5 minutes.

Tips

For information on *toor dal*, see the box on page 27.

In this recipe, the sambar spice mix is made from scratch to control the amount of salt added to the dish. If you purchase a store-bought sambar powder mix (which would replace the spices added in step 3), make sure to compare labels, as some brands contain 910 mg or more sodium in a $1\frac{1}{2}$-tsp (7 mL) serving.

This soup is traditionally relatively thick, but by adjusting the amount of water, you can make it thicker or thinner, as desired.

Sambar can also be eaten with brown rice or whole wheat roti (page 32), a side of raita (page 86 or 87) and a fresh fruit.

Nutrition Tip

Pulses (dried beans, peas and lentils), such as yellow pigeon peas, have lots of protein, are a source of fiber (especially soluble fiber) and have no fat. As a result, they may help to lower blood glucose and low-density lipoprotein (LDL) blood cholesterol.

Punjabi Lachha Salad

Makes 12 servings

This salad is fresh, crisp and tangy! *Lachha* is a Punjabi term meaning "groups of long strands." The very popular lachha paratha (a flatbread), for example, is made with long strands of dough. The vegetables for lachha salad, therefore, should be cut into long, thin strands. Lachha salads are meant to be simple, with just a lemon and salt dressing. I replaced the salt with chaat masala, for a real kick.

Preparation time: **25 minutes**

4	plum (Roma) tomatoes, seeded and finely julienned	4
2	medium green bell peppers, finely julienned	2
2	medium onions, finely julienned	2
1	large cucumber, peeled and finely julienned	1
1	medium carrot, finely julienned	1
1/4	cabbage, shredded	1/4
2 tbsp	chaat masala (see page 16)	30 mL
3 tbsp	freshly squeezed lemon juice	45 mL

1. In a large bowl, combine tomatoes, green peppers, onions, cucumber, carrot, cabbage, chaat masala and lemon juice. Serve immediately.

Tips

Plum tomatoes are the best choice for this recipe, as they do not release as much liquid as other varieties.

To "julienne" means to cut vegetables into long, thin pieces, similar to matchsticks. Although chefs disagree on the "proper" dimensions of these sticks, an easy rule of thumb is to make them 2 inches (5 cm) long and between $1/16$ and $1/8$ inch (2 and 3 mm) thick. If a recipe calls for "finely julienned" vegetables, tend toward the thinner side; if it calls for "julienned" vegetables, cut them a bit thicker.

Serve this salad soon after making it; otherwise, the vegetables will release water and the salad will be soggy.

Nutrition info per serving	
Calories	38
Fat, total	1 g
Fat, saturated	0.1 g
Cholesterol	0 mg
Sodium	224 mg
Carbohydrate	8 g
Fiber	2 g
Protein	2 g
Food Choices	
1	Extra

Tomato Mint Salad *(Kachumber)*

Makes 4 servings

This refreshing, colorful salad goes with everything! *Kachumber* means "small pieces, mixed together," so finely chop the vegetables. It can be made with or without chickpeas, but leaving them in is a great way to slip more legumes into your diet.

Make It a Meal

1 serving Bengali Yellow Lentil Curry (page 50)

1 serving Zucchini Curry (page 49)

1 Whole Wheat and Besan Flatbread (page 32)

1 serving Tomato Mint Salad

1 small papaya (1 Carbohydrate)

Nutrition info per serving

Calories	59
Fat, total	1 g
Fat, saturated	0.1 g
Cholesterol	0 mg
Sodium	375 mg
Carbohydrate	12 g
Fiber	3 g
Protein	3 g
Food Choices	
1	Extra

Preparation time: **15 minutes**

1	small green chile pepper, minced	1
1 ½ cups	finely chopped plum (Roma) tomatoes	375 mL
1 cup	finely chopped cucumber	250 mL
1 cup	packed fresh mint leaves, finely chopped	250 mL
½ cup	rinsed drained canned chickpeas	125 mL
½ cup	minced sweet onion	125 mL
2 tsp	freshly squeezed lemon juice	10 mL
¼ tsp	salt	1 mL

1. In a large bowl, combine chile pepper, tomatoes, cucumber, mint, chickpeas, onion, lemon juice and salt.

2. Serve immediately or cover and refrigerate for up to 2 days.

Tips

Store the remaining chickpeas in an airtight container in the refrigerator for up to 3 days. They make a great addition to salads and stir-fries.

Lemon juice and herbs are a flavorful way to dress a salad without adding salt or fat.

Nutrition Tip

Chickpeas are a good source of fiber, especially soluble fiber, which helps lower low-density lipoprotein (LDL) blood cholesterol. Although they contain carbohydrate, they have a low glycemic index, which may help maintain blood glucose levels.

Whole Wheat and Besan Flatbread *(Besan Roti)*

Makes 6 roti

This is a very healthy flatbread, quite different from regular roti, naan or paratha. It is great for people with diabetes, as it contains a lot of fiber and has a lower glycemic index than other South Asian flatbreads. The hot pepper flakes add a nice heat. Serve it alongside a mild curry, with a side of raita (page 86 or 87).

Make It a Meal

1 serving Okra and Tomato Curry (page 48)

1 serving Butter Chicken (page 74)

2 Whole Wheat and Besan Flatbread

¾ cup (175 mL) Mango Yogurt Smoothie (page 92)

½ small papaya (½ Carbohydrate)

Nutrition info per roti

Calories	121
Fat, total	4 g
Fat, saturated	0.4 g
Cholesterol	0 mg
Sodium	202 mg
Carbohydrate	19 g
Fiber	3 g
Protein	4 g

Food Choices

1	Carbohydrate
½	Fat

Preparation time: **30 minutes**
Cooking time: **20 minutes**

½ cup	finely chopped spinach	125 mL
¼ cup	minced onion	60 mL
4 tsp	finely chopped fresh cilantro	20 mL
1 cup	whole wheat flour	250 mL
½ cup	chickpea flour (besan)	125 mL
½ tsp	hot pepper flakes	2 mL
½ tsp	salt	2 mL
¼ tsp	baking powder	1 mL
4 tsp	vegetable oil, divided	20 mL
¼ cup	water (approx.)	60 mL
1 tbsp	whole wheat flour	15 mL

1. In a bowl, combine spinach, onion, cilantro, 1 cup (250 mL) whole wheat flour, chickpea flour, hot pepper flakes, salt, baking powder and 2 tsp (10 mL) oil. Knead in enough water to form a soft dough. Cover with plastic wrap or a damp towel and let rest for 15 minutes.

2. Divide dough into 6 equal balls. On a work surface lightly floured with 1 tbsp (15 mL) whole wheat flour, flatten balls into small discs, then roll out into 6-inch (15 cm) diameter circles. Lightly brush each circle with some of the remaining oil.

3. Heat a small skillet over medium heat. Working with one roti at a time, cook roti for about 1 minute per side or until lightly blistered on both sides. Transfer roti to a plate and keep warm. Repeat with the remaining roti, adjusting heat as necessary between roti to prevent burning.

Tips

Chickpea flour, also called besan flour, chana dal flour or gram flour, is made from ground *chana dal* (see page 51). It is gluten-free and is a good source of fiber.

The addition of whole wheat flour to this dough adds a nice texture and, thanks to the gluten, binds it together and keeps it soft.

The water in this and other dough recipes is a guideline, as some flours absorb water differently than others. For this recipe, you want dough that is soft but not sticky.

Chickpea and Potato Snack
(Aloo Cholay)

Makes 6 servings

This healthy snack is sold as street food in Pakistan and India. I remember, as a child in Pakistan, walking down the street with my tangy and spicy aloo cholay. There are many different versions of this snack; this one features tamarind and chaat masala.

Preparation time: **35 minutes**

1	can (19 oz/540 mL) chickpeas, drained and rinsed	1
2	small green chile peppers, minced	2
1	plum (Roma) tomato, chopped	1
1 cup	chopped green bell pepper	250 mL
½ cup	boiled chopped potato	125 mL
⅓ cup	Tamarind Purée (page 91)	75 mL
⅓ cup	minced sweet onion	75 mL
1 tsp	chaat masala (see page 16)	5 mL
¼ tsp	salt	1 mL
¼ cup	1% plain yogurt	60 mL
1 tsp	freshly squeezed lemon juice	5 mL
¼ cup	packed fresh cilantro leaves, finely chopped (optional)	60 mL

1. In a large bowl, combine chickpeas, chiles, tomato, green pepper, potato, tamarind purée, onion, chaat masala, salt, yogurt and lemon juice. Sprinkle with cilantro, if desired.

Tips

If you can only find 14- or 15-oz (398 or 425 mL) cans of chickpeas, buy two. You'll need about 2 cups (500 mL) rinsed drained chickpeas for this recipe.

The traditional version of this recipe uses a lot of potato. To reduce the amount of carbohydrate per serving, I've minimized the potato in favor of other vegetables and more chickpeas, which are fiber-rich and do not raise blood glucose levels.

Nutrition info per serving	
Calories	132
Fat, total	2 g
Fat, saturated	0.2 g
Cholesterol	0 mg
Sodium	302 mg
Carbohydrate	25 g
Fiber	7 g
Protein	6 g

Food Choices

1	Carbohydrate
½	Meat & Alternatives

South Indian Dosas

Makes 12 dosas

Dosas are a popular South Indian dish, often served for breakfast or sold as a street food, that resemble large crêpes. Made from fermented lentils and rice, they are usually served with spicy sides, such as rasam (page 26), sambar (page 28) or coconut chutney (page 89), or with a spicy potato filling. These homemade dosas are lower in sodium than store-bought versions and have added fiber from the brown rice.

Nutrition info per dosa	
Calories	82
Fat, total	2 g
Fat, saturated	0.2 g
Cholesterol	0 mg
Sodium	51 mg
Carbohydrate	15 g
Fiber	1 g
Protein	3 g
Food Choices	
1	Carbohydrate

Soaking time: **12 hours or overnight**
Fermenting time: **12 to 18 hours**
Preparation time: **20 minutes**
Cooking time: **4 minutes per dosa**

- **Blender**
- **Nonstick griddle or *tawa***
- **Palette knife**

1 cup	brown basmati rice, rinsed	250 mL
⅓ cup	dried white lentils (*urad dal*), rinsed	75 mL
	Hot water	
1¼ cups	water, divided (approx.)	300 mL
¼ tsp	salt	1 mL
1 tbsp	vegetable oil	15 mL

1. Place rice and lentils in separate bowls and add hot water to cover to each bowl. Cover bowls and let soak for 12 hours or overnight. (Both the rice and the lentils will increase in size.)

2. Drain rice and lentils, transfer to the blender and purée until smooth, adding about ½ cup (125 mL) water as needed to make a smooth paste.

3. Preheat oven to 200°F (100°C), then turn oven off. Transfer purée to a bowl, cover with a plate and place in oven for 12 to 18 hours to ferment or until batter rises and gets slightly bubbly on top.

4. Return purée to the blender and add salt; purée, adding up to ¾ cup (175 mL) water as needed, for about 1 minute to make a very thin, smooth batter (similar to a crêpe batter).

5. Heat griddle over medium heat and brush lightly with oil. Ladle about ¼ cup (60 mL) batter onto pan, using a circular motion. Using the bottom of the ladle, lightly make circles on the surface to spread the batter into a thin, even 8-inch (20 cm) diameter circle. Spread ¼ tsp (1 mL) oil on top of the circle. Cook for about 4 minutes or until bubbles form on top and dosa turns golden brown on the bottom. Do not flip dosa. Remove from heat using a palette knife and serve immediately, or wrap in a towel and keep warm in an insulated container (hot case). Repeat with the remaining batter, oiling pan and adjusting heat as necessary between dosa to prevent sticking and burning.

Tips

A *tawa* is a large flat pan, usually made of iron. They are inexpensive and can be purchased at South Asian markets.

When making dosas, always use a 3:1 ratio of rice to lentils to ensure proper leavening of the dough.

Making dosas is very similar to making crêpes and may take a bit of practice, but it is worth it to incorporate this healthy dish into your diet.

The best dosas are served immediately, right off the griddle. If they sit for a while (even in an insulated container), they lose their crispness and get soggy. To help bring back the crispness, sprinkle some water on top and microwave on High for 10 to 15 seconds.

Dosa batter can be stored in an airtight container in the refrigerator for up to 3 days, if you prefer to cook only a few dosas at a time.

Urad Dal

In South Asian cuisine, the word *dal* (or *dhal*) refers to dried beans, peas and lentils. Dal may or may not contain the outer husk and can be split or whole. Whole *urad dal* is a black lentil-like bean grown mainly in South Asia. It is also called black gram, black lentils or *kali dal*. When the beans are split and husked, the creamy white interiors are called white lentils, and are also just known as *urad dal* or as *maash ki daal*. Because of their creamy texture, white lentils are perfect for making dosas. Look for *urad dal* at South Asian grocery stores.

Potato and Pea Samosas

Makes 12 samosas

Samosas are by far the most popular street snack in South Asia. They can be vegetarian or meat-filled and are usually deep-fried. This baked vegetarian version turns out crispy and delicious. Serve the samosas with Cilantro Mint Chutney (page 88) or Pakistani Sweet Tamarind Chutney (page 90).

Preparation time: **45 minutes**
Cooking time: **20 minutes**

- **Preheat oven to 400°F (200°C)**
- **Baking sheet, lined with parchment paper**

Dough

1 1/2 cups	whole wheat flour, divided	375 mL
1/4 cup	chickpea flour (besan)	60 mL
2 tbsp	ground flax seeds (flaxseed meal)	30 mL
1/2 tsp	salt	2 mL
1/2 cup	skim milk (approx.), divided	125 mL
1	large egg, lightly beaten	1
1 tbsp	vegetable oil	15 mL

Filling

1/2	medium potato, diced	1/2
1 cup	small cauliflower florets	250 mL
1/3 cup	frozen green peas	75 mL
1 tsp	vegetable oil	5 mL
1	medium onion, minced	1
1	clove garlic, minced	1
1 1/4 cups	minced cabbage	300 mL
1 tsp	cumin seeds	5 mL
1/2 tsp	hot pepper flakes	2 mL
1 tsp	mango powder (*amchoor*)	5 mL
1/2 tsp	salt	2 mL
1/4 tsp	ground turmeric	1 mL
1/2 tsp	garam masala	2 mL
2 tbsp	water	30 mL
1/4 cup	finely chopped fresh cilantro	60 mL

1. *Dough:* In a large bowl, combine 1 1/4 cups (300 mL) whole wheat flour, chickpea flour, flax seeds and salt.

2. Reserve 1 tbsp (15 mL) milk. Add egg and oil to the flour mixture. Gradually stir in the remaining milk, using only enough to make a firm dough. Wrap in plastic wrap or cover with a damp towel and let rest while preparing filling.

3. *Filling:* Place potato and cauliflower in a small saucepan and cover with water. Bring to a boil over high heat. Reduce heat and boil for about 8 minutes or until tender. Drain.

4. Meanwhile, in another small saucepan of boiling water, boil peas for 2 minutes. Drain.

Nutrition info per samosa	
Calories	101
Fat, total	3 g
Fat, saturated	0.4 g
Cholesterol	16 mg
Sodium	219 mg
Carbohydrate	16 g
Fiber	3 g
Protein	4 g

Food Choices	
1	Carbohydrate
1/2	Fat

Variation

For a dairy- and egg-free version, replace the milk and egg in the dough with ½ cup (125 mL) unsweetened soy milk. Whisk the soy milk with the ground flax seeds and let stand for 5 minutes before adding it to the flour mixture.

5. In a large skillet, heat oil over medium heat. Add onion, garlic, cabbage, cumin and hot pepper flakes; cook, stirring, until cabbage is soft and golden. Add mango powder, salt and turmeric; cook, stirring, for 1 minute. Stir in garam masala.

6. Add water, scraping up any brown bits from bottom of pan. Remove from heat and stir in cauliflower and potatoes. Partially mash ingredients together. Gently stir in peas and cilantro until incorporated.

7. Divide dough into 6 equal balls. On a work surface floured with the remaining whole wheat flour, roll each ball out into a thin oval. Cut each oval in half crosswise, then form each half into a cone, pressing two edges together. Fill each cone with stuffing and seal the remaining edge, using a little water if necessary.

8. Place samosas at least 1 inch (2.5 cm) apart on prepared baking sheet and brush lightly with the reserved milk.

9. Bake in preheated oven for about 20 minutes or until golden and crisp. Serve hot or let cool to room temperature.

Tips

The traditional version of this recipe uses a lot of potatoes and green peas. To reduce the amount of carbohydrate per serving, I've minimized the role of those starchy vegetables in favor of cabbage and cauliflower, which will not affect blood glucose levels.

You can brush the samosas with oil instead of milk before baking, but use it sparingly to keep the fat low.

Extra samosas can be cooled on a wire rack, then refrigerated in an airtight container for up to 3 days. Reheat on a baking sheet in a 350°F (180°C) oven for 10 to 15 minutes, if desired.

South Indian Dhokla

Makes 8 wedges

Dhokla, a tasty and healthy vegetarian snack originally from the state of Gujarat in western India, is also popular in northern India. My friend Preety showed me how to make dhokla, and I was amazed by how easy it is! My version has less added sugar and salt than traditional recipes.

Soaking time: **4 hours or overnight**
Preparation time: **10 minutes**
Cooking time: **20 to 30 minutes**

- **Blender**
- **8-inch (20 cm) dhokla steamer (see tip, opposite)**

Dhokla

1 cup	dried husked mung beans (*moong dal*), rinsed	250 mL
	Water	
1/4 tsp	vegetable oil	1 mL
1/4 tsp	antacid powder (Eno)	1 mL
1/4 tsp	salt	1 mL

Syrup

2 tsp	vegetable oil	10 mL
1 tsp	large black mustard seeds	5 mL
5	small green chile peppers, sliced lengthwise	5
1 tbsp	granulated sugar	15 mL
1/2 tsp	salt	2 mL
1 cup	water	250 mL
3 tbsp	freshly squeezed lemon juice	45 mL

1. *Dhokla:* Place beans in a bowl with enough water to cover; let soak for at least 4 hours or overnight. Drain.

2. In blender, combine beans and 1/2 cup + 1 tbsp (140 mL) fresh water; blend until mixture becomes a thick liquid. Transfer batter to a bowl.

3. Add 1 to 1 1/2 cups (250 to 375 mL) water to the dhokla steamer and bring to a boil over high heat. Grease a dhokla pan with oil.

4. Just as the water in the steamer comes to a boil, stir antacid powder and salt into batter. It will rise instantly as you mix. Pour the batter into the pan and smooth the top with a spatula. Place the pan on the stand, and carefully place the stand in the steamer. Cover and steam over medium-high heat for 12 to 15 minutes or until a knife inserted in the center comes out clean. Remove from steamer and let cool for 10 to 15 minutes. Cut into 8 wedges and let cool completely.

Nutrition info per wedge

Calories	121
Fat, total	2 g
Fat, saturated	0.2 g
Cholesterol	0 mg
Sodium	224 mg
Carbohydrate	21 g
Fiber	5 g
Protein	7 g

Food Choices

1	Carbohydrate
1	Meat & Alternatives
1/2	Fat

Tips

A dhokla steamer includes a large, deep pot and circular pans stacked on a stand. It is very similar to an idli steamer (see tip, page 64); in fact, you can purchase steamers with pans for making both dhoklas and idlis. Look for them at South Asian grocery stores or online.

The size of your steamer pot will determine how much water you should add. For a smaller steamer pot, add 1 cup (250 mL) water. For a larger one, add 1½ cups (375 mL) water.

5. *Syrup:* Meanwhile, in a small saucepan, heat oil over medium heat. Add mustard seeds and cook, stirring, for about 2 minutes or until seeds pop. Add chiles and cook, stirring, until slightly softened. Stir in sugar, salt, water and lemon juice; bring to a boil over high heat. Reduce heat and simmer, stirring, for about 5 minutes or until sugar is dissolved. Be careful not to let the syrup get too thick. Let syrup cool for 10 to 15 minutes, then pour over dhokla wedges.

Moong Dal

In South Asian cuisine, the word *dal* (or *dhal*) refers to dried beans, peas and lentils. Dal may or may not contain the outer husk and can be split or whole. *Moong dal* is the Hindi term for the mung bean. Whole mung beans, with their husks intact, are green and are also known as green gram. When they have been split but still have their husk, they are known as split mung beans. When the husks are removed, the split beans within are yellow and are also known as golden gram or split yellow lentils. All three types of mung beans are used extensively in South Asian cuisines, in both savory and sweet dishes. Mung beans are high in folate and are a source of magnesium and fiber, especially soluble fiber, which has been shown to reduce blood glucose and low-density lipoprotein (LDL) blood cholesterol.

Pakistani Oven-Baked Shami Kebabs

Makes 14 patties

In North America, we think of kebabs as barbecued cubes of meat on a skewer. In South Asia, kebabs come in many different shapes, textures and flavors. Shami kebabs are circular patties made with lentils and ground meat. They are typically deep-fried, but this recipe bakes them instead. They can be served with chutney or raita as a snack or appetizer, or as part of a meal with rice and a vegetable curry.

Soaking time: **30 minutes or overnight**
Preparation time: **45 minutes**
Cooking time: **50 minutes**

- **Preheat oven to 350°F (180°C)**
- **Food processor**
- **Rimmed baking sheet, lined with foil**

½ cup	dried split Bengal gram (*chana dal*), rinsed	125 mL
	Water	
1 lb	lean ground chicken	500 g
1 ½ tsp	finely chopped gingerroot	7 mL
1 tsp	hot pepper flakes	5 mL
1 tsp	salt	5 mL
½	small green chile pepper, chopped (optional)	½
⅓ cup	finely chopped yellow onion	75 mL
1 tsp	garam masala	5 mL
2 tbsp	chopped fresh cilantro	30 mL
1	large egg, well beaten	1
1 tsp	freshly squeezed lemon juice	5 mL
1 tsp	vegetable oil, divided	5 mL

1. Place Bengal gram in a bowl with enough water to cover; let soak for at least 30 minutes or overnight.

2. Drain soaking water from Bengal gram and transfer Bengal gram to a large pot. Stir in chicken, ginger, hot pepper flakes, salt and 1 cup (250 mL) water; bring to a boil over high heat. Reduce heat to medium, cover and boil gently for 10 minutes. Uncover and boil gently, stirring often, for about 25 minutes or until chicken is no longer pink and mixture is very dry. Let cool slightly.

Nutrition info per patty (40 g)

Calories	81
Fat, total	3 g
Fat, saturated	0.8 g
Cholesterol	34 mg
Sodium	191 mg
Carbohydrate	6 g
Fiber	1 g
Protein	8 g

Food Choices

1	Meat & Alternative
1	Extra

Make It a Meal

2 servings Pakistani
Oven-Baked Shami
Kebabs

1 serving Okra and
Tomato Curry (page 48)

$2/3$ cup (150 mL) unsalted
cooked brown basmati
rice (2 Carbohydrate)

1 serving Cucumber
Yogurt (page 86) or
$1/4$ cup (60 mL) low-fat
plain yogurt (1 Extra)

$3/4$ cup (175 mL) Mango
Yogurt Smoothie
(page 92)

1 medium guava
($1/2$ Carbohydrate)

3. Transfer chicken mixture to food processor and process until finely ground.

4. In a large bowl, combine chicken mixture, chile, onion, garam masala, cilantro, egg and lemon juice. Using $1/4$ cup (60 mL) of the mixture for each patty, form 14 small patties, $2\frac{1}{2}$ inches (6 cm) in diameter and $1/4$ inch (0.5 cm) thick.

5. Brush prepared pan with $1/2$ tsp (2 mL) oil or less. Arrange patties on pan and brush tops lightly with the remaining oil.

6. Bake in preheated oven for 10 minutes, flipping halfway though, until browned on both sides. Drain off liquid.

Tips

Shami kebabs are smaller and a bit thicker than other types of South Asian kebabs, such as chappali or seekh kebabs.

For information on *chana dal*, see the box on page 51.

Fish Amritsari

Fish amritsari has its origins in Amritsar, in northern India. A fried fish with Indian spices, it is typically sold as street food or served as an appetizer or side dish. It is usually deep-fried, but in this recipe, the fish is pan-fried, then baked, and it still turns out crispy and delicious!

Nutrition info per serving

Calories	359
Fat, total	12 g
Fat, saturated	1.3 g
Cholesterol	96 mg
Sodium	*531 mg
Carbohydrate	18 g
Fiber	3 g
Protein	44 g

* This recipe is high in sodium. Balance it out by making lower-sodium choices for the rest of your meal and throughout the day.

Food Choices

1	Carbohydrate
4½	Meat & Alternatives
1	Fat

Preparation time: **15 minutes**
Cooking time: **25 to 30 minutes**

- **Preheat oven to 275°F (140°C)**
- **Rimmed baking sheet**

5	king mackerel steak pieces (each about 6 oz/175 g), rinsed and patted dry	5
3 tbsp	white vinegar	45 mL
½ tsp	salt	2 mL
1½ cups	chickpea flour (besan)	375 mL
2 tsp	carom seeds	10 mL
1½ tsp	minced garlic	7 mL
1½ tsp	minced ginger	7 mL
1 tsp	chaat masala (see page 16)	5 mL
½ tsp	ground turmeric	2 mL
⅓ cup	freshly squeezed lemon juice	75 mL
1 cup	water	250 mL
2 tbsp	vegetable oil, divided	30 mL
4	lemon wedges (optional)	4

1. Place fish in a shallow dish and sprinkle with vinegar and salt, turning to coat. Let stand while you prepare the batter.

2. In a bowl, combine chickpea flour, carom seeds, garlic, ginger, chaat masala and turmeric. Stir in lemon juice. Gradually add water, stirring after every addition, until a thick batter forms.

3. Remove fish from vinegar mixture and pat dry. Dip fish in batter, coating evenly. Discard any excess batter and vinegar mixture.

4. In a large nonstick skillet, heat half the oil over medium-high heat. Add fish, in batches as necessary to avoid crowding pan, and sear for 2 to 3 minutes per side or until golden brown on both sides. Transfer fish to baking sheet. Repeat with the remaining fish, adding oil and adjusting heat as necessary between batches.

5. Bake in preheated oven for 10 minutes or until fish is opaque and flakes easily when tested with a fork.

6. Serve garnished with lemon wedges, if desired.

Make It a Meal

½ serving Fish Amritsari

1 serving Okra and Tomato Curry (page 48)

⅔ cup (150 mL) unsalted cooked brown basmati rice (2 Carbohydrate)

1 serving Cucumber Yogurt (page 86) or ¼ cup (60 mL) low-fat plain yogurt (1 Extra)

½ cup (125 mL) Masala Tea (page 93)

½ medium mango (1 Carbohydrate)

Tips

King mackerel (also called kingfish) is used a lot in South Asian cooking. It is very high in heart-healthy omega-3 fatty acids — even higher than salmon. King mackerel steaks tend to be large, so cut them into smaller pieces (or ask your fishmonger to do so).

Eat only small portions of king mackerel, and don't eat it very often, as it is high in mercury. Women of childbearing age, pregnant women and children should not eat king mackerel.

Some studies suggest that baking and broiling are better cooking methods than frying for retaining fish's omega-3 content.

Chaat masala is often added on top of the cooked fish as seasoning, but doing so will increase the salt content of the dish.

Chickpea flour, also called besan flour, chana dal flour or gram flour, is made from ground *chana dal* (see page 51). It is gluten-free and is a good source of fiber.

Nonstick pans require good care to protect the nonstick coating. Buy good-quality, heavy pans and never heat an empty pan. And always use plastic, rubber, silicon or wood utensils; metal tools or those with a sharp edge can cause some of the nonstick coating to scrape off into your food.

Homemade Low-Fat Paneer

Makes
12 oz (375 g)

Paneer is a fresh cheese used in many northern Indian dishes. Traditionally, it is made with buffalo or goat milk. It has a texture much like cottage cheese, but is tarter in flavor. It goes well with many South Asian curries. Although paneer is now readily available, store-bought versions are high in fat and can have additives. So why not make your own? It does take some time, but the low-fat, high-protein, no-additive results will be worth it!

Preparation time: **5 minutes**
Cooking time: **40 minutes**
Standing time: **20 minutes**

- **Large strainer, lined with an 18-inch (45 cm) square piece of cheesecloth**

16 cups	1% milk	4 L
½ cup	freshly squeezed lemon juice	125 mL

1. In a large pot, slowly bring milk to a boil over medium heat, stirring occasionally. Add lemon juice and boil, stirring, for about 5 minutes or until milk curdles and lumps begin to settle to the bottom of the pot. Remove from heat and let stand for 5 minutes.

2. Pour curdled milk into lined strainer to drain off liquid, then use cheesecloth to shape curds into a ball. Wrap cheesecloth around the ball and leave on the bottom of the strainer. Place a heavy pan on the cheesecloth to press out the liquid gently. Let stand for 20 minutes.

3. Cut cheese into 1-inch (2.5 cm) cubes.

Tips

Store-bought paneer is made with full-fat milk. To keep the fat content low, this recipe uses 1% milk rather than homogenized, or whole (3.25%), milk.

Fresh paneer will not work with ultra-high temperature (UHT) milk (milk that does not need refrigeration), as the milk proteins are denatured and cheese will not form.

Do not use raw (unpasteurized) milk to make paneer. The U.S. Food and Drug Administration and Centers for Disease Control advise against the use of raw milk, to prevent foodborne illnesses and outbreaks.

Store cubed paneer in small airtight containers in the refrigerator for up to 3 days or in the freezer for up to 1 month.

Nutrition info per 1 oz (30 g)	
Calories	58
Fat, total	2 g
Fat, saturated	2.0 g
Cholesterol	9 mg
Sodium	11 mg
Carbohydrate	1 g
Fiber	0 g
Protein	8 g
Food Choices	
1	Meat & Alternatives

Sri Lankan Eggplant Curry *(Baigan)*

Makes 4 servings

Sri Lankans love their spice! Sri Lankan curry powder is essential for Sri Lankan cooking, giving dishes a distinctive flavor and (usually) a lot of heat. If you find this dish too spicy, you can omit the hot pepper flakes.

Make It a Meal

1 serving Sri Lankan Eggplant Curry

2 servings Bengali Fish Curry (page 82)

2/3 cup (150 mL) unsalted cooked brown basmati rice (2 Carbohydrate)

1 cup (250 mL) Masala Tea (page 93)

1/2 medium mango (1 Carbohydrate)

Nutrition info per serving

Calories	121
Fat, total	5 g
Fat, saturated	1.2 g
Cholesterol	0 mg
Sodium	309 mg
Carbohydrate	19 g
Fiber	6 g
Protein	3 g
Food Choices	
1	Fat
1	Extra

Preparation time: 15 minutes
Cooking time: 20 minutes

1 tbsp	vegetable oil	15 mL
1 1/2 cups	chopped onion	375 mL
3	cloves garlic, minced	3
1 tbsp	hot pepper flakes	15 mL
2 tsp	Sri Lankan curry powder (see tip, below)	10 mL
1/2 tsp	salt	2 mL
1/4 tsp	ground turmeric	1 mL
1 1/4 cups	water	300 mL
1/3 cup	light coconut milk	75 mL
4 tsp	Tamarind Purée (page 91)	20 mL
6 cups	chopped eggplant (1-inch/2.5 cm cubes)	1.5 L
3 tbsp	chopped fresh curry leaves	45 mL

1. In a large pot, heat oil over medium heat. Add onion and garlic; cook, stirring, for 1 minute. Add hot pepper flakes and cook, stirring, for 2 minutes. Stir in curry powder, salt, turmeric and water; cook for 1 minute. Stir in coconut milk and tamarind purée; cook for 1 minute.

2. Stir in eggplant and curry leaves; reduce heat to low, cover and simmer for about 12 minutes or until eggplant is tender. Check occasionally and, if mixture is too dry, add water, 1 tbsp (15 mL) at a time.

Tips

Sri Lankan curry powder is easy to find in South Asian grocery stores, including brands with no added salt. Ask a store clerk to point you in the right direction if you are unsure.

Although coconut milk is a good source of various vitamins, minerals and antioxidants, it is high in saturated fat and should be consumed in moderation. This recipe calls for less coconut milk than traditional versions, and uses light coconut milk.

If you don't have time to make your own tamarind purée, ready-to-use purées can be found in South Asian, Asian or Caribbean grocery stores. Read labels and buy a brand with no salt added.

Sri Lankan Bitter Melon Curry
(Karawila)

This simple but fiery Sri Lankan dish features bitter melon, which is popularly believed to cure many ailments, including diabetes. Research is ongoing to see whether bitter melon really does help lower blood glucose levels; in the meantime, it's worth adding this fruit to your diet for its distinctive flavor alone!

Preparation time: 15 minutes
Cooking time: 25 minutes

2 tsp	vegetable oil	10 mL
½ cup	chopped onion	125 mL
¼ cup	chopped fresh curry leaves	60 mL
½ cup	chopped tomato	125 mL
4 tsp	hot pepper flakes	20 mL
½ tsp	salt	2 mL
½ tsp	ground turmeric	2 mL
2	small green chile peppers, chopped	2
½	large bitter melon, seeded and cut into ¼-inch (0.5 cm) pieces	½
1½ cups	water	375 mL
2 tbsp	light coconut milk	30 mL

1. In a skillet, heat oil over medium heat. Add onion and curry leaves; cook, stirring, for 1 minute. Add tomato and cook, stirring, for 3 minutes. Add hot pepper flakes, salt and turmeric; cook, stirring, for 2 minutes.

2. Stir in chiles, bitter melon and water. Increase heat to high and cook for 15 minutes or until bitter melon is soft. Stir in coconut milk and remove from heat.

Tips

To tame the heat of this dish a bit, omit the hot pepper flakes or remove the seeds from the green chiles.

To reduce its bitter flavor, rub salt into the sliced melon, then soak it in water for 30 minutes or overnight. Squeeze out the liquid, then rinse well and drain before use.

Curry leaves and coconut milk are common ingredients in the south of India and in Sri Lanka, as curry trees are native to those regions. In northern Indian and Pakistani cooking, these ingredients are less commonly used.

I have made this dish healthier by reducing the amount of coconut milk and using light.

Nutrition info per serving	
Calories	74
Fat, total	4 g
Fat, saturated	0.7 g
Cholesterol	0 mg
Sodium	367 mg
Carbohydrate	10 g
Fiber	3 g
Protein	2 g
Food Choices	
½	Fat
1	Extra

Make It a Meal

1 serving Sri Lankan Bitter Melon Curry

1 serving Goan Fish Curry (page 80)

Two 6-inch (15 cm) plain whole wheat rotis (2 Carbohydrate)

1 serving Cucumber Yogurt (page 86) or ¼ cup (60 mL) low-fat plain yogurt (1 Extra)

1 cup (250 mL) Masala Tea (page 93)

½ medium mango (1 Carbohydrate)

Bitter Melon

Grown in tropical and subtropical climates, bitter melon (*Momordica charantia*), also known as bitter gourd, *karawila* or *karela*, is a fruit, although it's prepared and eaten like a vegetable. It is used all over Asia in curries, stir-fries and soups. It comes in different varieties, with different textures, size and shapes, so the bitter melon you see in a South Asian market may look different from the bitter gourd you see in a Chinese grocery store.

There is evidence in animal studies that bitter melon could perhaps be used for management of type 2 diabetes, though currently there is no conclusive evidence that bitter melon lowers blood glucose in people with diabetes. More human studies need to be done, but in the meantime, by all means enjoy bitter melon as part of a healthy diet.

Okra and Tomato Curry *(Bhindi)*

Makes 7 servings

Okra is a popular vegetable in South Asian cooking, and is included in many dishes, with and without meat. I chose one of my favorites, from when I was growing up. If you have never tried okra before, this recipe will make you love it!

Nutrition Tip

Okra is a good source of soluble fiber, which has been shown to lower low-density lipoprotein (LDL) blood cholesterol and blood glucose levels.

Nutrition info per serving

Calories	93
Fat, total	3 g
Fat, saturated	0.0 g
Cholesterol	0 mg
Sodium	403 mg
Carbohydrate	17 g
Fiber	6 g
Protein	4 g
Food Choices	
½	Fat

Preparation time: 20 minutes
Cooking time: 25 minutes

1 tbsp	vegetable oil	15 mL
2	medium onions, thinly sliced lengthwise	2
2	medium tomatoes, peeled (see tip, below) and chopped	2
1 tsp	hot pepper flakes	5 mL
1 tsp	salt	5 mL
½ tsp	ground turmeric	2 mL
2 lbs	okra, trimmed and sliced	1 kg
1 cup	water (approx.), divided	250 mL
¼ cup	freshly squeezed lemon juice	60 mL
1 cup	chopped fresh cilantro	250 mL

1. In a large skillet, heat oil over medium heat. Add onions and cook, stirring, for 2 minutes. Add tomatoes and cook, stirring, for about 2 minutes or until onions are translucent. Add hot pepper flakes, salt and turmeric; cook, stirring, for 2 minutes.

2. Add okra and stir well, adding 2 tbsp (30 mL) water if ingredients are sticking to pan. Add lemon juice and cook, stirring, for 2 minutes, adding another 2 tbsp (30 mL) water if ingredients are sticking.

3. Reserve 2 tbsp (30 mL) cilantro. Add the remaining cilantro to the pan, along with the remaining water; cover and cook for about 15 minutes or until okra is tender.

4. Serve garnished with the reserved cilantro.

Tips

When cooking with a small amount of oil, be sure to heat it well before adding the other ingredients; otherwise, they may simply absorb the oil, which can cause sticking and burning.

When fresh okra is not available, you can use frozen sliced okra in this recipe. You won't need to add the remaining water in step 3, because frozen okra is blanched before freezing.

To peel tomatoes, blanch them in a pot of boiling water for 1 minute, then, using a slotted spoon, immediately transfer them to a bowl of ice water. When the tomatoes are cool enough to handle, cut out the core with a sharp knife and peel off the skin.

Zucchini Curry *(Turaii)*

This spicy Pakistani-style vegetable dish is great served with any flatbread, especially roti (page 32), and raita (page 86 or 87). If you want to reduce the heat, you can omit the hot pepper flakes. The servings are large, to encourage you to eat more vegetable curries and less meat.

Make It a Meal

1 serving Zucchini Curry

1 serving Red Lentil Curry (page 52)

$2/3$ cup (150 mL) unsalted cooked brown basmati rice (2 Carbohydrate)

1 serving Cucumber Yogurt (page 86) or $1/4$ cup (60 mL) low-fat plain yogurt (1 Extra)

1 small papaya (1 Carbohydrate)

Nutrition info per serving

Calories	93
Fat, total	2 g
Fat, saturated	0.3 g
Cholesterol	0 mg
Sodium	258 mg
Carbohydrate	18 g
Fiber	4 g
Protein	2 g
Food Choices	
1	Extra

Preparation time: 15 minutes
Cooking time: 30 minutes

$1/2$ tsp	vegetable oil	2 mL
$1 1/4$ cups	thinly sliced onion (sliced lengthwise)	300 mL
1	small tomato, chopped	1
$1/2$ tsp	hot pepper flakes	2 mL
$1/2$ tsp	ground turmeric	2 mL
6 tbsp	water	90 mL
1 lb	zucchini (unpeeled), cut into $1/2$-inch (1 cm) wide strips	500 g
1	small green chile pepper, seeded and minced	1
$1/2$ tsp	carom seeds	2 mL
2 tsp	freshly squeezed lemon juice	10 mL
$1/2$ tsp	salt	2 mL

1. In a medium skillet, heat oil over medium heat. Add onion and cook, stirring, for about 5 minutes or until golden. Add tomato, hot pepper flakes and turmeric; cook, stirring, for about 2 minutes or until spices are fragrant.

2. Stir in water, increase heat to high and bring to a boil. Stir in zucchini, chile and carom seeds; reduce heat to low, cover and simmer for about 20 minutes or until water has evaporated and mixture is thickened. Remove from heat and stir in lemon juice and salt.

Tips

When cooking with a small amount of oil, be sure to heat it well before adding the other ingredients; otherwise, they may simply absorb the oil, which can cause sticking and burning.

The key to curries is to thoroughly cook the onions and spices. This helps to remove the raw taste and intensifies the flavors. Although very little oil is used in this recipe, be sure to cook the onion until golden; reduce the heat as necessary to soften and cook the onions to golden without letting them burn.

Bengali Yellow Lentil Curry
(Cholar Dal)

Makes 6 servings

This festive Bengali curry is made for celebrations, such as birthdays and weddings. It is meant to be sweet, savory and aromatic, with a crunch, so raisins, an array of spices, coconut and sometime nuts are added. It is usually served with a deep-fried bread such as puri or luchi, but I have suggested a healthier meal for you to enjoy. So go ahead — enjoy cholar dal any time!

Soaking time: **30 minutes**
Preparation time: **15 minutes**
Cooking time: **1 hour and 40 minutes**

2 cups	dried split Bengal gram (*chana dal*), rinsed	500 mL
	Water	
1 tsp	ground turmeric	5 mL
1½ tbsp	vegetable oil	22 mL
5	whole cloves	5
4	green cardamom pods	4
3	bay leaves	3
2	1-inch (2.5 cm) cinnamon sticks	2
2	small green chile peppers, slit	2
2	dried red chile peppers	2
⅓ cup	unsweetened desiccated or flaked coconut	75 mL
3 tbsp	raisins	45 mL
1 tbsp	ground coriander	15 mL
2 tsp	granulated sugar	10 mL
1 tsp	cumin seeds	5 mL
1 tsp	ground dried red chile peppers (*lal mirch*)	5 mL
1 tsp	salt	5 mL

1. Place Bengal gram in a bowl with enough water to cover; let soak for 30 minutes.

2. Drain soaking water from Bengal gram and transfer Bengal gram to a pot. Stir in 4 cups (1 L) fresh water and turmeric; bring to a boil over high heat, cook over medium heat for 30 minutes. Add 2 cups (500 mL) water and cook for 45 minutes.

3. In a small saucepan, heat oil over medium-high heat. Add cloves, cardamom, bay leaves, cinnamon, green chiles, red chiles, coconut, raisins, coriander, sugar, cumin seeds, ground chile peppers and salt; cook, stirring, for 3 minutes.

Nutrition info per serving

Calories	325
Fat, total	8 g
Fat, saturated	2.9 g
Cholesterol	0 mg
Sodium	409 mg
Carbohydrate	47 g
Fiber	12 g
Protein	18 g

Food Choices

2	Carbohydrate
2½	Meat & Alternatives
1	Fat

Make It a Meal

1 serving Bengali Yellow
Lentil Curry

1 serving Zucchini Curry
(page 49)

1 Whole Wheat and
Besan Flatbread
(page 32)

1 serving Tomato Mint
Salad (page 31)

1 small papaya
(1 Carbohydrate)

4. Add spice mixture to the cooked Bengal gram and stir in 2 cups (500 mL) water; bring to a boil over high heat. Reduce heat and simmer for 10 minutes. Discard cardamom, bay leaves and cinnamon.

Tips

Grated fresh or thawed frozen shredded coconut can also be used, and will add even more flavor to this recipe.

The traditional version of this recipe is quite high in fat and saturated fat. To make it suitable for a diabetes diet, I cut the amount of coconut in half, substituted vegetable oil for the ghee, and omitted the *tarka* (see tip, page 89) of ghee, bay leaves and garam masala that is typically added on top.

Chana Dal

In South Asian cuisine, the word *dal (or dhal)* refers to dried beans, peas and lentils. Dal may or may not contain the outer husk and can be split or whole. Whole *chana dal*, with the husks on, are also known as black chickpeas, black gram or *kala chana*. When they are split and husked, they are known as Bengal gram or yellow gram and are used to make a variety of dishes, from soups to desserts. *Chana dal* takes longer than other *dals* to cook. *Chana dal* is also used to make chickpea (besan) flour.

Red Lentil Curry *(Masoor Dal)*

There are many ways to prepare *masoor dal*, but this tasty one-pot recipe is my mom, Nargis's, favorite. She uses fresh tomatoes, but I use canned to save time. This dish is famous for its oily topping of fried onions. I kept the flavor of cooked onions with a limited amount of oil.

Tips

Many South Asian dishes call for a *tarka*, where onions, garlic and/or spices are cooked in oil or ghee. A *tarka* can be used as a topping or garnish, or added as you begin to cook a dish, to enhance the flavors. *Tarkas* are delicious, but they do add quite a bit of fat to a recipe.

This recipe is quite low in fat, but you can reduce it further by omitting the *tarka*.

Nutrition info per serving

Calories	213
Fat, total	2 g
Fat, saturated	0.2 g
Cholesterol	0 mg
Sodium	304 mg
Carbohydrate	36 g
Fiber	12 g
Protein	14 g

Food Choices

1	Carbohydrate
2	Meat & Alternatives
½	Fat

Preparation time: **30 minutes**
Cooking time: **1 hour and 15 minutes**

- **Food processor or blender**

2	cloves garlic, minced	2
1 cup	dried split red lentils (*masoor dal*), rinsed	250 mL
½ cup	finely chopped onion	125 mL
1 cup	no-salt-added canned diced tomatoes, drained	250 mL
1 tsp	salt	5 mL
½ tsp	ground turmeric	2 mL
¼ tsp	cayenne pepper	1 mL
3 cups	water	750 mL
2 tsp	freshly squeezed lemon juice	10 mL
2 tbsp	finely chopped fresh cilantro (optional)	30 mL

Tarka

1 ½ tsp	vegetable oil	7 mL
¼ cup	thinly sliced onion (sliced lengthwise)	60 mL

1. In a large saucepan, combine garlic, lentils, onion, tomatoes, salt, turmeric, cayenne and water. Bring to a boil over high heat. Reduce heat to medium-low, cover, leaving lid ajar, and cook, stirring occasionally, for 1 hour or until the mixture is thickened.

2. Transfer lentil mixture to food processor and purée until smooth (see tip, page 27). Pour into a serving dish and stir in lemon juice. Set aside.

3. *Tarka:* In a small skillet, heat oil over medium heat. Add onion and cook, stirring, until golden.

4. Garnish lentils with cilantro, onion and any remaining oil.

Masoor Dal

In South Asian cuisine, the word *dal (or dhal)* refers to dried beans, peas and lentils. Dal may or may not contain the outer husk and can be split or whole. *Masoor dal* is split red lentils (also called pink or orange lentils) with the husks removed. When whole, with the husks intact, they are black and are known as *sabut masoor dal*. When cooked, *masoor dal* turn yellow. They cook quickly and do not require soaking. Lentils are a source of protein, iron and fiber, do not increase blood glucose levels and help lower low-density lipoprotein (LDL) blood cholesterol.

Kidney Bean Curry *(Rajma)*

Makes 6 servings

This easy, delicious, saucy and hearty recipe originated in northern India and is a great alternative to meat-based dishes. Rajma, as it is known in Hindi, is very popular throughout India.

Make It a Meal

1 serving Kidney Bean Curry

1 serving Vegetable and Cheese Curry (page 56)

1 serving Chickpea Rice (page 62)

1 serving Cucumber Yogurt (page 86) or ¼ cup (60 mL) low-fat plain yogurt (1 Extra)

1 cup (250 mL) Masala Tea (page 93)

½ medium mango (1 Carbohydrate)

Nutrition info per serving

Calories	155
Fat, total	6 g
Fat, saturated	0.0 g
Cholesterol	0 mg
Sodium	208 mg
Carbohydrate	19 g
Fiber	7 g
Protein	6 g

Food Choices

½	Carbohydrate
½	Meat & Alternatives
1	Fat

Preparation time: 20 minutes
Cooking time: 55 minutes

2 tbsp	vegetable oil	30 mL
2	black cardamom pods	2
2	bay leaves	2
1	2-inch (5 cm) cinnamon stick	1
½ tsp	cumin seeds	2 mL
1½ cups	very finely chopped onion	375 mL
2 tsp	minced gingerroot	10 mL
2 tsp	minced garlic	10 mL
½ tsp	ground coriander	2 mL
½ tsp	ground turmeric	2 mL
½ tsp	ground dried red chile peppers (*lal mirch*)	2 mL
¾ cup	no-salt-added canned diced tomatoes, with juice	175 mL
1	can (19 oz/540 mL) red kidney beans, drained and rinsed	1
½ tsp	salt	2 mL
½ cup	water	125 mL

1. In a medium skillet, heat oil over medium heat. Add cardamom, bay leaves, cinnamon and cumin seeds; cook, stirring, for about 1 minute or until fragrant. Add onion and cook, stirring, for about 20 minutes or until onion is golden. Add ginger and garlic; cook, stirring for 1 minute. Add coriander, turmeric and ground chile peppers; cook, stirring, for 1 minute or until fragrant.

2. Stir in tomatoes and cook, stirring and breaking tomatoes up with a spoon, for 10 minutes. Stir in beans, salt and water; bring to a boil over high heat. Reduce heat to medium-low, cover and simmer for 15 minutes or until sauce is thickened. Discard cardamom, bay leaves and cinnamon.

Tips

If you can only find 14- or 15-oz (398 or 425 mL) cans of beans, buy two. You'll need about 2 cups (500 mL) rinsed drained beans for this recipe.

If you prefer, you can also purée the onion and the tomatoes, which will cut down on your cooking time and give you a smoother sauce.

Store-bought ready-to-eat rajma masalas can save time, but they can also have a lot of sodium, so avoid eating them on a regular basis.

Spinach and Tofu Curry *(Palak Tofu)*

Makes 6 servings

One of the most popular and delicious vegetarian dishes in India, this recipe will make you love eating green leafy vegetables! Traditionally, it is made with paneer, a fresh cheese common in Indian cuisine, and is called palak paneer. However, to reduce the saturated fat in this dish while keeping the same texture, I have replaced the paneer with light tofu. Serve with rice or roti and some raita (page 86 or 87) on the side, for a yummy combination.

Preparation time: **30 minutes**
Cooking time: **25 minutes**

- **Food processor**

3	medium tomatoes	3
4 cups	blanched finely chopped spinach leaves (see tip, opposite)	1 L
1 tbsp	vegetable oil	15 mL
2 cups	finely chopped onion	500 mL
1/4 cup	minced garlic	60 mL
2 tbsp	minced gingerroot	30 mL
2 tbsp	ground coriander	30 mL
2 tsp	ground cumin	10 mL
2 tsp	dried fenugreek leaves (*kasuri methi*)	10 mL
1 tsp	garam masala	5 mL
4	small green chile peppers, chopped (with seeds)	4
1/2 tsp	salt	2 mL
12 oz	firm light tofu, cut into 1/4-inch (1 cm) cubes	375 g

1. In food processor, purée tomatoes; set aside. Purée spinach until smooth. Set aside separately.

2. In a large skillet, heat oil over medium heat. Add onion, reduce heat to medium-low and cook, stirring, for about 10 minutes or until golden.

3. Add garlic and ginger; cook, stirring, for 1 minute. Add coriander, cumin, fenugreek and garam masala; cook, stirring, for 1 minute.

4. Add chiles, increase heat to medium and cook, stirring, for 1 minute. Add tomato purée and cook, stirring, for 2 minutes or until liquid has evaporated.

5. Add puréed spinach and salt; cook, stirring, for 5 minutes. Add tofu and cook, stirring, for 1 minute.

Nutrition info per serving

Calories	160
Fat, total	5 g
Fat, saturated	0.5 g
Cholesterol	0 mg
Sodium	400 mg
Carbohydrate	16 g
Fiber	5 g
Protein	15 g

Food Choices

1	Meat & Alternatives
1/2	Fat
1	Extra

Tips

For the spinach, you can use 3 lbs (1.5 kg) baby spinach or
4 large bunches of regular spinach. To blanch it, place it in a
large pot, add a pinch of salt and cover with cold water. Bring
to a boil, then quickly transfer spinach to a strainer.

When cooking with a small amount of oil, be sure to heat it
well before adding the other ingredients; otherwise, they may
simply absorb the oil, which can cause sticking and burning.

Ready-to-eat palak paneer is now readily available in grocery
stores, but can have a lot of fat and sodium and very little
protein. Why bother, when it's so easy to make fresh?

Nutrition Tip

Spinach is an excellent source of vitamins A, C and K,
folate, iron and magnesium, and is high in calcium and
fiber. Include dark green vegetables such as spinach in
your diet on a daily basis.

Vegetable and Cheese Curry
(Paneer Bhurji)

This spicy, colorful vegetarian dish from northern India is now a favorite across India and around the world. *Paneer bhurji* literally means "scrambled paneer," and the dish is a mixture of just about everything. It should be made just before serving or it gets soggy. Serve with flatbread, such as whole wheat roti (page 32).

Preparation time: **20 minutes**
Cooking time: **20 minutes**

1½ tsp	cumin seeds	7 mL
1½ tsp	hot pepper flakes	7 mL
1 tbsp	vegetable oil	15 mL
1½ cups	finely chopped green cabbage	375 mL
1 cup	finely chopped onion	250 mL
3	cloves garlic, minced	3
1 tbsp	minced gingerroot	15 mL
1 tbsp	tomato paste	15 mL
2 tbsp	water (optional)	30 mL
½ tsp	ground fenugreek	2 mL
½ tsp	ground turmeric	2 mL
¾ cup	no-salt-added canned diced tomatoes, with juice	175 mL
2 tbsp	nonfat plain yogurt	30 mL
7 cups	trimmed spinach (about 7 oz/210 g)	1.75 L
¼ cup	frozen green peas	60 mL
1 tsp	garam masala	5 mL
12 oz	low-sodium dry-pressed 0.5% cottage cheese, crumbled	375 g
½ cup	rinsed drained canned navy beans	125 mL
¼ cup	chopped fresh cilantro	60 mL
½ tsp	salt	2 mL

1. Heat a large skillet over medium heat. Toast cumin seeds and hot pepper flakes for about 1 minute or until fragrant. Add oil, swirling to coat. Add cabbage and onion; cook, stirring, for about 3 minutes or until softened. Add garlic, ginger and tomato paste; cook, stirring, for about 2 minutes or until garlic and ginger are golden.

2. Add water if needed to scrape up any brown bits from bottom of pan. Add fenugreek and turmeric; cook, stirring, for 1 minute. Stir in tomatoes and yogurt, scraping up any browned bits from bottom of pan. Add spinach and stir until wilted.

3. Stir in peas and garam masala; reduce heat to low, cover and simmer for about 5 minutes or until liquid has evaporated but mixture is not overly dry. Stir in cheese, beans, cilantro and salt; simmer until heated through. Serve immediately.

Nutrition info per serving

Calories	128
Fat, total	3 g
Fat, saturated	1.0 g
Cholesterol	7 mg
Sodium	254 mg
Carbohydrate	13 g
Fiber	4 g
Protein	13 g

Food Choices

1	Meat & Alternatives
1	Extra

Make It a Meal

1 serving Kidney Bean Curry (page 53)

1 serving Vegetable and Cheese Curry

1 serving Chickpea Rice (page 62)

1 serving Cucumber Yogurt (page 86) or ¼ cup (60 mL) low-fat plain yogurt (1 Extra)

1 serving Cilantro Mint Chutney (page 88)

1 medium mango (2 Carbohydrate)

Tips

You can substitute Homemade Low-Fat Paneer (page 44) or low-fat tofu for the cottage cheese.

When cooking with a small amount of oil, be sure to heat it well before adding the other ingredients; otherwise, they may simply absorb the oil, which can cause sticking and burning.

The traditional version of this recipe uses potatoes and a lot of green peas — starchy vegetables that can raise blood glucose levels. To reduce the amount of carbohydrate per serving, I've omitted the potatoes and reduced the amount of peas in favor of cabbage and spinach.

Homemade Garam Masala

6	green cardamom pods	6
4	black cardamom pods	4
4	2-inch (5 cm) cinnamon sticks	4
1	large bay leaf	1
2 tbsp	cumin seeds	30 mL
2 tsp	coriander seeds	10 mL
2 tsp	whole black peppercorns	10 mL
1 tsp	whole cloves	5 mL

In a spice grinder, combine green and black cardamom pods, cinnamon, bay leaf, cumin seeds, coriander seeds, peppercorns and cloves; grind into a fine powder. Store in an airtight jar in a cool, dark, dry place. (**Makes about 6 tbsp/90 mL.**)

Pakistani Potatoes and Cauliflower (Aloo Gobi)

Makes 4 servings

Aloo gobi is popular all over South Asia and around the world — it was even featured in a Hollywood movie! This Pakistani-style version is easy to make. I've cut back on the potato to lower the carbohydrate content so you can enjoy it with whole wheat roti (page 32).

Preparation time: 30 minutes
Cooking time: 50 minutes

2 tsp	vegetable oil	10 mL
1	large onion, cut into thin slices	1
2	plum (Roma) tomatoes, peeled (see tip, page 48) and chopped	2
2	green chile peppers, seeded and chopped	2
1 1/2 tsp	hot pepper flakes	7 mL
1 tsp	nigella seeds	5 mL
1/2 tsp	salt	2 mL
1/4 tsp	ground turmeric	1 mL
1 cup	chopped peeled red-skinned potato	250 mL
1/4 cup	water, divided (optional)	60 mL
6 cups	cauliflower florets	1.5 L
1 tsp	freshly squeezed lemon juice	5 mL
1	2-inch (5 cm) piece gingerroot, thinly sliced	1
2 tbsp	chopped fresh cilantro	30 mL

1. In a large skillet, heat oil over medium heat. Add onions and cook, stirring, for about 5 minutes or until translucent. Add tomatoes, green chiles, hot pepper flakes, nigella seeds, salt and turmeric; cook, stirring, for 5 minutes.

2. Add potato and cook, stirring, for 3 to 4 minutes, adding 2 tbsp (30 mL) water if mixture is sticking to pan. Reduce heat to low, cover and cook for about 10 minutes or until potatoes are starting to get tender.

3. Stir in cauliflower, cover and increase heat to medium. Cook, stirring occasionally and adding another 2 tbsp (30 mL) water if mixture is sticking, for 20 minutes or until potato and cauliflower are tender. Remove from heat and stir in lemon juice.

4. Serve garnished with ginger and cilantro.

Tips

Be precise when measuring the potato for this recipe, as even a little extra will raise the carbohydrate content.

When cooking with a small amount of oil, be sure to heat it well before adding the other ingredients; otherwise, they may simply absorb the oil, which can cause sticking and burning.

Nutrition info per serving

Calories	120
Fat, total	3 g
Fat, saturated	0.3 g
Cholesterol	0 mg
Sodium	346 mg
Carbohydrate	22 g
Fiber	5 g
Protein	5 g

Food Choices

1/2	Carbohydrate
1/2	Fat

Sri Lankan Red Rice Congee

Makes 7 servings

Congee is a type of porridge that is common in Asian cuisines. In this Sri Lankan recipe, it is made with red rice, which has a red husk and a nutty flavor. Red rice is a good source of fiber because it is a whole grain.

Variation

If you don't have a pressure cooker, place mung beans in a large saucepan and add 5 cups (1.25 L) water. Bring to a boil over high heat. Reduce heat to medium and boil gently for 1 hour. Proceed with step 2.

Preparation time: 10 minutes
Cooking time: 55 minutes

- **Pressure cooker (optional; see variation, at left)**

½ cup	dried husked mung beans (*moong dal*), rinsed (see page 39)	125 mL
9 cups	water, divided	2.25 L
1 cup	red rice, rinsed	250 mL
1 cup	skim milk	250 mL
1 tsp	salt	5 mL
3 cups	drumstick leaves	750 mL

1. In pressure cooker, combine beans and 5 cups (1.25 L) water. Cover and cook on high for 20 minutes. Open the lid, being cautious of the steam.

2. Stir in rice and the remaining water; bring to a boil over high heat. Reduce heat to medium, cover with a lid (not the pressure cooker lid, but a lid that fits on top of the pot) and simmer for 15 minutes.

3. Stir in milk and salt; simmer, uncovered, for 5 minutes or until rice is tender. Stir in drumstick leaves and simmer for 1 minute.

Tips

If fresh drumstick leaves are not available, look for frozen drumstick leaves at South Asian grocery stores. Thaw and drain before using. If you cannot find drumstick leaves at all, substitute 1 cup (250 mL) baby spinach leaves, stems removed.

To reduce the saturated fat in this dish, I replaced the traditional coconut milk with skim milk.

Drumstick Pods and Leaves

The drumstick tree (*Moringa oleifera*) grows in tropical and subtropical climates, such as India, and its pods and leaves are common ingredients in South Asian cuisine. The long, slender pod contains a soft, edible pulp that is used to make dishes such as sambar. The leaves are used much like spinach and are high in magnesium, iron and calcium, an excellent source of vitamins A, C and K, and a source of fiber.

Nutrition info per serving

Calories	183
Fat, total	1 g
Fat, saturated	0.0 g
Cholesterol	1 mg
Sodium	347 mg
Carbohydrate	37 g
Fiber	2 g
Protein	7 g

Food Choices

2	Carbohydrate
½	Meat & Alternatives

Pakistani Spicy Vegetable Rice
(Tahari)

Makes 6 servings

Tahari (also known as *masala chawal*) is a style of rice that is popular in India and Pakistan. True tahari is made with layers of basmati rice, potatoes and vegetables. This is my mom's everyday version, which is easier to make. It's delicious with a side of raita (page 86 or 87). This dish is meant to have a lot of heat, but if you prefer, you can reduce the number of green chiles and/or remove the seeds.

Preparation time: 20 minutes
Cooking time: 35 minutes

1 ½ cups	white basmati rice, rinsed	375 mL
	Water	
2 tbsp	vegetable oil	30 mL
⅓ cup	sliced onion	75 mL
½ cup	diced peeled tomato (see tip, opposite)	125 mL
2	3-inch (7.5 cm) cinnamon sticks	2
2	black cardamom pods, cracked	2
1 tbsp	ground coriander	15 mL
1 ¼ tsp	salt	6 mL
1 tsp	cumin seeds	5 mL
1 tsp	cayenne pepper	5 mL
½ tsp	whole cloves	2 mL
½ tsp	whole black peppercorns	2 mL
½ tsp	ground turmeric	2 mL
2	small green chile peppers, minced	2
2 tbsp	thinly sliced gingerroot	30 mL
2 cups	frozen mixed vegetables (carrots, peas, beans)	500 mL

1. Place rice in a small bowl with enough water to cover; let soak while following steps 2 and 3.

2. In a medium skillet, heat oil over medium-high heat. Add onion and cook, stirring, for about 3 minutes or until golden.

3. Add tomato, cinnamon, cardamom, coriander, salt, cumin seeds, cayenne, cloves, peppercorns and turmeric; reduce heat to medium and cook, stirring, for about 5 minutes or until tomato liquid has evaporated. Add chiles and ginger; cook, stirring and adding 2 tbsp (30 mL) water if mixture is sticking, for 8 to 10 minutes or until tomato has turned into a paste. Stir in frozen vegetables.

Nutrition info per serving

Calories	250
Fat, total	7 g
Fat, saturated	0.7 g
Cholesterol	0 mg
Sodium	*523 mg
Carbohydrate	45 g
Fiber	5 g
Protein	6 g

* This recipe is high in sodium. Balance it out by making lower-sodium choices for the rest of your meal and throughout the day.

Food Choices

2	Carbohydrate
1	Fat

Make It a Meal

1 serving Easy Pakistani Veal Stew (page 66)

1 serving Pakistani Spicy Vegetable Rice

1 serving Cucumber Yogurt (page 86) or ¼ cup (60 mL) low-fat plain yogurt (1 Extra)

1 serving Tomato Mint Salad (page 31)

¾ cup (175 mL) Mango Yogurt Smoothie (page 92)

1 medium guava (½ Carbohydrate)

4. Drain and rinse rice, then add to pan along with 3¼ cups (800 mL) fresh water. The water should cover the rice mixture by ½ inch (1 cm); use more or less water as needed. Stir, increase heat to high and bring to a boil. Boil until the water has evaporated enough that the top of the rice is visible. Reduce heat to low, cover and simmer for 10 to 12 minutes or until rice is tender.

Tips

To peel tomatoes, blanch them in a pot of boiling water for 1 minute, then, using a slotted spoon, immediately transfer them to a bowl of ice water. When the tomatoes are cool enough to handle, cut out the core with a sharp knife and peel off the skin.

I used more vegetables than the traditional version, to increase the fiber, and omitted the potatoes to reduce the carbohydrate content.

This dish is traditionally eaten with a side of chutney or pickled vegetables or fruit (*achar*), which tend to have a lot of added salt. This dish is already relatively high in sodium, so use these condiments sparingly. Or make your own chutney at home (pages 88–90).

Nutrition Tip

Currently there is no conclusive evidence that cinnamon helps to lower blood glucose levels. Studies are ongoing, but in the meantime, its great taste alone is enough reason to add cinnamon to your cooking.

Chickpea Rice *(Chana Chawal)*

Makes 8 servings

I grew up on this rice and still make it all the time. This version uses brown basmati rice and has more chickpeas than the traditional recipe, for added nutrition, but the flavor and aroma are just as I remember from my childhood. This dish goes with everything: raita (page 86 or 87), chutney (pages 88–90), Tomato Mint Salad (page 31) or any vegetable curry.

Preparation time: **25 minutes**
Cooking time: **1 hour**

1 cup	brown basmati rice, rinsed	250 mL
	Water	
20	whole black peppercorns	20
10	whole cloves	10
2	black cardamom pods, cracked	2
2	1-inch (2.5 cm) cinnamon sticks	2
1 ½ tsp	cumin seeds	7 mL
1 tbsp	vegetable oil	15 mL
½ cup	minced onion	125 mL
2 tbsp	minced garlic	30 mL
2 tbsp	minced gingerroot	30 mL
1 tbsp	water	15 mL
1	can (19 oz/540 mL) chickpeas, drained and rinsed	1
½ tsp	salt	2 mL

1. Place rice in a small bowl with enough water to cover; let soak for 20 minutes.

2. Meanwhile, heat a medium saucepan over medium heat. Toast peppercorns, cloves, cardamom, cinnamon and cumin seeds for about 1 minute or until fragrant. Add oil and swirl to coat. Add onion and cook, stirring, for about 5 minutes or until golden brown. Add garlic, ginger and 1 tbsp (15 mL) water; cook, stirring, for 3 minutes.

3. Drain and rinse rice, then add to pan along with chickpeas and 2 cups (500 mL) water. The water should be level with the rice mixture; use more or less water as needed. Stir, increase heat to high and bring to a boil. Stir in salt, reduce heat to low, cover and simmer for 40 minutes or until water is absorbed and rice is tender. Remove from heat and fluff rice with a fork. Cover and let stand for 5 minutes before serving.

Nutrition info per serving

Calories	158
Fat, total	4 g
Fat, saturated	0.4 g
Cholesterol	0 mg
Sodium	266 mg
Carbohydrate	27 g
Fiber	4 g
Protein	5 g

Food Choices

1½	Carbohydrate
½	Meat & Alternatives
½	Fat

Make It a Meal

1 serving Pakistani Lamb Stew (page 68)

1 serving Pakistani Potatoes and Cauliflower (page 58)

1 serving Chickpea Rice (page 62)

1 serving Mixed Vegetable Yogurt (page 87)

1 cup (250 mL) Masala Tea (page 93)

$\frac{1}{2}$ small papaya ($\frac{1}{2}$ Carbohydrate)

Tips

If you can only find 14- or 15-oz (398 or 425 mL) cans of chickpeas, buy two. You'll need about 2 cups (500 mL) rinsed drained chickpeas for this recipe.

Using spices and herbs means you won't need as much salt in a recipe.

Leftover rice can be stored in airtight containers in the refrigerator for up to 3 days or in the freezer for up to 3 months. Thaw frozen rice overnight in the refrigerator, drain off any excess liquid and microwave on High for 3 to 5 minutes or until hot and fluffy.

Nutrition Tip

Many research studies suggest that eating three or more servings of whole grains a day can help manage or prevent diabetes and heart disease, thanks to the phytochemicals and fiber in whole grains. (Phytochemicals, such as flavonoids and beta-glucans, are compounds found in foods that, while not considered nutrients, can still have health benefits.) Higher whole-grain intake has also been linked to lower weight and waist circumference. Whole grains include foods such as brown, black or red rice, whole-grain bread and pasta, buckwheat noodles, barley and millet. If you are accustomed to eating processed grains, try to replace them with whole grains as much as possible.

Savory South Indian Semolina Cakes *(Rava Idlis)*

Makes 24 idlis

An idli (or idly) is a healthy South Indian savory cake that is steamed in a specialty steamer. Idlis make a great snack, on their own or with chutney, but they are most commonly served for breakfast, paired with sambar (page 28), rasam (page 26), a vegetable curry or coconut chutney (page 89).

Preparation time: **20 minutes**
Cooking time: **20 minutes**

- **Idli steamer with 4 six-cup idli plates (see tips, opposite)**

2 cups	fine semolina (*rava* or *suji*)	500 mL
1 ½ cups	nonfat plain yogurt, well beaten	375 mL
¾ cup	water	175 mL
2	small green chile peppers, finely chopped (optional)	2
½	medium onion, finely chopped	½
½ cup	chopped fresh cilantro	125 mL
1 ½ tsp	minced gingerroot	7 mL
1 tsp	salt	5 mL
2 tsp	vegetable oil	10 mL
1 ½ tsp	antacid powder (Eno)	7 mL

1. In a bowl, combine semolina and yogurt. Stir in water. Stir in chiles (if using), onion, cilantro, ginger and salt.

2. Add 1 to 1½ cups (250 to 375 mL) water to the idli steamer and bring to a boil over high heat. Oil the idli cups.

3. Stir antacid powder into batter. It will rise instantly as you mix. Add 3 tbsp (45 mL) batter to each idli cup. Place the idli plates on the stand, and carefully place the stand in the steamer. Cover and steam over medium-high heat for about 15 minutes or until a tester inserted into an idli comes out clean.

Tips

An idli steamer includes a large, deep pot and circular plates stacked on a stand. Each plate has four to six cups to hold batter, and most idli steamers come with either three or four plates (so they make anywhere from 12 to 24 idli at a time). Look for them at South Asian markets or online.

If you have an idli steamer that makes fewer than 24 idli at a time, you'll need to steam the idli in two batches of 12. Divide the batter in half, and stir half of the antacid powder into each half of the batter just before adding it to the idli cups in each batch.

If you only have an idli stand and no steamer, you can use a large pot with a tight-fitting lid to steam the idlis.

Nutrition info per 2 idlis	
Calories	125
Fat, total	1 g
Fat, saturated	0.1 g
Cholesterol	1 mg
Sodium	370 mg
Carbohydrate	24
Fiber	1 g
Protein	5 g
Food Choices	
1½	Carbohydrate

Make It a Meal

3 Savory South Indian
  Semolina Cakes
  (page 64)

1 serving Spicy South
  Indian Soup (page 26)

1 serving Spinach and
  Tofu Curry (page 54)

1 serving Coconut
  Chutney (page 89)

2 medium guava
  (1 Carbohydrate)

Tips

The size of your steamer pot will determine how much water you should add. For a smaller steamer pot, add 1 cup (250 mL) water. For a larger one, add 1½ cups (375 mL) water.

Idli batter must be fermented before steaming. The antacid powder ferments the batter quickly, but if you prefer to omit it and use ¼ tsp (1 mL) of baking soda instead, the batter will need to ferment in a warm place for at least 8 hours or overnight.

Ready-to-eat rava idli mixes can be found in South Asian grocery stores, but they contain a lot of sodium and fat. It is worth the time to make your own rava idlis and enjoy them fresh.

Semolina

Semolina is a flour made from the endosperm of the durum wheat grain, a type of hard wheat that is high in protein. Semolina is off-white or yellow and has a coarse texture. It has a special place in Indian culture, where it is used for many things, such as religious ceremonies. It is also used across South Asia in many savory dishes and desserts. Semolina has no fat but is high in carbohydrates, so eat it sparingly.

Easy Pakistani Veal Stew
(Karahi Ghosht)

Makes 4 servings

In Pakistan, this is a special-occasion dish, popular at weddings and when dining out. It is traditionally cooked in a large cast-iron, wok-like pan called a *karahi*, and can be prepared with any meat or meat alternative. I am sharing an easy version, meant to be made at home. It is typically eaten with a flatbread, such as whole wheat roti (page 32), but it can also be eaten with rice.

Preparation time: **30 minutes**
Cooking time: **1½ hours**

1 lb	lean bone-in veal shoulder, cut into 1-inch (2.5 cm) cubes (see tips, opposite)	500 g
1½ cups	thinly sliced onions (sliced lengthwise)	375 mL
18	whole black peppercorns	18
12	whole cloves	12
2	black cardamom pods, cracked	2
2	plum (Roma) tomatoes, peeled (see tip, opposite) and chopped	2
2	5-inch (12.5 cm) cinnamon sticks	2
1 tsp	minced garlic	5 mL
1 tsp	minced gingerroot	5 mL
1 tsp	crushed coriander seeds	5 mL
1 tsp	cumin seeds	5 mL
¾ tsp	paprika	3 mL
½ tsp	hot pepper flakes	2 mL
½ tsp	salt	2 mL
⅛ tsp	ground turmeric	0.5 mL
1 cup	water	250 mL
2 tbsp	nonfat plain yogurt	30 mL
1	small green chile pepper, with stem	1
1 tbsp	chopped fresh cilantro	15 mL
1 tbsp	thinly sliced gingerroot	15 mL

1. In a medium pot, combine veal, onion, peppercorns, cloves, cardamom, tomatoes, cinnamon, garlic, minced ginger, coriander seeds, cumin seeds, paprika, hot pepper flakes, salt, turmeric and water. Bring to a boil over high heat (this will take about 7 minutes). Reduce heat to low, cover and simmer for 1 hour or until veal is tender.

2. Stir in yogurt and cook, uncovered, stirring occasionally, for 20 minutes or until stew is thickened and liquid is reduced. Stir in chile, cilantro and sliced ginger.

Nutrition info per serving	
Calories	132
Fat, total	2 g
Fat, saturated	0.7 g
Cholesterol	71 mg
Sodium	377 mg
Carbohydrate	9 g
Fiber	2 g
Protein	19 g
Food Choices	
2	Meat & Alternatives

Tips

For ease of preparation, ask your local butcher to cut the veal into 1-inch (2.5 cm) cubes for you if precut meat is not available. Ask for any visible fat to be trimmed as well.

If you cannot find veal shoulder, a lean simmering cut of beef can be substituted in this dish.

To peel tomatoes, blanch them in a pot of boiling water for 1 minute, then, using a slotted spoon, immediately transfer them to a bowl of ice water. When the tomatoes are cool enough to handle, cut out the core with a sharp knife and peel off the skin.

What makes karahi dishes distinct from other curry- or gravy-based dishes, such as kormas, is the spice blend, the richness of the gravy or sauce and the cooking vessel.

Nutrition Tip

Turmeric has a bioactive compound called curcumin, which has been shown, in animal and some human studies, to have anti-inflammatory and antioxidant properties. It has demonstrated potential in the future treatment of certain cancers, arthritis pain and Alzheimer's disease, and it may lower low-density lipoprotein (LDL) blood cholesterol and triglycerides. These findings are still preliminary, and more long-term human clinical trials are needed.

Pakistani Lamb Stew *(Mutton Korma)*

Makes 4 servings

This traditional recipe was passed down from my grandmother to my mom to me, and now to you. I have made some adjustments, such as cutting back on the oil, using a small amount of low-fat yogurt and choosing a lean cut of lamb. But the results are as tasty as ever! Serve with a flatbread, such as whole wheat roti (page 32).

Preparation time: **20 minutes**
Cooking time: **1 hour**

- **Small food processor**

Masala Paste

1	plum (Roma) tomato, peeled (see tip, opposite) and coarsely chopped	1
¼ cup	coarsely chopped onion	60 mL
1 tbsp	ground coriander	15 mL
1 tsp	puréed garlic (see tips, opposite)	5 mL
1 tsp	puréed gingerroot	5 mL
½ tsp	cayenne pepper	2 mL
½ tsp	salt	2 mL
½ tsp	paprika	2 mL
¼ tsp	ground turmeric	1 mL
2 tbsp	1% plain yogurt	30 mL
2 tbsp	water	30 mL

Stew

2 tsp	vegetable oil	10 mL
1 cup	finely chopped onion	250 mL
12	whole black peppercorns	12
8	whole cloves	8
1 lb	lean bone-in lamb shoulder, trimmed and cut into 2-inch (5 cm) cubes (see tip, below)	500 g
2½ cups	water, divided (approx.)	625 mL
2 tbsp	chopped fresh cilantro	30 mL

1. *Masala:* In food processor, combine tomato, onion, coriander, garlic, ginger, cayenne, salt, paprika, turmeric, yogurt and water; process until blended. Set aside.

2. *Stew:* In a large saucepan, heat oil over medium heat. Add onion, peppercorns and cloves; cook, stirring, for about 6 minutes or until onions are light golden.

3. Add lamb and stir well. Stir in masala and cook, stirring, for 2 minutes. Reduce heat to medium-low, cover and simmer, stirring occasionally, for 25 minutes. If masala is sticking, add 2 tbsp (30 mL) water and reduce heat to low.

Nutrition info per serving	
Calories	246
Fat, total	12 g
Fat, saturated	3.5 g
Cholesterol	86 mg
Sodium	406 mg
Carbohydrate	8 g
Fiber	2 g
Protein	27 g

Food Choices

2½	Meat & Alternatives
1	Fat
1	Extra

Tip

Ready-to-use korma pastes are sold at well-stocked grocery stores, but they can be quite high in sodium — 400 mg or more for 2 tbsp (30 mL)! I recommend making your own korma paste.

4. Stir in 2 cups (500 mL) water and bring to a boil over high heat. Reduce heat to low, cover and simmer for 5 minutes. Uncover and simmer for 10 minutes.

5. Add the remaining water, increase heat to medium and cook, stirring, for about 5 minutes, adding more water if lamb is drying out, until meat is tender. If the stew is still quite liquidy, simmer longer, but there should be enough gravy to nicely coat lamb.

6. Serve garnished with cilantro.

Tips

Purée the garlic and ginger in a mini food processor. You can do a small amount and refrigerate in a jar for up to 2 days for garlic or up to 5 days for ginger. If you prefer to purée a large amount, store it in an airtight container or jar in the freezer for up to 3 months.

Premade garlic and ginger purées can have a lot of added sodium, so avoid them in favor of homemade.

For ease of preparation, ask your local butcher to cut the lamb into 2-inch (5 cm) cubes for you if precut meat is not available. Ask for any visible fat to be trimmed as well.

To peel tomatoes, blanch them in a pot of boiling water for 1 minute, then, using a slotted spoon, immediately transfer them to a bowl of ice water. When the tomatoes are cool enough to handle, cut out the core with a sharp knife and peel off the skin.

Goan Pork Vindaloo

When the Portuguese colonized India over 400 years ago, they left their mark on the cuisine, especially in what is now the state of Goa. One dish that bears the marks of this influence is vindaloo. Vindaloos are distinctive for their spicy, sweet and sour flavor. They require marinating, usually with a masala paste, as in this recipe.

Tip

Ready-to-use vindaloo masala pastes are sold at well-stocked grocery stores, but they can be quite high in sodium — 400 mg or more for 2 tbsp (30 mL)! I recommend making your own vindaloo paste.

Nutrition info per serving	
Calories	198
Fat, total	9 g
Fat, saturated	2.7 g
Cholesterol	65 mg
Sodium	268 mg
Carbohydrate	9 g
Fiber	2 g
Protein	20 g
Food Choices	
2	Meat & Alternatives
½	Fat
1	Extra

Preparation time: **30 minutes**
Marinating time: **1 hour**
Cooking time: **1 hour and 15 minutes**

- **Spice grinder, mortar and pestle or mini chopper**
- **Small food processor**

Masala Paste

20	whole black peppercorns	20
14	whole cloves	14
10	small dried Kashmiri chile peppers, broken in half	10
6	green cardamom pods	6
1	1-inch (2.5 cm) cinnamon stick	1
2 tbsp	minced garlic	30 mL
1 tbsp	minced gingerroot	15 mL
1 tsp	ground dried red chile peppers (*lal mirch*)	5 mL
½ tsp	cumin seeds	2 mL
¼ tsp	ground turmeric	1 mL
¼ cup	malt or white vinegar	60 mL
¼ cup	water (approx.)	60 mL

Vindaloo

1½ lbs	lean boneless pork shoulder, cut into ½-inch (1 cm) cubes	750 g
1 tbsp	vegetable oil	15 mL
2 cups	finely chopped red onions	500 mL
	Water	
½ tsp	granulated sugar	2 mL
½ tsp	salt	2 mL
1 tbsp	Tart Tamarind Paste (see box, opposite)	15 mL

1. *Masala Paste:* In spice grinder or using a mortar and pestle, grind peppercorns, cloves, Kashmiri chiles, cardamom, cinnamon, garlic, ginger, ground chile peppers (if using), cumin seeds and turmeric. Transfer to food processor and add vinegar and water; process until blended.

2. *Vindaloo:* In a large bowl, combine pork and masala paste, coating evenly. Cover and refrigerate for 1 hour.

3. In a large skillet, heat oil over medium heat. Add onions and cook, stirring, for 30 minutes or until golden. Add up to ⅓ cup (75 mL) water if onions are sticking.

4. Stir in pork with masala paste; reduce heat to medium-low, cover and cook, stirring occasionally, for 8 to 10 minutes or until browned on all sides.

Make It a Meal

1 serving Goan Pork Vindaloo

²/₃ cup (150 mL) unsalted cooked brown basmati rice (2 Carbohydrate)

1 serving Cucumber Yogurt (page 86) or ¼ cup (60 mL) low-fat plain yogurt (1 Extra)

1 serving Punjabi Lachha Salad (page 30) or 1 cup (250 mL) mixed green salad (1 Extra) with 1 tbsp (15 mL) low-fat dressing (½ Fat)

¾ cup (175 mL) Mango Yogurt Smoothie (page 92)

1 medium guava (½ Carbohydrate)

5. Stir in 1½ cups (375 mL) water and bring to a boil over high heat. Reduce heat to low, cover and simmer, stirring occasionally, for about 20 minutes or until pork is tender and sauce is thickened. Stir in sugar, salt and tamarind paste; cover and simmer for 5 minutes to blend the flavors.

Tips

The key to vindaloo dishes is the dried Kashmiri chiles, which add a distinctive color and do not fade with the addition of vinegar. However, they do not add heat. If you like heat, add the optional ground dried red chile peppers. For more information on Kashmiri chilies, see page 18.

Traditionally, coconut toddy vinegar is used in vindaloos and many other dishes to add the sour flavor Goan cuisine is known for. Since this vinegar may not be readily available in North America, I have substituted malt or white vinegar.

Tart Tamarind Paste

The recipes for Spicy South Indian Soup (page 26), Goan Pork Vindaloo (opposite) and Goan Pork with Liver (page 72) use a tamarind paste created especially for them. Here's the recipe.

3½ oz	piece tamarind block (see page 18)	100 g
½ cup	warm water	125 mL

In a bowl, combine tamarind and warm water; soak for 30 minutes, stirring pulp periodically. Stir to make a paste. Strain through a fine-mesh sieve and discard pits and solids. (**Makes about ¾ cups/175 mL paste.**)

Tip

Leftover tamarind block can be stored in an airtight container in the refrigerator for up to 3 months or in the freezer for up to 1 year. Extra tamarind paste can be frozen in ice cube trays until solid, then stored in freezer bags or small airtight containers for up to 6 months. Use in other Goan, South Asian, Caribbean or Thai dishes.

Goan Pork with Liver *(Sorpotel)*

Makes 6 servings

This rich, spicy dish is made with pork and organ meats, such as heart and liver. I used just a small amount of liver, to keep the saturated fat low. The dish is often eaten the day after it is prepared, to give the flavors time to develop. A savory, fermented rice cake called sanna is the traditional accompaniment, but idlis (page 64) would make a suitable replacement.

Nutrition info per serving

Calories	221
Fat, total	8 g
Fat, saturated	1.2 g
Cholesterol	103 mg
Sodium	289 mg
Carbohydrate	16 g
Fiber	3 g
Protein	23 g

Food Choices

2½	Meat & Alternatives
1	Fat
1	Extra

Preparation time: **30 minutes**
Cooking time: **1 hour**

- **Small food processor or mini chopper**

Masala Paste

8	dried Kashmiri chile peppers	8
6	whole cloves	6
6	whole black peppercorns	6
4	green cardamom pods	4
2	2-inch (5 cm) cinnamon sticks	2
1½ tbsp	minced garlic	22 mL
1 tbsp	minced gingerroot	15 mL
1 tsp	cumin seeds	5 mL
1 tsp	ground dried red chile peppers (*lal mirch*)	5 mL
¼ tsp	ground turmeric	1 mL
⅓ cup	water	75 mL
2 tbsp	malt or white vinegar	30 mL

Sorpotel

3 cups	water, divided	750 mL
1 lb	lean boneless pork shoulder, cut into ¼-inch (0.5 cm) cubes	500 g
3½ oz	pork liver, cut into ¼-inch (0.5 cm) cubes	100 g
2 tbsp	vegetable oil	30 mL
1½ cups	chopped red onions	375 mL
½ tsp	granulated sugar	2 mL
½ tsp	salt	2 mL
1 tbsp	Tart Tamarind Paste (see box, page 71)	15 mL

1. *Masala Paste:* In food processor, combine Kashmiri chiles, cloves, peppercorns, cardamom, cinnamon, garlic, ginger, cumin seeds, ground chile peppers, turmeric, water and vinegar; process until blended. Set aside.

2. *Sorpotel:* In a small pot, bring ½ cup (125 mL) water to a boil over high heat. Add pork, reduce heat to medium, cover and boil for 10 minutes or until no longer pink inside. Drain and set aside.

3. Meanwhile, in another small pot, bring ½ cup (125 mL) water to a boil over high heat. Add pork liver, reduce heat to medium, cover and boil for 5 minutes or until no longer pink inside. Drain and set aside.

Make It a Meal

1 serving Goan Pork with Liver

3 Savory South Indian Semolina Cakes (page 64)

1 serving Cucumber Yogurt (page 86) or 1/4 cup (60 mL) low-fat plain yogurt (1 Extra)

1 serving Punjabi Lachha Salad (page 30) or 1 cup (250 mL) mixed green salad (1 Extra)

3/4 cup (175 mL) Mango Yogurt Smoothie (page 92)

1 medium guava (1/2 Carbohydrate)

4. In a large pot, heat oil over medium-high heat. Add onions, reduce heat to low and cook, stirring occasionally, for 25 minutes or until soft and golden. Add pork and liver; cook, stirring, for 2 minutes. Stir in masala paste and cook for 2 minutes.

5. Stir in the remaining water and bring to a boil over high heat. Reduce heat to low, cover and simmer, stirring occasionally, for about 12 minutes or until pork is tender and sauce is thickened. Stir in sugar, salt and tamarind paste; cover and simmer for 5 minutes.

Tips

Ready-to-eat vindaloo masala pastes are available, but they have a lot of added sodium. It is best to make your own masala paste at home and use store-bought pastes sparingly.

Traditionally, coconut toddy vinegar is used in vindaloos and many other dishes to add the sour flavor Goan cuisine is known for. Since this vinegar is not readily available outside India, I have substituted malt or white vinegar.

You may be accustomed to eating richer, fattier versions of this dish, but be cautious about adding more organ meat or oil, as they will increase the fat and saturated fat content.

This recipe is fairly mild; if you would like more heat, increase the amount of ground dried red chile peppers. Kashmiri chile peppers add a nice dark red color, but do not add heat.

Nutrition Tip

Ginger has been shown to have an anti-inflammatory effect, but it is unclear whether it is effective in inflammatory diseases such as rheumatoid arthritis or osteoarthritis. Short-term studies have shown that ginger can be beneficial in alleviating nausea and vomiting during pregnancy. Studies are ongoing in animals to assess ginger's potential as a treatment option for diabetes, cancer and heart disease.

Butter Chicken *(Makhani Murgh)*

Makes 6 servings

Many traditional versions of this popular recipe from northern India include ghee (clarified butter) and a large amount of cream and nuts. To significantly reduce the total fat and saturated fat, I eliminated the ghee, replaced much of the cream with nonfat yogurt and cut back on the nuts. The results are still outstanding!

Nutrition info per serving

Calories	113
Fat, total	4 g
Fat, saturated	0.7 g
Cholesterol	42 mg
Sodium	*534 mg
Carbohydrate	3 g
Fiber	1 g
Protein	15 g

* This recipe is high in sodium. Balance it out by making lower-sodium choices for the rest of your meal and throughout the day.

Food Choices

2	Meat & Alternatives
½	Fat

Preparation time: **20 minutes**
Marinating time: **30 minutes**
Cooking time: **35 minutes**

- **Rimmed baking sheet**
- **Blender or food processor**

Chicken and Marinade

½ tsp	paprika	2 mL
½ tsp	ground dried red chile peppers (*lal mirch*)	2 mL
2 tbsp	nonfat plain yogurt	30 mL
1 lb	boneless skinless chicken breasts, cut into 1-inch (2.5 cm) cubes	500 g

Curry Sauce

1½ tsp	vegetable oil	7 mL
1 tsp	minced garlic	5 mL
1 tsp	minced gingerroot	5 mL
2 tbsp	tomato paste	30 mL
2 cups	no-salt-added canned diced tomatoes, with juice	500 mL
1 tbsp	finely ground unsalted dry-roasted cashews	15 mL
1 cup	water	250 mL
⅓ cup	nonfat plain yogurt	75 mL
2 tsp	dried fenugreek leaves (*kasuri methi*)	10 mL
1½ tsp	garam masala	7 mL
½ tsp	salt	2 mL
¼ cup	half-and-half (10%) cream	60 mL

1. *Chicken and Marinade:* In a medium bowl, combine paprika, ground chile peppers and yogurt. Add chicken and stir to coat. Cover and refrigerate for 30 minutes.

2. Meanwhile, preheat oven to 350°F (180°C).

3. Arrange chicken, with all the marinade, in a single layer on baking sheet. Bake for 10 minutes.

4. *Curry Sauce:* Meanwhile, in a large pot, heat oil over medium heat. Add garlic and ginger; cook, stirring, for about 1 minute or until golden brown. Add tomato paste and cook, stirring, for 2 minutes.

5. Stir in tomatoes, cashews and water; bring to a boil. Stir in yogurt, reduce heat and simmer, stirring often, for 10 minutes or until sauce is reduced by about one-quarter.

When cream is necessary for a traditional dish, use a lower-fat cream such as half-and-half (10%) instead of heavy or whipping (35%) cream. Add it at the end of the recipe to avoid curdling.

6. Transfer sauce to blender and purée until smooth. Return to pot and keep warm.

7. Heat a small dry skillet over medium heat. Toast fenugreek leaves, stirring constantly, for about 1 minute or until fragrant. Using your fingers, crush leaves into powder.

8. Stir baked chicken into the sauce, along with crushed fenugreek, garam masala and salt; bring to a boil over medium heat. Reduce heat and simmer, stirring often, until sauce is slightly thickened. Stir in cream and immediately remove from heat.

Tips

Use no-salt-added canned tomatoes so you can control the amount of salt in your dishes. Leftover tomatoes can be stored in an airtight container in the refrigerator for up to 3 days or in the freezer for up to 3 months, and are a great addition to any curry (see pages 52 and 53, for example) or tomato sauce.

Premade curry powders and pastes can be found in South Asian grocery stores, but they can have a lot of added salt. For example, 2 tbsp (30 mL) of butter chicken paste can have as much as 460 mg of sodium. I recommend you use your own blend of spices.

Nutrition Tip

A few small studies have found that fenugreek may help lower blood glucose levels in diabetes. Some of these studies used fenugreek in supplement form and others used whole fenugreek seeds. Some studies have also shown fenugreek to lower low-density lipoprotein (LDL) blood cholesterol and triglycerides. However, the studies are few, none have been long-term, and the dose and form of fenugreek varies greatly. More studies are needed to conclude whether fenugreek can be used as an alternative treatment in diabetes.

Pakistani Chicken Stew *(Murgh Korma)*

Korma is a Punjabi dish from northern India or Pakistan and is known for its creamy texture, rich color and spice! I have kept the heat mild, so if you want more, add more cayenne. To make this dish properly does take some time, but the flavors and aromas will not disappoint! Serve with a flatbread, such as whole wheat roti (page 32).

Preparation time: **20 minutes**
Cooking time: **1 hour**

- **Small food processor**

Masala Paste

⅓ cup	finely chopped white onion	75 mL
2½ tbsp	ground coriander	37 mL
1½ tsp	puréed garlic (see tips, opposite)	7 mL
1½ tsp	paprika	7 mL
1 tsp	cayenne pepper	5 mL
1 tsp	salt	5 mL
⅛ tsp	ground turmeric	0.5 mL
¼ cup	nonfat plain yogurt	60 mL

Chicken Korma

1	whole bone-in chicken (about 2 lbs/1 kg)	1
1½ tsp	vegetable oil	7 mL
½ cup	finely chopped white onion	125 mL
4	green cardamom pods, cracked	4
3	whole black peppercorns	3
3	whole cloves	3
1¾ cups	water, divided	425 mL
2 tbsp	finely chopped fresh cilantro	30 mL

1. *Masala Paste:* In food processor, combine onion, coriander, garlic, paprika, cayenne, salt, turmeric and yogurt; process until blended. Transfer to a bowl and set aside.

2. *Chicken Korma:* Cut backbone from chicken and cut chicken into 10 pieces. Remove skin and discard, along with any excess fat.

3. In a pot, heat oil over medium heat. Add onion, cardamom, peppercorns and cloves; reduce heat to medium-low and cook, stirring, for about 2 minutes or until onions are softened.

Nutrition info per serving	
Calories	187
Fat, total	6 g
Fat, saturated	1.0 g
Cholesterol	86 mg
Sodium	323 mg
Carbohydrate	6 g
Fiber	2 g
Protein	27 g

Food Choices

2	Meat & Alternatives
1	Extra

Purée the garlic in a mini food processor. You can do a small amount and refrigerate in a jar for up to 2 days. If you prefer to purée a large amount, store it in an airtight container or jar in the freezer for up to 3 months.

Premade garlic purées can have a lot of added sodium, so avoid them in favor of homemade.

4. Stir in chicken, reduce heat and simmer, stirring occasionally, for 10 minutes. Reduce heat to low, cover and cook for about 3 minutes or until chicken is browned on all sides.

5. Stir $\frac{1}{4}$ cup (60 mL) water into masala paste. Add to pot, stirring well, increase heat and simmer, uncovered, stirring occasionally, for 20 minutes.

6. Add the remaining water, increase heat to medium and bring to a boil. Cover and boil, stirring occasionally, for 15 minutes or until chicken is no longer pink inside and a meat thermometer inserted in the thickest part of a thigh registers 165°F (74°C). If the curry has extra liquid, leave lid half on and cook over high heat to evaporate some liquid. Remove from heat and stir in cilantro.

Tips

Thoroughly cooking the masala paste and onions before adding other ingredients is the key to developing the flavors of the sauce. The flavors should not be raw-tasting and the texture of the final sauce should be dark, thick and smooth.

Ready-to-use korma pastes are sold at many grocery stores, but they can be quite high in sodium — 400 mg or more for 2 tbsp (30 mL)! I recommend making your own korma paste.

Pakistani Chicken Pilaf *(Murgh Pulao)*

Makes 8 servings

Pilaf is meant to be a meal on its own but can be high in carbohydrates and fat if you don't watch your portion size. My dad, who has diabetes, created a balanced meal that includes a smaller serving of this favorite dish, and I am sharing it with you in the meal suggestions opposite.

Nutrition info per serving

Calories	368
Fat, total	9 g
Fat, saturated	1.8 g
Cholesterol	92 mg
Sodium	*500 mg
Carbohydrate	48 g
Fiber	2 g
Protein	21 g

* This recipe is high in sodium. Balance it out by making lower-sodium choices for the rest of your meal and throughout the day.

Food Choices

3	Carbohydrate
1½	Meat & Alternatives
1	Fat

Preparation time: **30 minutes**
Cooking time: **45 minutes**

2½ cups	white basmati rice, rinsed	625 mL
	Water	
1 tbsp	vegetable oil	15 mL
¾ cup	thinly sliced onion	175 mL
20	whole black peppercorns	20
15	whole cloves	15
4	½-inch (1 cm) cinnamon sticks	4
8	green cardamom pods, cracked	8
2	black cardamom pods, cracked	2
1½ tsp	minced garlic	7 mL
1½ tsp	minced gingerroot	7 mL
8	bone-in skinless chicken thighs and drumsticks (about 2 lbs/1 kg total)	8
1½ tsp	salt	7 mL
1½ tsp	cumin seeds	7 mL
3 tbsp	nonfat plain yogurt	45 mL
1 to 2	drops kewra essence (optional)	1 to 2
⅛ tsp	zarda orange food coloring (optional)	0.5 mL

1. Place rice in a medium bowl with enough water to cover; let soak while following steps 2 through 5.

2. In a large saucepan, heat oil over medium heat. Add onion, peppercorns, cloves, cinnamon, green cardamom and black cardamom; cook, stirring, for about 5 minutes or until onions are golden. Reduce the heat if necessary to prevent sticking.

3. Stir in ginger and garlic, then add chicken. Cook, stirring occasionally, for 5 minutes or until chicken is golden on all sides.

4. Stir in salt, cumin seeds and yogurt; cook, stirring occasionally, for 5 minutes.

5. Stir in 2 cups (500 mL) water and bring to a boil. Cover and boil for 10 minutes. Discard whole spices, if desired.

Make It a Meal

1 serving Pakistani
Chicken Pilaf

1 serving Pakistani Oven-
Baked Shami Kebabs
(page 40)

1 serving Mixed Vegetable
Yogurt (page 87)

1 medium guava
($\frac{1}{2}$ Carbohydrate)

6. Drain and rinse rice, then add to the pan, along with $2\frac{1}{2}$ cups (625 mL) water. Stir, increase heat to high and bring to a boil. Reduce heat to low, cover and simmer for 10 to 12 minutes or until rice is tender and juices run clear when chicken is pierced and a meat thermometer inserted in the thickest part of a thigh registers 165°F (74°C). If desired, stir in kewra in the last 5 minutes of cooking.

7. Combine food coloring and 3 tbsp (45 mL) water; drizzle evenly over rice.

Tips

Kewra essence, derived from pandan flowers, is used to add aroma to meat or rice dishes and desserts. Be careful not to use too much, as it has a very strong, concentrated flavor. It is sold in small bottles at South Asian stores, and is not the same as kewra water.

Zarda is a bright orange powdered food coloring used to add visual appeal to rice dishes and sweets. When mixed with water, it turns yellow. Be careful to use only a small amount unless you want your rice to be bright orange. Zarda is available at most South Asian grocery stores.

For food safety, cooked rice should be stored in the refrigerator for no longer than 2 days.

There are a variety of rice dishes in South Asian cuisine. Two of the most popular are biryani and pulao. Both are made with meat or vegetables and basmati rice. Biryanis have layers of meat and/or vegetables, rice and fried onions, and are spicier. They take more time to make and are usually served on special occasions. With pulaos, the meat and/or vegetables and rice are cooked all together in one pot and served as a mixture.

Goan Fish Curry *(Machhi Curry)*

Makes 4 servings

Fish, coconut milk and spicy chiles are popular ingredients in Goa, India, and this traditional Goan dish is frequently eaten for lunch or dinner, with a side of rice. Okra, while not a customary addition, adds even more flavor and nutrients and is a great way to sneak in some vegetables.

Preparation time: **20 minutes**
Cooking time: **55 to 60 minutes**

- **Preheat oven to 400°F (200°C)**
- **2 rimmed baking sheets, lined with parchment paper**
- **Steamer basket (optional)**
- **Blender**

1 lb	skinless cod fillets, rinsed and cut into 4 equal pieces	500 g
¼ tsp	freshly ground black pepper	1 mL
1 ½ cups	sliced okra	375 mL
2 tsp	coriander seeds	10 mL
1 ½ tsp	cumin seeds	7 mL
1 tsp	ground dried red chile peppers (*lal mirch*)	5 mL
1 tsp	ground turmeric	5 mL
1 cup	chopped tomato	250 mL
⅓ cup	light coconut milk	75 mL
2 tbsp	vegetable oil	30 mL
1 ½ cups	finely chopped red onion	375 mL
1 ½ tbsp	minced garlic	22 mL
2 tsp	Tamarind Paste (see box, opposite)	10 mL
½ tsp	salt	2 mL
1 cup	water	250 mL

1. Place fish on one prepared baking sheet and season with black pepper. Bake in preheated oven for about 20 minutes or until fish is firm and flakes easily when tested with a fork. Remove from oven and keep warm.

2. Spread okra in a single layer on the other prepared baking sheet and bake for 15 to 20 minutes or until okra is al dente and not shriveled.

3. Meanwhile, heat a small skillet over medium heat. Toast coriander seeds, cumin seeds, ground chile peppers and turmeric for about 1 minute, being careful not to burn them. Remove from pan.

4. In blender, combine toasted spices, tomato and coconut milk; purée until smooth. Set aside.

5. In a large skillet, heat oil over medium heat. Add onion and cook, stirring, for about 5 minutes or until golden. Add garlic and cook, stirring, for about 1 minute or until fragrant.

Nutrition info per serving

Calories	246
Fat, total	9 g
Fat, saturated	1.6 g
Cholesterol	59 mg
Sodium	382 mg
Carbohydrate	14 g
Fiber	4 g
Protein	27 g

Food Choices

3	Meat & Alternatives
1½	Fat
1	Extra

Make It a Meal

1 serving Goan Fish Curry

1 serving Pakistani Potatoes and Cauliflower (page 58)

⅔ cup (150 mL) unsalted cooked brown basmati rice (2 Carbohydrate)

1 cup (250 mL) Masala Tea (page 93)

¼ medium mango (½ Carbohydrate)

6. Stir in tomato purée and bring to a boil over high heat. Stir in okra, tamarind paste, salt and water; reduce heat and simmer for 2 minutes or until sauce is thickened.

7. Carefully place fish in the skillet and simmer for 1 minute, spooning sauce over fish to help it warm through.

Tips

Okra is a good source of soluble fiber, which has been shown to lower low-density lipoprotein (LDL) blood cholesterol and blood glucose levels.

When cooking with a small amount of oil, be sure to heat it well before adding the other ingredients; otherwise, they may simply absorb the oil, which can cause sticking and burning.

Tamarind Paste

The recipe for Goan Fish Curry (opposite) uses a tamarind paste created especially for it. Here's the recipe.

7 oz	piece tamarind block (see page 18)	200 g
3½ cups	warm water	875 mL

In a bowl, combine tamarind and warm water; soak for 15 to 30 minutes, stirring pulp periodically. Stir to make a paste. Strain through a fine-mesh sieve and discard pits and solids. (**Makes about 4 cups/1 L paste.**)

Tip

Leftover tamarind block can be stored in an airtight container in the refrigerator for up to 3 months or in the freezer for up to 1 year. Extra tamarind paste can be frozen in ice cube trays until solid, then stored in freezer bags or small airtight containers for up to 6 months. Use in other Goan, South Asian, Caribbean or Thai dishes.

Bengali Fish Curry *(Doi Maach)*

Makes 6 servings

Doi maach, which translates literally as "yogurt fish," is a very popular spicy fish dish in Bangladesh. It is usually eaten with a side of hot white rice on festive occasions. The serving of fish in this dish is small, so be sure to balance your meal with enough proteins, as in the sample meal below.

Make It a Meal

2 servings Bengali Fish Curry

1 cup (250 mL) unsalted cooked brown basmati rice (3 Carbohydrate)

1 serving Punjabi Lachha Salad (page 30)

½ medium mango (1 Carbohydrate)

Nutrition info per serving

Calories	93
Fat, total	4 g
Fat, saturated	0.5 g
Cholesterol	23 mg
Sodium	363 mg
Carbohydrate	8 g
Fiber	2 g
Protein	8 g

Food Choices

1	Meat & Alternatives
½	Fat
1	Extra

Preparation time: 15 minutes
Cooking time: 10 minutes

⅓ cup	nonfat plain yogurt	75 mL
2 tbsp	water	30 mL
¾ tsp	salt	3 mL
¾ tsp	ground turmeric	3 mL
10 oz	skinless sole fillets (see tip, below), rinsed and patted dry	300 g
1 tbsp	mustard oil	15 mL
1	large yellow onion, finely chopped	1
1 tbsp	minced gingerroot	15 mL
1 tbsp	minced garlic	15 mL
1	large bay leaf	1
1	1½-inch (4 cm) cinnamon stick	1
4 tsp	ground green cardamom seeds	20 mL
1 tsp	ground cumin	5 mL
2	dried red chile peppers, broken in half	2
2	small green chile peppers, finely chopped	2

1. In a bowl, combine yogurt and water until smooth. Set aside.

2. Combine salt and turmeric and rub over fish. Set aside.

3. In a skillet, heat oil over medium-high heat. Add onion, ginger and garlic; cook, stirring, for about 3 minutes or until onions are starting to turn golden. Add bay leaf, cinnamon, cardamom, cumin and dried red chiles; cook, stirring, for 30 seconds.

4. Stir in yogurt mixture and green chiles. Place fish on top, reduce heat and simmer, gently moving the fish in the sauce occasionally, for about 5 minutes or until fish is firm and flakes easily when tested with a fork. Discard bay leaf and cinnamon.

Tips

In Bangladesh, this dish is traditionally made with a sweet-tasting fish called *rohu* or *rui maach* (a species of carp) or with *hilsa* or *ilish* (oily fish that are rich in omega-3s). These fish may be difficult to find and expensive in North America, so I've substituted sole. If sole is not available, any other carp species, haddock or salmon will also work in this recipe.

Rinse fish thoroughly under cold water before cooking it, to remove as much salt as possible, especially if it is frozen.

Mustard oil is the key ingredient in this dish, but because it has a high fat content, I reduced the amount used.

South Indian Coconut Shrimp Curry (Jhinga Malai Curry)

Southern India is known for its seafood and coconut, and this recipe makes great use of both. The traditional version uses a lot of coconut milk. To reduce the saturated fat content, I used a smaller amount and chose light coconut milk.

Preparation time: 15 minutes
Cooking time: 25 minutes

10	whole cloves	10
7	green cardamom pods	7
2	1 1/2-inch (4 cm) cinnamon sticks	2
1 tbsp	vegetable oil	15 mL
1	medium red onion, chopped	1
1 1/2 tbsp	minced gingerroot	22 mL
1 tsp	ground turmeric	5 mL
	Water	
2	medium green chile peppers, slit	2
1 tsp	granulated sugar	5 mL
1/2 tsp	salt	2 mL
1 lb	medium shrimp, peeled, deveined and tail removed, rinsed	500 g
1/2	can (14 oz/400 mL) light coconut milk	1/2

1. Using the broad side of a knife, smash cloves, cardamom and cinnamon.

2. In a skillet, heat oil over medium-low heat. Add smashed spices and cook, stirring, for 2 minutes or until fragrant.

3. Add onion and cook, stirring, for 5 to 10 minutes or until golden. Add ginger and turmeric; cook, stirring and adding 1 to 2 tbsp (15 to 30 mL) water if mixture is sticking to pan, for 2 minutes.

4. Add chiles, sugar and salt; increase heat to medium and cook, stirring, for 1 minute. Add shrimp and cook, stirring, for 1 minute.

5. Stir in coconut milk and 1/2 cup (125 mL) water; bring to a boil over high heat. Reduce heat to low, cover and simmer, stirring occasionally, for about 5 minutes or until shrimp are pink, firm and opaque and sauce has thickened slightly.

Tips

Rinse shrimp thoroughly under cold water before cooking them, to remove as much salt as possible, especially if they are frozen.

The key to curries is to thoroughly cook the onions and spices. This helps to remove the raw taste and intensifies the flavors. Although very little oil is used in this recipe, be sure to cook the onion until golden; reduce the heat as necessary to soften and cook the onions to golden without letting them burn.

Nutrition info per serving

Calories	178
Fat, total	6 g
Fat, saturated	2.3 g
Cholesterol	162 mg
Sodium	429 mg
Carbohydrate	9 g
Fiber	1 g
Protein	22 g

Food Choices

2 1/2	Meat & Alternatives
1/2	Fat
1	Extra

Goan Shrimp Vindaloo

Makes 6 servings

Goa is known for its great seafood, and this dish, typically served with rice, is no exception! It can be made with or without potatoes; I used just a small amount, to keep the carbohydrate content low. Since shrimp are high in cholesterol, the serving size is small, so you'll want to add other dishes to balance out your meal, as in the example on page 85.

Preparation time: 20 minutes
Cooking time: 40 minutes

½ tsp	salt	2 mL
¼ tsp	ground turmeric	1 mL
2 tbsp	malt or white vinegar	30 mL
1 lb	medium shrimp, peeled, deveined and tail removed, rinsed	500 g
2 cups	cubed peeled potatoes (1-inch/2.5 cm cubes)	500 mL
	Water	
2 tbsp	vegetable oil	30 mL
½ tsp	cumin seeds	2 mL
½ tsp	brown mustard seeds	2 mL
1½ cups	chopped red onion	375 mL
1 tbsp	minced gingerroot	15 mL
1 tbsp	minced garlic	15 mL
3	medium tomatoes, chopped	3
4	small dried Kashmiri chile peppers (see page 18)	4
½ tsp	ground dried red chile peppers (*lal mirch*) (optional)	2 mL

1. In a large bowl, combine salt, turmeric and vinegar. Add shrimp, tossing to coat. Cover and refrigerate until ready to use.

2. Place potatoes in a pot and cover with water. Bring to a boil over high heat. Reduce heat and boil for about 8 minutes or until starting to get tender. Drain and set aside.

3. In a large skillet, heat oil over medium heat. Add cumin seeds and mustard seeds; cook, stirring, for about 1 minute or until seeds crackle and brown.

4. Add onion, reduce heat to low and cook, stirring, for about 10 minutes or until golden. Add ginger and garlic; cook, stirring, for 2 minutes. Add 2 tbsp (30 mL) water if mixture is sticking.

5. Add tomatoes, increase heat to medium and cook, stirring, for 5 minutes or until tomatoes are breaking down into a paste.

Nutrition info per serving

Calories	162
Fat, total	5 g
Fat, saturated	0.4 g
Cholesterol	87 mg
Sodium	262 mg
Carbohydrate	16 g
Fiber	3 g
Protein	13 g

Food Choices

1	Carbohydrate
1½	Meat & Alternatives
1	Fat

Make It a Meal

1 serving Goan Shrimp Vindaloo

1 serving Spinach and Tofu Curry (page 54)

⅔ cup (150 mL) unsalted cooked brown basmati rice (2 Carbohydrate)

1 serving Punjabi Lachha Salad (page 30) or 1 cup (250 mL) mixed green salad (1 Extra) with 1 tbsp (15 mL) low-fat dressing (½ Fat)

1 serving Cucumber Yogurt (page 86) or ¼ cup (60 mL) low-fat plain yogurt (1 Extra)

2 medium guavas (1 Carbohydrate)

6. Stir in parboiled potatoes, Kashmiri chiles and ground chile peppers; reduce heat to medium-low and cook, stirring, for 3 minutes.

7. Stir in marinated shrimp (with liquid) and simmer, stirring, for 5 minutes or until shrimp are pink, firm and opaque. Serve immediately.

Tips

Rinse shrimp thoroughly under cold water before cooking them, to remove as much salt as possible, especially if they are frozen.

The key to this dish (as with many South Asian dishes) is to cook the onions well. With very little oil to work with, you will have to be patient and cook them on low heat for a longer time, so that they color nicely without burning.

Nutrition Tip

Some evidence indicates that as little as one to two cloves of garlic a day may modestly lower low-density lipoprotein (LDL) blood cholesterol and triglycerides. There is also some evidence that garlic is associated with anti-clotting effects and a modest reduction in blood pressure in people with high blood pressure. More long-term human studies are necessary to determine how much garlic is needed, and in what form, for it to be a safe and effective alternative treatment option. In the meantime, in its fresh form, it is an incredibly flavorful addition to recipes.

Cucumber Yogurt *(Keera Raita)*

Makes 6 servings

Raita is a traditional yogurt condiment served as an accompaniment to South Asian curries and rice dishes. It can help tame the heat of the frequently spicy meals. There are many varieties of raita, made from spinach, eggplant, potato, carrot… the list goes on! I am showcasing the ones I like best (of course)! Raita is a great way to sneak a milk and alternatives serving into your meal.

Preparation time: **15 minutes**

- **Sieve, lined with cheesecloth**

2 cups	grated English cucumber (unpeeled), excess water squeezed out	500 mL
1/2 tsp	minced garlic	2 mL
1/4 tsp	salt	1 mL
1/4 tsp	cayenne pepper	1 mL
1 cup	nonfat plain yogurt	250 mL

1. In a medium bowl, combine cucumber, garlic, salt, cayenne and yogurt.

2. Serve immediately or cover and refrigerate for up to 3 days. Drain off any excess liquid before serving.

Tip

Raita is a great way to increase calcium and vitamin D in the traditional South Asian diet, but keep the fat low by using nonfat or low-fat dairy products.

Nutrition info per serving

Calories	23
Fat, total	0 g
Fat, saturated	0.0 g
Cholesterol	1 mg
Sodium	217 mg
Carbohydrate	5 g
Fiber	0 g
Protein	2 g
Food Choices	
1	Extra

Mixed Vegetable Yogurt *(Sabzi Raita)*

Makes 6 servings

This version of raita contains a variety of vegetables and can be served as a dip or eaten with spicy rice, curry or lentil dishes.

Preparation time: **20 minutes**

• **Sieve, lined with cheesecloth**

1 cup	minced cucumber (unpeeled), excess water squeezed out	250 mL
1/2 cup	minced seeded plum (Roma) tomato	125 mL
1/4 cup	minced red onion	60 mL
1 tbsp	minced fresh mint	15 mL
1/2 tsp	salt	2 mL
1/4 tsp	minced garlic	1 mL
1/8 tsp	cayenne pepper	0.5 mL
2 cups	nonfat plain yogurt	500 mL

1. In a medium bowl, combine cucumber, tomato, onion, mint, salt, garlic, cayenne and yogurt.

2. Serve immediately or cover and refrigerate for up to 3 days. Drain off any excess liquid before serving.

Tip

Red onions are usually a good size, so you will have quite a bit left over after mincing 1/4 cup (60 mL). Use chopped red onion to add flavor to sandwiches and salads so you don't need to add as much fat or salt.

Nutrition Tip

Yogurt is a source of magnesium and a good source of calcium. Make sure to purchase one that is fortified with vitamin D. It also has probiotics, which are good bacteria that, among other benefits, help to keep your digestive tract healthy.

Nutrition info per serving

Calories	43
Fat, total	0 g
Fat, saturated	0.0 g
Cholesterol	2 mg
Sodium	241 mg
Carbohydrate	8 g
Fiber	1 g
Protein	4 g

Food Choices

1/2	Carbohydrate

Cilantro Mint Chutney
(Hara Dhania Chutney)

Sure, jars of mint chutney are available at South Asian grocery stores, but they contain a lot of sodium. This homemade version has a delightfully fresh flavor and the added health benefits of cilantro, garlic and cumin. It's another one of my mom's secret recipes, and it works well with almost anything.

Preparation time: **20 minutes**

• **Food processor or blender**

8	small green chile peppers, chopped	8
5	large cloves garlic, minced	5
1	plum (Roma) tomato, chopped	1
1 cup	packed fresh cilantro (with stems)	250 mL
1 cup	packed mint leaves	250 mL
1/4 cup	chopped onion	60 mL
2 1/2 tsp	ground cumin	12 mL
1/4 tsp	salt	1 mL
2 tbsp	freshly squeezed lemon juice	30 mL

1. In food processor, combine chiles, garlic, tomato, cilantro, mint, onion, cumin, salt and lemon juice; purée until smooth.

2. Transfer to a bowl and serve immediately, or transfer to an airtight container and refrigerate for up to 3 days.

Tips

Small green chile peppers, also known as Thai chile peppers, can be very spicy. If you prefer, you can substitute milder chiles, or reduce the number of green chiles, to adjust the heat level.

Chutneys are a great complement to many dishes, but use them sparingly and remember to factor in the amount of salt, sugar and fat they add to your daily intake, particularly if using store-bought chutneys.

Nutrition info per serving	
Calories	12
Fat, total	0 g
Fat, saturated	0.0 g
Cholesterol	0 mg
Sodium	128 mg
Carbohydrate	3 g
Fiber	1 g
Protein	1 g
Food Choices	
1	Extra

Coconut Chutney *(Nariyal Chutney)*

Makes 12 servings

Coconut is a popular ingredient throughout South Asia, especially in India and Sri Lanka. This easy South Indian chutney goes with everything, especially dosas (page 34) and idlis (page 64). Coconut is a source of fiber and is packed with vitamins, minerals and antioxidants. Nevertheless, this chutney should be enjoyed sparingly, as coconut is high in saturated fat.

Preparation time: **30 minutes**
Cooking time: **12 minutes**

• Blender

3	small green chile peppers, chopped	3
1 ¼ cups	grated fresh coconut (see tip, below)	300 mL
2 tsp	chopped gingerroot	10 mL
1 tsp	salt	5 mL
½ cup	water	125 mL
3 tbsp	nonfat plain yogurt	45 mL
1 ½ tsp	freshly squeezed lemon juice	7 mL

Tarka

1 tsp	vegetable oil	5 mL
2 tbsp	dried curry leaves	30 mL
1 tsp	mustard seeds	5 mL
½	medium onion, finely chopped	½

1. In blender, combine chiles, coconut, ginger, salt, water, yogurt and lemon juice; blend to the consistency of a thick smoothie. Transfer to a bowl.

2. *Tarka:* In a small skillet, heat oil over medium heat. Add curry leaves and mustard seeds; cook, stirring, for about 30 seconds or until seeds crackle. Add onion, reduce heat to low and cook, stirring, for 5 to 10 minutes or until onion is well browned.

3. Stir the *tarka* into the coconut mixture. Serve immediately (preferably) or cover and refrigerate for up to 3 days.

Tips

Fresh coconut is the traditional and best choice for this recipe, but it can be time-consuming to clean and grate it. If you do put in the effort, grate a whole coconut and freeze the remainder in an airtight container for up to 3 months. Alternatively, substitute thawed frozen shredded coconut, available at South Asian grocery stores and many supermarkets. Choose a brand that has coconut as the only ingredient.

Chutneys are a great complement to many dishes, but use them sparingly and remember to factor in the amount of salt, sugar and fat they add to your daily intake, particularly if using store-bought chutneys.

Many South Asian dishes call for a *tarka*, where onions, garlic and/or spices are cooked in oil or ghee. A *tarka* can be used as a topping or garnish, or added as you begin to cook a dish, to enhance the flavors. *Tarkas* are delicious, but they do add quite a bit of fat to a recipe.

Nutrition info per serving

Calories	65
Fat, total	6
Fat, saturated	4.6 g
Cholesterol	0 mg
Sodium	192 mg
Carbohydrate	4 g
Fiber	2 g
Protein	1 g

Food Choices

½	Fat

Pakistani Sweet Tamarind Chutney *(Imali Chutney)*

Makes 18 servings

As the name suggests, this chutney is meant to be sweet, so a lot of sugar is needed to offset the tartness of the tamarind. Even though this recipe has less added sugar than the traditional version, you'll still want to use it sparingly, but it's great on top of snacks such as Chickpea and Potato Snack (page 33).

Soaking time: **Overnight**
Preparation time: **20 minutes**
Cooking time: **1 hour and 15 minutes**

3½ oz	piece tamarind block (see page 18)	100 g
4 cups	water, divided	1 L
10	dates (about 8 oz/250 g)	10
2 cups	packed brown sugar	500 mL
1 tsp	cayenne pepper	5 mL
1 tsp	ground cumin	5 mL
¼ tsp	salt	1 mL

1. In a bowl, soak tamarind in 2 cups (500 mL) water overnight.

2. Strain tamarind through a fine-mesh sieve into a bowl, to remove pulp and small pieces of skin. Add 2 cups (500 mL) water to help strain the tamarind. Discard pulp and skin. You should have about 4 cups (1 L) tamarind liquid.

3. In a medium skillet, combine tamarind liquid, dates, brown sugar, cayenne, cumin and salt. Cook over medium-low heat for 1 hour, stirring occasionally and breaking dates apart, until liquid is thickened.

4. Using a slotted spoon, sift through the chutney to strain out any skin (from dates) and date seeds.

5. Return the liquid to high heat and bring to a boil, stirring often. Remove from heat. Chutney should be a smooth liquid.

6. Transfer to a bowl and let cool before serving, or transfer to small airtight containers and store in the refrigerator for up to 3 months or in the freezer for up to 6 months.

Tips

Look for a brand of tamarind block with no added salt or sugar.

Dates are fat-free, cholesterol-free and sodium-free, and are a good source of fiber. They can be stored in an airtight container at room temperature for several months or in the refrigerator for up to a year.

Tamarind chutneys are available in stores, but can have additives and as much as 65 mg of sodium per 1 tsp (5 mL). This chutney, with 35 mg of sodium per 2 tbsp (30 mL), will keep for a long time, so it is worth making a large batch.

Nutrition info per serving

Calories	108
Fat, total	0 g
Fat, saturated	0.0 g
Cholesterol	0 mg
Sodium	35 mg
Carbohydrate	29 g
Fiber	2 g
Protein	0 g
Food Choices	
3	Carbohydrate

Tamarind Purée *(Imali)*

**Makes about
1 cup (250 mL)**

This tart purée is used in Split Yellow Pigeon Pea Soup (page 28), Chickpea and Potato Snack (page 33) and Sri Lankan Eggplant Curry (page 45). It can be stored for quite a while in the freezer, so feel free to double the ingredients and make a big batch!

Preparation time: **15 minutes**
Cooking time: **45 minutes**

8 oz	piece tamarind block (see page 18)	250 g
2 cups	water	500 mL

1. In a small saucepan, combine tamarind block and water. Bring to a boil over high heat. Reduce heat and simmer gently, mashing occasionally as tamarind breaks down, for about 30 minutes or until tamarind is very soft.

2. Press tamarind mixture through a fine-mesh sieve into a bowl, to separate pulp from pods and fiber. Discard pods and fiber.

Tips

Look for a brand of tamarind block with no added salt or sugar.

Store tamarind purée in small portions (1 tbsp/15 mL to ¼ cup/60 mL, or the amount used in your favorite recipes) in the freezer for up to 6 months.

Nutrition info per serving	
Calories	130
Fat, total	0 g
Fat, saturated	0.0 g
Cholesterol	0 mg
Sodium	19 mg
Carbohydrate	36 g
Fiber	8 g
Protein	2 g
Food Choices	
2	Carbohydrate

Mango Yogurt Smoothie *(Aam Lassi)*

Makes about 4 cups (1 L)

Lassi is a yogurt-based cold drink that is popular in India and Pakistan. Traditionally, it is made with a large amount of added sugar, but fully ripe or frozen mangos provide a naturally sweet flavor, so there's no need to add more than a small touch of honey.

Preparation time: **5 to 20 minutes**

- **Blender**

4 cups	chopped fresh or frozen mangos	1 L
1 cup	nonfat plain yogurt	250 mL
1 cup	skim milk	250 mL
1 tbsp	liquid honey	15 mL
Pinch	ground cardamom (optional)	Pinch

1. In blender, combine mangos, yogurt, milk and honey; blend until smooth.
2. Pour into glasses and sprinkle with cardamom, if desired.

Tips

The best way to tell whether a mango is ripe is to smell it. If the fruit has a distinctive aroma, it is ready for eating. Another good sign is if the fruit yields slightly to gentle pressure.

It is best to use fresh, ripe mangos, but frozen will work if fresh are not available.

To keep this recipe low in fat, make sure to use nonfat yogurt and skim milk.

Variation

Substitute chopped fresh or frozen peaches for the mangos.

Nutrition info per ¾ cup (175 mL)

Calories	106
Fat, total	0 g
Fat, saturated	0.2 g
Cholesterol	2 mg
Sodium	45 mg
Carbohydrate	24 g
Fiber	2 g
Protein	4 g

Food Choices

1½	Carbohydrate

Masala Tea *(Masala Chai)*

Masala chai is a spiced tea blended with aromatic herbs. It is very popular not only in South Asia, but also in the United States, Canada, the United Kingdom and Australia. In India, unlike in the Western countries, tea is never served cold.

Preparation time: **5 minutes**
Cooking time: **15 minutes**

10	whole black peppercorns	10
10	whole cloves	10
6	green cardamom pods, cracked	6
2	2-inch (5 cm) cinnamon sticks	2
2 tbsp	granulated sugar	30 mL
1/4 tsp	minced gingerroot	1 mL
4 cups	1% milk	1 L
2	black tea bags	2

1. In a deep pot, combine peppercorns, cloves, cardamom, cinnamon, sugar, ginger and milk. Bring to a boil over medium heat. Reduce heat to low, add tea bags and steep for 10 minutes (or longer for stronger tea).

2. Remove from heat and strain out spices and tea bags.

Tips

In India, people prefer a strong tea flavor, so they boil tea leaves in the tea for few minutes rather than use tea bags.

Any type of black tea can be used in the recipe. Green teas can also be used, but they do not hold up well to strong spices and must not be steeped for more than 3 minutes or you will end up with a bitter brew.

Nutrition info per 1 cup
(250 mL)

Calories	130
Fat, total	2 g
Fat, saturated	1.7 g
Cholesterol	13 mg
Sodium	111 mg
Carbohydrate	19 g
Fiber	0 g
Protein	9 g

Food Choices

1	Carbohydrate

Chinese Cuisine

Sichuan, Hakka and Cantonese Recipes

Soups, Salads and Snacks

Wonton Soup *(Yun Tun Tang)* 96

Chicken Corn Soup *(Ji Rong Su Mi Tang)* 97

Sichuan Vegetarian Hot-and-Sour Soup *(Suan La Tang)* 98

Chayote Salad *(Liang Ban Fo Shou Gua)* 100

Homemade Wontons *(Xian Hun Tun)* 101

Hakka Bamboo Shoot Dumplings *(Sun Gan Jiao)* 102

Vegetarian Tofu Rolls *(Dou Fu Juan)* 104

Chinese Tea Eggs *(Cha Ye Dan)* . . . 106

Vegetarian Dishes

Baby Bok Choy and Mushrooms with Oyster Sauce *(Qing Cai Chao Xiang Gu)* 107

Bamboo Shoots with Mushrooms *(Mo Gu Chao Sun)* 108

Hakka Stir-Fried Soybean Sprouts *(Chao Dou Ya)* 109

Stir-Fried Mixed Vegetables *(Chao Shi Jin)*. 110

Sichuan Noodles *(Dan Dan Mian)* 112

Hakka Choi Bo and Chives Omelet *(Jiu Cai Dan Bing)* 114

Braised Tofu and Eggplant *(Qie Xiang Dou Fu)* 116

Crispy Tofu with Vegetables *(Jia Zha Dou Fu)* 118

Sichuan Vegetarian Ma-Po Tofu *(Ma Po Dou Fu)* 120

Braised Seitan with Peanuts and Black Fungus *(Lao Hua Sheng Dou Fu)*. 122

Meat, Poultry, Fish and Seafood Dishes

Sichuan Beef Stir-Fry *(Si Chuan Jiang Bao Niu Rou)* 124

Stir-Fried Lamb with Scallions *(Cong Bao Yang Rou)*. 126

Steamed Egg with Ground Pork *(Zheng Dan)*. 127

Ma-Po Tofu with Pork
(Rou Jiang Ma Po Dou Fu)..... 128

Tofu with Spicy Meat and
Vegetables (Ma Po Dou Fu)... 129

Sautéed Chicken with
Onions and Balsam Pear
(Ku Gua Ji)................. 130

Hot-and-Spicy Chicken
(La Zi Ji).................. 132

Kung Pao Chicken
(Gong Bao Ji Din)........... 134

Hakka Chicken Curry (Ga Li Ji)... 136

Hakka Chicken Bao
(Ke Jia Ji Bao) 138

Hakka Braised Duck with
Lily Flower (Jin Zhen
Zheng Ya)................. 140

Cantonese Mushroom, Vegetable
and Scallop Stir-Fry (Xing Bao
Gu Chao Dai Zi) 142

Cantonese Fried Shrimp with
Cashews and Cucumber
(Yao Guo Xia Ren) 144

Beverages

Asian Pear Drink (Li Tang)....... 145

Hawthorn Drink
(Hong Guo Tang) 146

Red Date, Longan and
Ginger Tea (Zhao Zi Cha) 147

Wonton Soup *(Yun Tun Tang)*

Makes 4 servings

If you have been to a Chinese restaurant in North America, you have likely tried wonton soup. Now a popular dish worldwide, its Cantonese name literally means "swallowing clouds," referring to the tender wonton dumplings floating on top. Premade wonton soups in grocery stores usually have a lot of sodium and carbohydrates and no fresh vegetables. Here is a simple, quick recipe you can make at home that is far more healthy!

Tip

Premade wontons are available in the frozen section of Asian grocery stores if you don't have time to make your own. Read the labels and choose a brand with the lowest possible sodium and fat. That is still a healthier choice than buying premade wonton soup.

Nutrition info per serving	
Calories	134
Fat, total	3 g
Fat, saturated	0.5 g
Cholesterol	29 mg
Sodium	339 mg
Carbohydrate	17 g
Fiber	2 g
Protein	11 g
Food Choices	
1	Carbohydrate

Preparation time: 10 minutes
Cooking time: 15 minutes

12	Homemade Wontons (page 101), prepared through step 2	12
8	heads baby bok choy, trimmed	8
8	stalks Chinese broccoli, trimmed	8
½ cup	bean sprouts	125 mL
2 cups	ready-to-use reduced-sodium chicken broth	500 mL
1 tsp	natural rice vinegar	5 mL
½ tsp	toasted sesame oil	2 mL
½ tsp	reduced-sodium soy sauce	2 mL
¼ tsp	freshly ground black pepper	1 mL
2 tbsp	chopped green onions (optional)	30 mL

1. Bring a large pot of water to a boil over high heat. Add wontons, one by one, and boil for 6 to 8 minutes or until wontons float to the surface. Transfer wontons to a large bowl of cold water to stop the cooking. Drain.

2. Meanwhile, in another pot of boiling water, cook bok choy, broccoli and bean sprouts for 1 minute. Transfer vegetables to a large bowl of cold water to stop the cooking. Drain.

3. In a pot, combine wontons, vegetables, broth, vinegar, oil, soy sauce and pepper; bring to a boil over high heat. Reduce heat and simmer for 1 minute.

4. Serve garnished with green onions, if desired.

Tips

To reduce the sodium in this recipe, use ready-to-use no-salt-added chicken broth or, for more flavor, make your own chicken stock at home (see recipe, page 246).

If Chinese broccoli is not available, substitute additional baby bok choy or rapini.

Chinese Broccoli

Chinese broccoli (*gai lan*) belongs to the mustard green family. This green leafy vegetable is long and slender, with a stalk, leaves and tiny white-yellow flowers, all of which are edible. Blanching Chinese broccoli before adding it to recipes enhances its flavor.

Split Yellow Pigeon Pea Soup (page 28) with South Indian
Dosas (page 34) and Coconut Chutney (page 89)

Vegetable and Cheese Curry (page 56)

South Indian Coconut Shrimp Curry (page 83)

Wonton Soup (page 96)

Sichuan Beef Stir-Fry (page 124)

Cantonese Mushroom, Vegetable
and Scallop Stir-Fry (page 142)

Chicken Corn Soup *(Ji Rong Su Mi Tang)*

Makes 5 servings

This recipe is meant to be simple: just creamed sweet corn, chicken and egg. If you like some heat, stir in ¼ tsp (1 mL) garlic chile sauce (sambal) to the pot before serving. While this addition is not traditional, it will add more flavor to this sodium-reduced recipe.

Tips

If you have homemade chicken stock on hand (see recipe, page 246), use it in place of the chicken broth: the flavor of this soup will be noticeably improved.

Browning the chicken adds flavor, but if you prefer, you can skip that part of step 1 and simply add the chicken in step 2.

To lower the cholesterol in this dish, use 4 egg whites in place of the whole eggs.

Nutrition info per serving

Calories	187
Fat, total	5 g
Fat, saturated	1.0 g
Cholesterol	109 mg
Sodium	465 mg
Carbohydrate	14 g
Fiber	1 g
Protein	20 g

Food Choices

1	Carbohydrate
2½	Meat & Alternatives

Preparation time: **15 minutes**
Cooking time: **25 minutes**

- **Blender, food processor or immersion blender (optional)**

1½ tsp	vegetable oil	7 mL
1 tbsp	finely chopped shallot	15 mL
1 lb	boneless skinless chicken breast, finely chopped	500 g
4	slices gingerroot (⅛ inch/3 mm thick and 1 inch/2.5 cm wide)	4
1	can (14 oz/398 mL) cream-style corn	1
4 cups	ready-to-use no-salt-added chicken broth	1 L
1 tbsp	reduced-sodium soy sauce	15 mL
1½ tsp	natural rice vinegar	7 mL
¼ tsp	freshly ground white pepper	1 mL
2 tbsp	cornstarch	30 mL
¼ cup	cold water	60 mL
2	large eggs, well beaten	2
¼ cup	chopped green onions	60 mL

1. In a large skillet, heat oil over medium heat. Add shallots and cook, stirring, for 1 minute. Add chicken and cook, stirring, for about 3 minutes or until browned on all sides.

2. Meanwhile, in a medium pot, combine ginger, corn and broth. Bring to a boil over medium-high heat. Stir in chicken mixture, soy sauce, vinegar and pepper; reduce heat and simmer for 5 minutes.

3. In a small bowl, quickly stir together cornstarch and cold water to form a paste. Add to soup and simmer for about 5 minutes or until soup is thickened and chicken is no longer pink inside.

4. Increase heat to medium and, using one hand to slowly stir the soup in a circular motion, with the other hand gradually drizzle the eggs in a circular motion in the opposite direction; cook, stirring, for about 2 minutes or until all cooked egg floats to surface. Remove from heat and discard ginger.

5. If you would like a smoother soup, transfer soup to blender in batches (or use immersion blender in pot), and purée to desired consistency. Return to pot, if necessary, and reheat over medium heat, stirring often, until steaming.

6. Serve garnished with green onions.

Sichuan Vegetarian Hot-and-Sour Soup *(Suan La Tang)*

Makes 6 servings

Sichuan cuisine is known for its use of mouth-numbing spices and the Sichuan pepper. This soup is a great mix of hot (from the chile oil) and sour (from the rice vinegar). Most Chinese chile oil is made from Sichuan peppers, but make sure to check, as that is what imparts the great flavor.

Nutrition info per serving	
Calories	86
Fat, total	2 g
Fat, saturated	0.4 g
Cholesterol	31 mg
Sodium	241 mg
Carbohydrate	12 g
Fiber	3 g
Protein	6 g
Food Choices	
½	Meat & Alternatives
1	Extra

Soaking time: **30 minutes**
Preparation time: **25 minutes**
Cooking time: **15 minutes**

⅓ cup	dried wood ear mushrooms (see box, page 105)	75 mL
	Cold water	
5 cups	ready-to-use reduced-sodium vegetable broth	1.25 L
1 cup	finely julienned firm tofu (see tips, opposite)	250 mL
½ cup	finely julienned rinsed drained canned bamboo shoots (see box, page 108)	125 mL
½ cup	finely julienned fresh water chestnuts (see tip, opposite)	125 mL
½ cup	finely julienned enoki mushrooms (see box, opposite)	125 mL
⅓ cup	finely julienned carrots	75 mL
¼ cup	shredded Sichuan pickled cabbage (see tip, opposite)	60 mL
2 tsp	minced gingerroot	10 mL
⅛ tsp	freshly ground black pepper	0.5 mL
2 tbsp	natural rice vinegar	30 mL
1 tbsp	chile oil	15 mL
1 tsp	dark soy sauce	5 mL
¼ tsp	toasted sesame oil	1 mL
2 tbsp	cornstarch	30 mL
1	large egg, well beaten	1

1. Place wood ear mushrooms in a small bowl with enough cold water to cover; let soak for 30 minutes. Drain and cut into strips.

2. In a pot, bring broth to a boil over medium heat. Stir in wood ear mushrooms, tofu, bamboo shoots, water chestnuts, enoki mushrooms, carrots and cabbage; increase heat to high and bring to a boil. Stir in ginger, pepper, vinegar, chili oil, soy sauce and sesame oil. Reduce heat to medium.

3. In a small bowl, quickly stir together cornstarch and 2 tbsp (30 mL) cold water to form a paste. Add to soup and cook, stirring, until thickened.

4. Using one hand to slowly stir the soup in a circular motion, with the other hand gradually drizzle the egg in a circular motion in the opposite direction; cook, stirring, for about 2 minutes or until all cooked egg floats to surface.

Tips

To reduce the sodium in this recipe, use ready-to-use no-salt-added vegetable broth or, for more flavor, make your own vegetable stock at home (see recipe, page 245).

Chinese tofu, sold at Asian grocery stores, tends to be moister and smoother than the tofu sold in regular grocery stores. It's a good choice for this recipe if you can find it.

To reduce the total fat content of this dish, use low-fat tofu.

To "julienne" means to cut vegetables into long, thin pieces, similar to matchsticks. Although chefs disagree on the "proper" dimensions of these sticks, an easy rule of thumb is to make them 2 inches (5 cm) long and between $\frac{1}{16}$ and $\frac{1}{8}$ inch (2 and 3 mm) thick. If a recipe calls for "finely julienned" vegetables, tend toward the thinner side; if it calls for "julienned" vegetables, cut them a bit thicker.

If fresh water chestnuts are not available, you can use canned. Canned water chestnuts are readily available and contain very little or no added salt.

Sichuan pickled cabbage (*si chuan pao cai*) is pickled stems of mustard cabbage. It has a pungent aroma and is very salty, so it should be used sparingly.

Enoki Mushrooms

Enoki mushrooms (*jin zhen gu*), also known as enokitake, golden needle or lily mushrooms, are long, thin white mushrooms with small, shiny caps. Look for them at Asian grocery stores. To prepare them, first cut off the bottom end, where dirt and sand accumulate. Then wash the mushrooms gently under cold water. If fresh enoki mushrooms are not available, canned can be used; just be sure to drain and rinse them thoroughly before use. Alternatively, substitute white button mushrooms.

Chayote Salad *(Liang Ban Fo Shou Gua)*

Makes 4 servings

In Cantonese, chayote are known as *fo shou gua*, which literally translates to "Buddha's fists," because they resemble hands clasped in prayer. Chayote is also known as vegetable pear or chayote squash and can be eaten raw or cooked. The original recipe for this salad calls for pine nuts, but walnuts also work nicely.

Preparation time: 15 minutes

1	chayote, peeled, seeded and julienned	1
1/2 cup	julienned carrot	125 mL
1/2 cup	julienned red bell pepper	125 mL
2 tbsp	drained Japanese pickled ginger (see box, below), cut into thin strips	30 mL
2 tsp	pine nuts or chopped walnuts, toasted (see tip, below)	10 mL
1 tsp	granulated sugar	5 mL
1/4 tsp	salt	1 mL
1 tsp	Japanese pickled ginger juice	5 mL
1 tsp	natural rice vinegar	5 mL

1. In a medium bowl, combine chayote, carrot, red pepper, ginger and pine nuts.
2. In a small bowl, combine sugar, salt, ginger juice and vinegar. Pour over salad and toss to coat.

Tips

To "julienne" means to cut vegetables into long, thin pieces, similar to matchsticks. Although chefs disagree on the "proper" dimensions of these sticks, an easy rule of thumb is to make them 2 inches (5 cm) long and between 1/16 and 1/8 inch (2 and 3 mm) thick. If a recipe calls for "finely julienned" vegetables, tend toward the thinner side; if it calls for "julienned" vegetables, cut them a bit thicker.

If you cannot find Japanese pickled ginger, use any pickled ginger or pickled vegetable for flavor.

Toast nuts in a small dry skillet over medium heat, stirring constantly for 3 to 4 minutes or until golden and fragrant. Immediately transfer to a bowl and let cool.

Nutrition info per serving

Calories	44
Fat, total	1 g
Fat, saturated	0.1 g
Cholesterol	0 mg
Sodium	207 mg
Carbohydrate	8 g
Fiber	2 g
Protein	1 g
Food Choices	
1	Extra

Japanese Pickled Ginger

Japanese pickled ginger (*gari*) is a young ginger that is pickled with sugar and vinegar. It can be pink or white, and is usually eaten with sushi. Always measure pickled ginger juice precisely, as it adds sodium to your dishes. It can also add a bitter quality if not used sparingly.

Homemade Wontons *(Xian Hun Tun)*

Makes 24 wontons

Wontons are a type of dumpling similar to ravioli. They are stuffed with filling — often minced pork, but I've used a mixture of chicken and shrimp. Wontons are usually fried, but boiling them reduces the fat. Add them to Wonton Soup (page 96) or serve with hoisin sauce or a dipping sauce made of 1 tsp (5 mL) hoisin sauce, ½ tsp (2 ml) garlic chile sauce (sambal) and 2 tsp (10 mL) red wine vinegar.

Tip

Wontons can be prepared through step 2 and frozen in airtight containers, layered with parchment paper as necessary, for up to 3 months. Before making soup (page 96), thaw them overnight in the refrigerator, making sure they are not touching each other, as they can stick together as they thaw.

Nutrition info per 2 wontons

Calories	69
Fat, total	1 g
Fat, saturated	0.1 g
Cholesterol	10 mg
Sodium	183 mg
Carbohydrate	10 g
Fiber	0 g
Protein	5 g

Food Choices

½	Carbohydrate

Preparation time: **30 minutes**
Marinating time: **30 minutes**
Cooking time: **8 minutes**

- **Food processor (optional)**

1	boneless skinless chicken breast (4 oz/125 g), finely chopped	1
½ cup	finely chopped peeled shrimp	125 mL
1 tbsp	finely chopped green onions	15 mL
½ tsp	finely chopped gingerroot	2 mL
1½ tsp	cornstarch	7 mL
1	large egg white	1
1 tbsp	natural rice vinegar	15 mL
1½ tsp	reduced-sodium soy sauce	7 mL
¼ tsp	toasted sesame oil	1 mL
24	3½-inch (8.5 cm) wonton wrappers (see tip, below)	24

1. In a food processor (or in a large bowl), combine chicken, shrimp, green onions, ginger, cornstarch, egg white, vinegar, soy sauce and oil; process to form a smooth paste (or stir to thoroughly combine). Cover and refrigerate for 30 minutes.

2. Work with 3 or 4 wonton wrappers at a time and keep the remaining wrappers under a damp cloth to prevent them from drying out. Place about 1 tsp (5 mL) filling in the center of each wonton wrapper. Dampen the edges of the wrapper with a little water. Fold one corner across to the opposite corner to make a triangle. Press all of the edges firmly together to seal tightly. Bring the two farthest edges of the triangle together and cross them over, adding a bit of water between them to seal.

3. Bring a large pot of water to a boil over high heat. Add wontons, one by one, and boil for 6 to 8 minutes or until wontons float to the surface. Transfer wontons to large bowl of cold water to stop the cooking. Drain.

Tips

To reduce the saturated fat in your cooking, always purchase skinless chicken or remove the skin yourself. Trim off any excess fat before cooking.

Wonton wrappers, both fresh and frozen, are readily available at local grocery stores. Frozen wrappers need to be thawed before use or they will stick together.

Hakka Bamboo Shoot Dumplings
(Sun Gan Jiao)

Dumplings are famous in Chinese cuisine. These dumplings are from the Hakka style of cooking, which originated in the province of Guangdong and is similar to Cantonese cuisine in many ways. Hakka cuisine is meant to be simple: mainly vegetarian dishes with little in the way of extra flavoring.

Soaking time: **20 minutes**
Preparation time: **45 minutes**
Cooking time: **55 minutes**

- **Bamboo steamer (see tip, opposite), lined with parchment paper**

2 tbsp	dried shrimp	30 mL
	Water	
2 tbsp	vegetable oil, divided	30 mL
1 tbsp	chopped onion	15 mL
1 tbsp	minced garlic	15 mL
$\frac{1}{2}$ cup	chopped stemmed shiitake mushrooms	125 mL
$1\frac{1}{2}$ tsp	fish sauce	7 mL
$3\frac{1}{2}$ oz	lean ground chicken ($\frac{1}{2}$ cup/125 mL)	100 g
1 cup	shredded rinsed drained canned bamboo shoots (see box, page 108)	250 mL
1 cup	shredded medium-firm tofu	250 mL
1 tsp	freshly ground black pepper	5 mL
$\frac{1}{4}$ tsp	toasted sesame oil	1 mL
36	$3\frac{1}{2}$-inch (8.5 cm) round dumpling wrappers	36

1. Place shrimp in a bowl with enough cold water to cover; let soak for 20 minutes. Drain and mince (or grind in a mini food processor).

2. In a skillet, heat half the vegetable oil over medium heat. Add onion and garlic; cook, stirring, for about 1 minute or until golden. Stir in shrimp, mushrooms and fish sauce. Push mixture to edges of the pan, leaving the center empty. Add remaining oil to center, followed by chicken. Combine all ingredients and cook, stirring, for 3 minutes.

3. Add bamboo shoots and cook, stirring, for 2 minutes. Stir in tofu, pepper and sesame oil. Remove from heat.

4. Place about $1\frac{1}{2}$ tbsp (22 mL) filling in the center of each dumpling wrapper. Dampen the edges of the wrapper with a little water and fold one edge over to meet the other, forming a semicircle. Seal the dumpling by pressing the edges firmly together.

Nutrition info
per 3 dumplings

Calories	114
Fat, total	4 g
Fat, saturated	0.4 g
Cholesterol	7 mg
Sodium	131 mg
Carbohydrate	13 g
Fiber	1 g
Protein	6 g

Food Choices

$\frac{1}{2}$	Carbohydrate
$\frac{1}{2}$	Meat & Alternatives
$\frac{1}{2}$	Fat

Tips

Chinese tofu, sold at Asian grocery stores, tends to be moister and smoother than the tofu sold in regular grocery stores. It's a good choice for this recipe if you can find it.

To reduce the total fat content of this dish, use low-fat tofu.

Dumplings are traditionally eaten with soy sauce and therefore tend to be simple in flavor. Since the sodium content of this dish is already high, make sure to use reduced-sodium soy sauce, and try to use as little as possible.

5. In a large skillet, bring 2 to 3 inches (5 to 7.5 cm) of water to a boil. Add 9 dumplings to the bamboo steamer, leaving space between them. Cover the steamer and place it in the skillet, making sure the sides of the steamer do not touch the pan. Steam for 10 minutes or until tender and filling is hot. Repeat with the remaining dumplings.

Tip

Widely used in Asian cuisine, a bamboo steamer is designed to fit inside a large skillet. It is circular and has a slotted bottom where the food sits and is cooked by the steam rising from the boiling water below. It has a tight lid to prevent steam from escaping. Bamboo steamers can be stacked on top of each other in tiers, making it easier to cook several items at once. Bamboo steamers can be purchased at any Asian market or grocery store. If you can't find one, a regular kitchen steamer can be used.

Fresh Shiitake Mushrooms

Shiitake mushrooms (*xiang gu*) have been used in Asian cuisines for centuries and are a staple in Chinese medicine. They provide antioxidants, fiber, vitamins and minerals, and some studies have shown that they may have immune-boosting properties that might prove helpful in the fight against cancer. These mushrooms have recently become popular in Western cuisines due to their unique smoky flavor. Look for mushrooms that are firm, plump and clean, and avoid those that are wrinkled or have wet, slimy spots. The stems of shiitake mushrooms are tough, so they should be removed before cooking but can be used to flavor stocks. If fresh shiitake mushrooms are not available, dried can be used; for information on dried shiitake mushrooms, see box, page 111.

Vegetarian Tofu Rolls *(Dou Fu Juan)*

Makes 18 rolls

This tasty vegetarian snack is typically deep-fried, but here the rolls are lightly pan-fried in a small amount of oil to keep the fat low. Serve with Worcestershire sauce or Chinese red vinegar.

Soaking time: **30 minutes**
Preparation time: **30 minutes**
Cooking time: **20 minutes**

- **18 toothpicks**

8	dried shiitake mushrooms, stems removed	8
1/4 cup	dried wood ear mushrooms (see box, opposite)	60 mL
	Cold water	
3 tbsp	vegetable oil, divided	45 mL
3/4 cup	finely julienned carrots	175 mL
1 tsp	minced gingerroot	5 mL
1 1/2 cups	bean sprouts	375 mL
6 tbsp	shredded seitan (see box, page 121)	90 mL
3/4 cup	finely julienned celery	175 mL
1 tsp	salt	5 mL
1/2 cup	ready-to-use reduced-sodium vegetable broth	125 mL
1/2 tsp	granulated sugar	2 mL
3/4 cup	finely julienned rinsed drained canned bamboo shoots (see box, page 108)	175 mL
1 tsp	freshly ground black pepper	5 mL
1 1/2 tsp	vegetarian red soybean paste	7 mL
1/2 tsp	toasted sesame oil	2 mL
2	fresh tofu skin sheets (see tip, opposite), cut into 6-inch (15 cm) squares	2

1. Place shiitake and wood ear mushrooms in a bowl with enough cold water to cover; let soak for 30 minutes. Drain and rinse well. Shred mushrooms and set aside.

2. In a medium nonstick saucepan, heat 2 tbsp (30 mL) vegetable oil over medium heat. Add carrots and ginger; reduce heat to medium-low and cook for 1 minute. Add mushrooms and bean sprouts; cook, stirring, for 1 minute. Add seitan and cook, stirring, for 30 seconds. Add celery and salt; cook, stirring, for 2 minutes.

3. Stir in 2 tbsp (30 mL) broth and cook for 1 minute. Stir in sugar and cook for 1 minute. Stir in bamboo shoots and cook for 2 minutes. Stir in black pepper and the remaining broth; cook for 2 minutes. Stir in bean paste and cook for 30 seconds. Remove from heat and stir in sesame oil.

Nutrition info per roll	
Calories	64
Fat, total	3 g
Fat, saturated	0.2 g
Cholesterol	0 mg
Sodium	159 mg
Carbohydrate	4 g
Fiber	1 g
Protein	5 g
Food Choices	
1/2	Fat
1	Extra

Tips

To "julienne" means to cut vegetables into long, thin pieces, similar to matchsticks. Although chefs disagree on the "proper" dimensions of these sticks, an easy rule of thumb is to make them 2 inches (5 cm) long and between $\frac{1}{16}$ and $\frac{1}{8}$ inch (2 and 3 mm) thick. If a recipe calls for "finely julienned" vegetables, tend toward the thinner side; if it calls for "julienned" vegetables, cut them a bit thicker.

To reduce the sodium in this recipe, use ready-to-use no-salt-added vegetable broth or, for more flavor, make your own vegetable stock at home (see recipe, page 245).

4. Place about $\frac{1}{4}$ cup (60 mL) filling in the center of each tofu skin square. Fold the right side of the skin over the filling into the center of the square. Fold the bottom and top sides of the skin. Fold the left side of the skin over to the right edge of the roll, forming a rectangle. Secure the folds with a toothpick, threading the toothpick in and out in such a way that the toothpick does not pierce through the entire roll.

5. In a skillet, heat the remaining vegetable oil over medium-high heat. Add rolls, folded side down, in batches as necessary, and cook for 1 minute or until golden brown on the bottom. Remove the toothpicks (the heat will have sealed the openings), turn the rolls over and cook for 1 minute or until golden brown. Transfer rolls to a plate lined with paper towels to drain. Adjust heat as necessary between batches to prevent burning.

Tips

Tofu skin sheets, also called bean curd sheets, are yet another soybean product. When soy milk is boiled, a skin forms on the surface that can be skimmed off, hung and dried to form sheets. Like tofu, the sheets do not have an aroma or flavor of their own, but will absorb the flavor of ingredients they are cooked with. Tofu skin sheets are available dried or fresh. The sheets used in this recipe can be found in the freezer section of Asian grocery stores.

Oyster sauce and soy sauce (see page 20) are common inclusions in this recipe, but they add a considerable amount of sodium.

Wood Ear Mushrooms

Wood ear mushrooms (*mu er*) derived their name from their resemblance to the shape of an ear. Dried wood ears should be soaked in cold water for at least 30 minutes before use, but can also be soaked overnight so that they are soft and ready to cook the next day. If soaked long enough, they eventually expand to at least double in size. If dried wood ear mushrooms are not available, dried shiitake mushrooms can be used.

Chinese Tea Eggs *(Cha Ye Dan)*

In China, tea eggs are sold as a savory street snack, but they are also a common breakfast food, particularly in northern China. They are also known as marbled eggs because of the unique marbled pattern on the surface of the egg. The longer you steep the eggs, the stronger the flavor, the deeper the color and the more pronounced the marbled effect. They are usually eaten with rice or congee and soy milk.

Tip

Tea eggs can be stored in an airtight container in the refrigerator for to 3 days.

Nutrition info per serving

Calories	66
Fat, total	4 g
Fat, saturated	1.4 g
Cholesterol	154 mg
Sodium	76 mg
Carbohydrate	1 g
Fiber	0 g
Protein	5 g

Food Choices

½	Meat & Alternatives
½	Fat

Preparation time: 10 minutes
Cooking time: 1 hour
Marinating time: 4 hours or overnight

3½ cups	cold water (approx.)	875 mL
6	large eggs (in shell)	6
3	star anise pods (see page 21)	3
3	1-inch (2.5 cm) pieces gingerroot, thinly sliced	3
2	bay leaves	2
2	black tea bags	2
2	strips dried mandarin peel (optional)	2
1	1-inch (2.5 cm) cassia cinnamon stick	1
1 tbsp	reduced-sodium soy sauce	15 mL
1 tbsp	dark soy sauce	15 mL
1 tbsp	salt	15 mL
1 tbsp	granulated sugar	15 mL
2 tsp	crushed Sichuan peppercorns	10 mL
1½ tsp	whole cloves	7 mL
1½ tsp	cumin seeds	7 mL

1. Place cold water in a saucepan, then carefully place eggs in the water. The water should be at least ½ inch (1 cm) higher than the eggs. Gently stir in star anise, ginger, bay leaves, tea bags, mandarin peel, cassia, soy sauce, dark soy sauce, salt, sugar, peppercorns, cloves and cumin seeds. Bring to a boil over high heat. Boil for 20 minutes or until eggs are hard-cooked.

2. Using a slotted spoon, remove the eggs (do not drain the cooking liquid). Using the edge of a knife or spoon, tap each egg to lightly crack the shells all around, keeping the egg intact inside. Return the eggs to the cooking liquid.

3. Cover and simmer over low heat for 20 minutes, adding more water if necessary. Remove from heat and let cool, then cover and refrigerate for at least 4 hours or (preferably) overnight. Drain and serve cold.

Tips

You can use loose black tea leaves in place of the tea bags, if you prefer. They will impart a stronger flavor and color, so use no more than 1½ tbsp (22 mL) unless you like a really strong tea flavor.

For this recipe, use whole spices, not ground — the flavor of whole spices is much stronger.

Baby Bok Choy and Mushrooms with Oyster Sauce
(Qing Cai Chao Xiang Gu)

Shiitake mushrooms are widely used in Chinese cuisine, partly because they are believed to increase longevity. They are also an excellent source of vitamin D if cultured in the sun. The soy sauce and oyster sauce are reduced in this dish to keep the sodium low, but it still tastes fabulous.

Preparation time: **20 minutes**
Cooking time: **10 minutes**

2 tsp	vegetable oil	10 mL
3	cloves garlic, minced	3
1 tsp	minced gingerroot	5 mL
4 oz	shiitake mushrooms, stems removed and caps halved	125 g
1 lb	baby bok choy	500 g
1 tsp	cornstarch	5 mL
2 tsp	oyster sauce	10 mL
2 tsp	reduced-sodium soy sauce	10 mL

1. In a wok or nonstick skillet, heat oil over medium heat. Add garlic and ginger; stir-fry until fragrant and golden. Add mushrooms and stir-fry for 1 to 2 minutes or until tender. Add bok choy and stir-fry until just wilted.

2. In a small bowl, combine cornstarch, oyster sauce and soy sauce. Add to wok and cook, stirring, for about 2 minutes or until sauce is thickened.

Tip

When cooking with a small amount of oil, be sure to heat it well before adding the other ingredients; otherwise, they may simply absorb the oil, which can cause sticking and burning.

Bok Choy

Officially classified as a cabbage, bok choy (you cai) is popular in Asian cuisines. Look for smaller bok choy, such as baby bok choy, as they are usually more tender and can be eaten raw. Try to use bok choy as soon as you can; the leaves will start to wilt and will not last more than 2 to 3 days.

Nutrition info per serving

Calories	106
Fat, total	5 g
Fat, saturated	0.0 g
Cholesterol	0 mg
Sodium	393 mg
Carbohydrate	13 g
Fiber	4 g
Protein	5 g

Food Choices

1	Fat
1	Extra

Bamboo Shoots with Mushrooms
(Mo Gu Chao Sun)

Dried shiitake mushrooms impart an intense umami flavor to dishes that makes it worth the added time it takes to soak them. In this simple dish, I have called for winter bamboo shoots, which are canned when bamboo is at its best.

Tip

One tablespoon (15 mL) of regular soy sauce contains 1000 mg or more sodium. The reduced-sodium variety is a better option, but even then, always measure the amount you use: reduced-sodium soy sauce still has 580 mg or more sodium per tablespoon. Too much sodium can lead to high blood pressure, heart disease, stroke and kidney disease.

Nutrition info per serving

Calories	73
Fat, total	3 g
Fat, saturated	0.5 g
Cholesterol	0 mg
Sodium	234 mg
Carbohydrate	10 g
Fiber	2 g
Protein	3 g
Food Choices	
½	Fat
1	Extra

Soaking time: **20 minutes**
Preparation time: **15 minutes**
Cooking time: **10 minutes**

12	dried shiitake mushrooms, stems removed	12
	Cold water	
1	can (10¾ oz/304 g) winter bamboo shoots (see box, below)	1
1 tbsp	peanut oil	15 mL
1½ tsp	granulated sugar	7 mL
3 tbsp	reduced-sodium soy sauce	45 mL
2 tsp	Chinese cooking wine (see page 19)	10 mL
2 tsp	finely chopped green onion	10 mL

1. Place mushrooms in a bowl with enough cold water to cover; let soak for 20 minutes. Drain and rinse well. Cut into ¼-inch (0.5 cm) slices.

2. Drain bamboo shoots, reserving 2 tbsp (30 mL) liquid. Rinse bamboo shoots, then cut into ⅛-inch (3 mm) slices.

3. In a wok or nonstick skillet, heat oil over medium heat. Add mushrooms and bamboo shoots; stir-fry for about 3 minutes or until starting to brown. Stir in sugar, bamboo liquid, soy sauce and wine; reduce heat to low, cover and simmer for 5 minutes.

4. Serve garnished with green onion.

Bamboo Shoots

Used in many Asian dishes as a vegetable, bamboo shoots (zhu sun) are the edible shoots of the bamboo plant. Fresh bamboo shoots can be difficult to find, and need to be parboiled before use, as certain types contain a highly toxic acid and are very bitter. Canned bamboo shoots are available year-round at Asian grocery stores and well-stocked supermarkets, and are precooked. Many brands have no sodium, but it's still a good idea to drain and rinse them before use. Once opened, leftover bamboo shoots can be stored in an airtight container in the refrigerator for up to 3 weeks, as long as they are covered in fresh water that is changed every 2 days. In Asian stores, you may also find vacuum-packed bamboo, which is also precooked, but it must be used up right away after opening.

Hakka Stir-Fried Soybean Sprouts
(Chao Dou Ya)

Here's another fabulously simple Hakka-style dish. Tofu is a complete protein and hence a great vegetarian replacement for meat. It is also a source of calcium.

Preparation time: **15 minutes**
Cooking time: **15 minutes**

1 ½ tsp	peanut oil, divided	7 mL
3 cups	bean sprouts	750 mL
2 tsp	minced garlic	10 mL
2 tsp	minced gingerroot	10 mL
1	red bell pepper, cut into 1-inch (2.5 cm) slices	1
¼ cup	chopped Chinese celery (see tip, below)	60 mL
4 cups	chopped leeks (white and light green parts only)	1 L
1 to 2 tbsp	water (optional)	15 to 30 mL
¾ cup	julienned firm tofu (see tips, page 103)	175 mL
1 tbsp	sherry	15 mL
2 ¼ tsp	fish sauce	11 mL
½ tsp	toasted sesame oil	2 mL

1. In a nonstick skillet, heat half the peanut oil over medium heat. Add bean sprouts and cook, stirring, for about 3 minutes or until tender. Transfer bean sprouts to a plate and set aside.

2. Add the remaining peanut oil to the pan and heat over medium heat. Add garlic and ginger; cook, stirring, for about 30 seconds or until fragrant. Add red pepper and celery; cook, stirring, for about 4 minutes or until tender. Add leeks and cook, stirring, for 2 minutes. If vegetables are sticking to the pan, stir in 1 to 2 tbsp (15 to 30 mL) water.

3. Add tofu and cook, stirring, for 1 minute. Return bean sprouts to the pan, along with sherry and fish sauce, stirring to combine. Remove from heat and stir in sesame oil.

Tips

Chinese celery (*tang qin*), a variety grown in East Asian countries, has thinner stems and a stronger flavor than regular celery. It is not eaten raw, but is added to soups and stir-fries. It can be found in most Asian grocery stores. If it is not available, regular celery can be substituted.

Sherry is a common addition to vegetarian Chinese dishes. If you don't have any on hand, you can use dry red wine instead.

Nutrition info per serving

Calories	110
Fat, total	4 g
Fat, saturated	0.5 g
Cholesterol	0 mg
Sodium	278 mg
Carbohydrate	15 g
Fiber	3 g
Protein	5 g

Food Choices

½	Meat & Alternatives
½	Fat
1	Extra

Stir-Fried Mixed Vegetables
(Chao Shi Jin)

Makes 6 servings

This simple dish is popular all over China, and may be served hot or cold. There are many variations, so feel free to experiment! It is usually served with a side of rice. For a complete meal, you can add some pan-fried tofu, fruit and soy milk. I cut back on the typical amount of soy sauce to reduce the sodium content.

Soaking time: 20 minutes
Preparation time: 20 minutes
Cooking time: 15 minutes

5	dried shiitake mushrooms, stems removed	5
	Cold water	
1	large carrot, cut diagonally into 1/4-inch (0.5 cm) thick slices	1
1/2 cup	snow peas, trimmed	125 mL
1 tbsp	vegetable oil	30 mL
3/4 cup	rinsed drained canned bamboo shoots (see box, page 108), cut into 1 1/2-inch (4 cm) strips	175 mL
1 tbsp	minced gingerroot	30 mL
1	cucumber, cut diagonally into 1/4-inch (0.5 cm) thick slices	1
1/2 tsp	salt	2 mL
1 tsp	granulated sugar	5 mL
2 tbsp	reduced-sodium soy sauce	30 mL
3 tbsp	water (optional)	45 mL
1 cup	finely chopped cabbage	250 mL
1 tbsp	finely chopped green onion	15 mL

1. Place mushrooms in a bowl with enough cold water to cover; let soak for 20 minutes. Drain, rinse well and slice.

2. In a pot of boiling water, cook carrot and snow peas for 1 to 2 minutes or until snow peas are bright green. Drain and set aside.

3. In a wok or nonstick skillet, heat oil over medium-high heat. Add mushrooms, bamboo shoots and ginger; stir-fry for 1 minute, reducing heat if vegetables are sticking. Add cucumber and stir-fry over medium heat for 2 minutes.

4. Stir in salt, sugar and soy sauce; cook, stirring for 1 minute. If mixture is drying out, add 3 tbsp (45 mL) water and cook, stirring, for 2 minutes. Add cabbage and stir-fry for 1 minute. Add carrot and snow peas; stir-fry for 1 minute.

5. Serve garnished with green onion.

Nutrition info per serving	
Calories	61
Fat, total	2 g
Fat, saturated	0.2 g
Cholesterol	0 mg
Sodium	325 mg
Carbohydrate	9 g
Fiber	2 g
Protein	2 g
Food Choices	
1/2	Fat
1	Extra

Tips

Because only a small amount of oil is used in this dish, you'll need to keep a careful eye on the vegetables while they are cooking in steps 3 and 4. If they start to stick, reduce the heat and/or add a bit of water to the pan.

Nonstick pans require good care to protect the nonstick coating. Buy good-quality, heavy pans and never heat an empty pan. And always use plastic, rubber, silicon or wood utensils; metal tools or those with a sharp edge can cause some of the nonstick coating to scrape off into your food.

Dried Shiitake Mushrooms

Dried shiitake mushrooms, also known as dried Chinese mushrooms or black mushrooms, have an intense flavor and meaty texture. They are also sometimes labeled "fragrant mushrooms" because of their dusky aroma and fragrant flavor, which intensifies when they are dried. They are popular in Chinese cuisine and are used in soups, stir-fries and meat dishes. Despite one of their names, they are not always black; there are also brown, gray and beige varieties.

Look for dried shiitake mushrooms in Asian grocery stores. If they have stems attached, remove them before soaking. Soak in cold water for at least 20 minutes or overnight. Do not soak them in hot water or they will lose their fragrance. After soaking, gently rinse the mushrooms to remove any dirt from the gills. Leftover soaking liquid can be strained and used to enhance the flavor of stocks, soups and braising liquids.

Thanks to their unique flavor and texture, there is no true substitution for dried shiitake mushrooms, but if you cannot find them, substitute fresh shiitake, oyster, king oyster or portobello mushrooms and omit the soaking step. You can also buy canned shiitake or oyster mushrooms at Asian grocery stores; choose a brand with very little added sodium and rinse well.

Sichuan Noodles *(Dan Dan Mian)*

Makes 6 servings

This traditional Sichuan dish is sold in China as a popular street food. I toned down the heat a bit, but it is meant to have a lot of spice, so feel free to increase the amount of Sichuan pepper. *Dan dan* means "a carrying pole," and in years past, street vendors carried premade noodles and sauces on poles. Sichuan noodles can be served hot or cold.

Preparation time: 20 minutes
Cooking time: 10 to 15 minutes

½ cup	finely diced peeled English cucumber	125 mL
3 tbsp	minced green onion	45 mL
1 tbsp	minced garlic	15 mL
1 tbsp	finely diced Sichuan vegetable preserves	15 mL
1 tsp	granulated sugar	5 mL
1 tsp	ground Sichuan pepper	5 mL
1 cup	ready-to-use reduced-sodium chicken or vegetable broth	250 mL
3 tbsp	Asian sesame paste (see tip, opposite)	45 mL
2 tbsp	reduced-sodium soy sauce	30 mL
2 tbsp	natural rice vinegar	30 mL
1 tbsp	chile oil	15 mL
5 oz	fresh egg noodles	150 g
12	small heads baby bok choy, cut in half lengthwise	12
¼ tsp	toasted sesame oil	1 mL
3 tbsp	unsalted roasted peanuts, crushed	45 mL

1. In a saucepan, combine cucumber, green onion, garlic, preserves, sugar, Sichuan pepper, broth, sesame paste, soy sauce, vinegar and chile oil. Set aside.

2. In a pot of boiling water, cook noodles for about 3 minutes or until tender. Drain, rinse and transfer to a serving bowl.

3. Meanwhile, in another pot of boiling water, cook bok choy for 1 minute. Drain and set aside.

4. Bring cucumber mixture to a boil over high heat. Stir in sesame oil.

5. Pour sauce over noodles and arrange baby bok choy on top. Garnish with peanuts.

Nutrition info per serving	
Calories	171
Fat, total	10 g
Fat, saturated	1.3 g
Cholesterol	7 mg
Sodium	220 mg
Carbohydrate	17 g
Fiber	3 g
Protein	7 g

Food Choices

½	Carbohydrate
½	Meat & Alternatives
1½	Fat

Make It a Meal

1 serving Wonton Soup
(page 96)

2 servings Sichuan
Noodles

3 oz (90 g) regular firm
tofu, pan-fried in ½ tsp
(2 mL) vegetable oil
(1 Meat & Alternatives;
½ Fat)

1 cup (250 mL)
fortified plain soy milk
(1 Carbohydrate)

1 large Asian pear
(1 Carbohydrate)

Tips

The traditional inclusion of pork would add more fat to this recipe, but the vegetarian version is just as delicious as the original.

The amount of Sichuan vegetable preserves was reduced in this recipe to lower the sodium. Be sure to finely dice the preserves so that they are well distributed within the dish.

To reduce the sodium in this recipe, use ready-to-use no-salt-added broth or, for more flavor, make your own stock at home (see recipes, pages 245 and 246).

Look for Asian sesame paste at Asian grocery stores. It is made with toasted sesame seeds and imparts a different flavor than tahini.

If the dish is to be served cold, simply put it in the refrigerator for 30 minutes after it has cooled.

Sichuan Vegetable Preserves

The importance of preserved and pickled ingredients in Asian cuisine began in the days before refrigeration, when food had to be preserved but also traveled long distances. Sichuan vegetable preserves (*si chuan pao cai*) originated in Sichuan province, but are now available everywhere in Asia and even in well-stocked North American supermarkets. Sichuan preserves have a pungent aroma and are very salty, so they should be used sparingly. Before use, you can rinse them if desired to remove some salt and gritty bits.

Hakka Choi Bo and Chives Omelet
(Jiu Cai Dan Bing)

Although in North America we're accustomed to eating omelets for breakfast, in China, this dish is also often eaten for lunch or dinner. At breakfast, it's served with congee; at lunch or dinner, it's served with rice or noodles. I've adapted the traditional recipe by using egg whites in place of some of the whole eggs, to reduce the fat and cholesterol content of the dish.

Soaking time: **1 hour and 15 minutes**
Preparation time: **10 minutes**
Cooking time: **15 to 20 minutes**

1/4 cup	diced dried sweet daikon radish	60 mL
	Cold water	
3	large egg whites	3
1	large egg	1
1/4 tsp	salt	1 mL
1/2 tsp	fish sauce	2 mL
1/2 tsp	oyster sauce	2 mL
1/8 tsp	toasted sesame oil	0.5 mL
1 cup	chopped Chinese chives (1/2-inch/1 cm pieces)	250 mL
1 1/2 tsp	peanut oil, divided	7 mL
1/4 cup	chopped onion	60 mL

1. Place radish in a bowl with enough cold water to cover; let soak for 1 hour. Drain and pat dry with a towel. Return to the bowl and cover with more cold water; let soak for 15 minutes. Drain and pat dry with a towel. Set aside.

2. In a bowl, whisk together egg whites and egg. Stir in salt, fish sauce, oyster sauce and sesame oil. Stir in chives.

3. In a wok or nonstick skillet, heat half the peanut oil over medium heat. Add onion and cook, stirring, for 3 to 4 minutes or until golden. Add radish and cook, stirring, for 3 to 4 minutes or until softened. Stir onion mixture into egg mixture.

4. Add the remaining peanut oil to the wok and heat over medium-low heat. Pour in the egg mixture, swirling the eggs so they coat the pan evenly. Cook for 4 to 5 minutes or until lightly browned on the bottom. Flip the omelet over and cook for 2 to 3 minutes or until lightly browned on the other side.

Nutrition info per serving

Calories	75
Fat, total	3 g
Fat, saturated	0.7 g
Cholesterol	47 mg
Sodium	305 mg
Carbohydrate	6 g
Fiber	2 g
Protein	5 g

Food Choices

1/2	Meat & Alternatives
1/2	Fat

Tips

Daikon radish (*choi bo* or *luo bo gan*), also known as Chinese radish or Oriental radish, imparts a strong flavor to dishes. Dried daikon radish should always be soaked before use to remove the bitter flavor. Asian grocery stores sell both salty and sweet dried daikon radish. Choose sweet more often, as the salty version is high in sodium.

Fish sauce and oyster sauce (see page 20) have a high sodium content and should be used sparingly.

Nonstick pans require good care to protect the nonstick coating. Buy good-quality, heavy pans and never heat an empty pan. And always use plastic, rubber, silicon or wood utensils; metal tools or those with a sharp edge can cause some of the nonstick coating to scrape off into your food.

Chinese Chives

Also known as garlic chives, Chinese chives (*jiu cai*) are dark green with white flowers and broad leaves. Otherwise, they look very similar to regular chives and can be used and stored in the same way. As the name suggests, they have a delicate garlic flavor. If Chinese chives are not available, regular chives or green onions can be used.

Braised Tofu and Eggplant
(Qie Xiang Dou Fu)

Makes 6 servings

Here's another great way to enjoy a helping of tofu. One serving provides 2 oz (60 g) of soy protein. Add some more pan-fried tofu on the side, and you are on your way to 10 oz (300 g) of soy protein, an amount that has been shown to reduce LDL ("bad") blood cholesterol if consumed on a daily basis. Add in the benefits of eggplant, and this recipe is loaded with heart health!

Preparation time: **20 minutes**
Cooking time: **35 minutes**

● **Preheat oven to 425°F (220°C)**

12 oz	low-fat extra-firm tofu, drained and cut into 1/2-inch (1 cm) cubes	375 g
1/2 tsp	vegetable oil	2 mL
5	cloves garlic, minced	5
2	bird's eye chile peppers, seeded and minced	2
1	medium onion, coarsely chopped	1
2 tsp	minced gingerroot	10 mL
1 1/2 lbs	Chinese or Japanese eggplant, cut into 1 1/2-inch (4 cm) spears	750 g
1 1/2 cups	water	375 mL
2 tbsp	freshly squeezed lemon juice	30 mL
2 tbsp	reduced-sodium soy sauce	30 mL
1 1/2 tbsp	oyster sauce	22 mL
1 tbsp	natural rice vinegar	15 mL
1 tsp	cornstarch	5 mL
1/4 cup	cold water	60 mL
2	green onions, thinly sliced	2
1/8 tsp	freshly ground white pepper	0.5 mL

1. Arrange tofu in a single layer on a baking sheet. Bake in preheated oven for about 20 minutes or until lightly browned.

2. Meanwhile, in a wok or large nonstick skillet, heat oil over medium-high heat. Add garlic, chiles, onion and ginger; cook, stirring, until fragrant. Add eggplant and cook, stirring, for 2 minutes.

3. Stir in 1 1/2 cups (375 mL) water and lemon juice; bring to a boil over high heat. Reduce heat to low, cover and simmer for 10 minutes. Stir in tofu.

4. In a small bowl, combine soy sauce, oyster sauce and vinegar. Add to wok and simmer for 3 to 5 minutes or until eggplant is tender.

5. In a small bowl, quickly stir together cornstarch and cold water to form a paste. Add to wok and cook, stirring, until sauce is thickened. Stir in green onions and pepper.

Nutrition info per serving

Calories	109
Fat, total	2 g
Fat, saturated	0.1 g
Cholesterol	0 mg
Sodium	381 mg
Carbohydrate	16 g
Fiber	5 g
Protein	7 g

Food Choices

1/2	Meat & Alternatives
1	Extra

Make It a Meal

2 servings Sichuan Beef Stir-Fry (page 124)

1 serving Braised Tofu and Eggplant

2/3 cup (150 mL) unsalted cooked white or brown short-grain rice (2 Carbohydrate)

1 cup (250 mL) fortified plain soy milk (1 Carbohydrate)

1/2 cup (125 mL) chopped jackfruit (1 Carbohydrate)

Tips

Tofu is high in fat, though it is mostly polyunsaturated fats. To keep the overall fat down in the dish, low-fat tofu is used. If you can't find low-fat tofu, use regular extra-firm or firm tofu.

Compared to the common eggplant, Asian eggplants (*xie zi*) are longer and narrower, with a sweeter taste.

This recipe calls for natural rice vinegar. Be careful not to use seasoned rice vinegar, as it has added sugar and salt, and 1 tbsp (15 mL) can have as much as 250 mg of sodium.

Nutrition Tip

Eggplant is a good source of soluble fiber, which has been shown to lower low-density lipoprotein (LDL) blood cholesterol and blood glucose levels.

Crispy Tofu with Vegetables
(Jia Zha Dou Fu)

This popular Cantonese dish is usually eaten with rice noodles, but I suggest substituting buckwheat noodles so you can enjoy the benefits of a whole grain. Add more pan-fried tofu to your plate to increase the amount of soy protein, serve some soy milk and a fruit on the side, and you have a wholesome, healthy meal.

Nutrition info per serving	
Calories	180
Fat, total	4 g
Fat, saturated	0.2 g
Cholesterol	0 mg
Sodium	492 mg
Carbohydrate	24 g
Fiber	6 g
Protein	15 g
Food Choices	
1	Carbohydrate
1½	Meat & Alternatives

Soaking time: **20 minutes**
Preparation time: **15 minutes**
Cooking time: **30 to 35 minutes**

6	dried shiitake mushrooms, stems removed	6
	Cold water	
1 tsp	vegetable oil, divided	5 mL
11 oz	low-fat firm tofu, cut into 2-inch (5 cm) slices	330 g
1 tsp	minced gingerroot	5 mL
½ cup	dried TVP chunks (see box, opposite)	125 mL
½ cup	sliced rinsed drained canned bamboo shoots (see box, page 108)	125 mL
½ cup	sliced celery	125 mL
½ cup	julienned carrot	125 mL
6	baby bok choy	6
1 tsp	granulated sugar	5 mL
¼ tsp	salt	1 mL
2 tsp	sweet soybean paste (see tip, opposite)	10 mL
2 tsp	reduced-sodium soy sauce	10 mL
¼ tsp	toasted sesame oil	1 mL
½ cup	ready-to-use reduced-sodium vegetable broth	125 mL
1 tsp	cornstarch	5 mL
1 tsp	cold water	5 mL

1. Place mushrooms in a bowl with enough water to cover; let soak for 20 minutes. Drain and rinse well. Set aside.

2. In a wok or nonstick skillet, heat half the vegetable oil over medium-low heat. Add tofu and cook, turning once, for 10 to 15 minutes or until golden brown on both sides. Transfer tofu to a plate lined with paper towels to drain.

3. Add the remaining vegetable oil to the wok and heat over medium heat. Add mushrooms and ginger; stir-fry for about 3 minutes or until fragrant. Add TVP, bamboo shoots, celery, carrot and bok choy; stir-fry for about 5 minutes or until vegetables are slightly softened.

4. Stir in sugar, salt, bean paste, soy sauce and sesame oil. Stir in tofu and broth; increase heat to high and bring to a boil. Reduce heat and simmer for 5 minutes.

5. In a small bowl, quickly stir together cornstarch and cold water to form a paste. Add to wok and cook, stirring, for about 5 minutes or until slightly thickened.

Tips

Sweet soybean paste, also called sweet bean paste, is a dark-colored paste made mainly of flour, soybeans, sugar and salt. It goes well with meat and vegetable dishes, but use it sparingly. I have seen some brands with 3 g of carbohydrate and 650 mg of sodium per 1 tbsp (15 mL)! This recipe uses much less sweet soybean paste than the traditional version.

One tablespoon (15 mL) of regular soy sauce contains 1000 mg or more sodium. The reduced-sodium variety is a better option, but even then, always measure the amount you use: reduced-sodium soy sauce still has 580 mg or more sodium per tablespoon.

To reduce the sodium in this recipe, use ready-to-use no-salt-added vegetable broth or, for more flavor, make your own vegetable stock at home (see recipe, page 245).

Textured Vegetable Protein (TVP)

Textured vegetable protein (TVP), made from soybeans, mushrooms and seasonings, is used as a vegetarian meat replacement in many Asian dishes. Use it sparingly, as it can have a lot of added salt. Look for it in the tofu section of Asian grocery stores or well-stocked supermarkets.

Sichuan Vegetarian Ma-Po Tofu
(Ma Po Dou Fu)

Makes 5 servings

This spicy dish is popular in Chinese restaurants all over North America. The heat comes from the Sichuan pepper and chile bean paste. If you want even more heat, add more Sichuan pepper and not more chile bean paste, as the latter has a lot of added sodium.

Preparation time: **15 minutes**
Cooking time: **10 to 15 minutes**

1 1/2 tsp	vegetable oil	7 mL
1/2 cup	finely chopped seitan (see box, opposite)	125 mL
1/2 cup	minced stemmed shiitake mushrooms	125 mL
1 tsp	minced gingerroot	5 mL
1/4 cup	frozen green peas	60 mL
1/8 tsp	ground Sichuan pepper	0.5 mL
1/4 tsp	salt	1 mL
1/2 cup	ready-to-use reduced-sodium vegetable broth	125 mL
1 tbsp	chile bean paste (see page 19)	15 mL
1 tsp	reduced-sodium soy sauce	5 mL
1/2 tsp	toasted sesame oil	2 mL
1 1/2 cups	cubed low-fat firm tofu (1-inch/2.5 cm cubes)	375 mL
1 tsp	cornstarch	5 mL
1 tsp	cold water	5 mL

1. In a saucepan, heat vegetable oil over medium heat. Add seitan, mushrooms and ginger; cook, stirring, for about 2 minutes or until fragrant.

2. Stir in peas, Sichuan pepper, salt, broth, bean paste, soy sauce and sesame oil; bring to a boil. Add tofu, reduce heat and simmer for 3 minutes.

3. In a small bowl, quickly stir together cornstarch and cold water to form a paste. Add to pan and cook, stirring, until thickened.

Nutrition info per serving

Calories	192
Fat, total	5 g
Fat, saturated	0.6 g
Cholesterol	0 mg
Sodium	355 mg
Carbohydrate	7 g
Fiber	1 g
Protein	30 g

Food Choices

4	Meat & Alternatives
1/2	Fat
1	Extra

Make It a Meal

½ serving Sichuan Vegetarian Ma-Po Tofu

1 cup (250 mL) unsalted cooked buckwheat or soba noodles (2 Carbohydrate)

2 cups (250 mL) unsalted steamed vegetables, such as Chinese broccoli (1 Extra)

1 cup (250 mL) fortified plain soy milk (1 Carbohydrate)

1 large Asian pear (1 Carbohydrate)

Tips

If seitan is not available, omit it from step 1 and add another ½ cup (125 mL) tofu in step 2.

To reduce the sodium in this recipe, use ready-to-use no-salt-added vegetable broth or, for more flavor, make your own vegetable stock at home (see recipe, page 245).

Although tofu contains healthy polyunsaturated fats, you'll still want to keep an eye on the amount you eat, to keep track of your total fat intake over the course of the day.

Seitan

Seitan (*mian jin*), also known as "wheat meat" or wheat gluten, is made by washing wheat flour dough with water until all the starch dissolves. This process leaves layers of insoluble, sponge-like gluten, which is then formed into different shapes. Seitan is used as a meat substitute in many Chinese vegetarian dishes. Always check the label and choose a brand with no added salt. Once opened, seitan will keep in the refrigerator for up to 1 week.

Braised Seitan with Peanuts and Black Fungus *(Lao Hua Sheng Dou Fu)*

Makes 4 servings

Black fungus (*mu er*), also known as cloud ear, has been a staple in Chinese cuisine for several hundred years. In Shanghai, this dish is typically served cold, along with Chinese liquor or beer. It can be made vegetarian, as in this recipe, or with added pork.

Soaking time: **2 hours**
Preparation time: **20 minutes**
Cooking time: **25 minutes**
Chilling time: **2 hours**

1 1/4 cups	cubed seitan (see box, page 121)	300 mL
	Cold water	
1 cup	dried black fungus	250 mL
1/3 cup	dried daylily flowers (see box, opposite)	75 mL
5	dried shiitake mushrooms, stems removed	5
1 1/2 tbsp	vegetable oil	22 mL
1	star anise pod (see page 21)	1
1 tsp	minced gingerroot	5 mL
1/3 cup	unsalted peanuts	75 mL
2 tbsp	granulated sugar	30 mL
1 cup	water	250 mL
2 tbsp	ready-to-use reduced-sodium vegetable broth	30 mL
1 tbsp	reduced-sodium soy sauce	15 mL
1 tbsp	dark soy sauce	15 mL
1/4 tsp	toasted sesame oil	1 mL

1. Place seitan in a bowl with enough cold water to cover; let soak for 2 hours or until fully soft. Drain and set aside.

2. Meanwhile, place fungus and daylilies in another bowl with enough cold water to cover; let soak for 30 minutes. Soak mushrooms in a separate bowl of cold water for 20 minutes. Drain and rinse well. Dice mushrooms and fungus. Cut daylilies in half.

3. In a saucepan, heat vegetable oil over medium heat. Add star anise and ginger; cook, stirring, for about 1 minute or until fragrant. Add mushrooms, fungus, daylilies and peanuts; cook, stirring, for about 4 minutes or until mushrooms are softened.

Nutrition info per serving

Calories	278
Fat, total	11 g
Fat, saturated	1.0 g
Cholesterol	0 mg
Sodium	377 mg
Carbohydrate	30 g
Fiber	9 g
Protein	19 g

Food Choices

1	Carbohydrate
2 1/2	Meat & Alternatives
1 1/2	Fat

⅔ cup (150 mL) unsalted
cooked white or
brown short-grain rice
(2 Carbohydrate)

½ cup (125 mL)
fortified plain soy milk
(½ Carbohydrate)

½ large Asian pear
(½ Carbohydrate)

4. Stir in seitan, sugar, water, broth, soy sauce and dark soy sauce; bring to a boil over high heat. Reduce heat to low, cover and simmer, stirring occasionally, for 12 minutes, adding a little bit of water if it starts to get too dry. Remove from heat and stir in sesame oil. Let cool completely, then refrigerate for about 2 hours, until chilled, and serve cold.

Tips

The soaking water from the black fungus and daylilies, and from the mushrooms, can be used to make stock.

To reduce the sodium in this recipe, use ready-to-use no-salt-added vegetable broth or, for more flavor, make your own vegetable stock at home (see recipe, page 245).

Daylilies

Daylilies (*huang hua*), also called yellow flowers or golden needles, are commonly used in both Chinese cuisine and traditional Chinese medicine. Dried daylilies will keep for a long time as long as they are kept in an airtight container, away from strong light, heat and moisture. They have a unique fragrance and are often combined with dried black fungus in Chinese cooking. Look for daylilies at Chinese grocery stores.

Sichuan Beef Stir-Fry
(Si Chuan Jiang Bao Niu Rou)

Makes 4 servings

This dish originated in the Sichuan province, in southwestern China, and is popular, in various incarnations, in restaurants around the world. This version is spicy, but if you are heat-averse, you can omit the dried red chiles. Serve with a side of rice and some steamed vegetables for a delicious meal.

Preparation time: 15 minutes
Marinating time: 10 minutes
Cooking time: 10 minutes

1 tsp	cornstarch	5 mL
1/2 tsp	granulated sugar	2 mL
1/4 tsp	freshly ground black pepper	1 mL
2 tbsp	reduced-sodium soy sauce	30 mL
8 oz	beef flank steak, cut into 1/4-inch (0.5 cm) thick strips	250 g
1 tsp	vegetable oil	5 mL
2	cloves garlic, minced	2
2	dried red chile peppers, cut into 1-inch (2.5 cm) pieces	2
1 tbsp	minced gingerroot	15 mL
8	stalks asparagus, cut into 2-inch (5 cm) pieces	8
1 cup	snow peas, trimmed	250 mL
1 cup	chopped red bell pepper (1-inch/2.5 cm pieces)	250 mL
1 tbsp	water	15 mL

1. In a bowl, combine cornstarch, sugar, pepper and soy sauce. Stir in beef. Marinate for 10 minutes.

2. In a wok or large nonstick skillet, heat oil over medium-high heat. Add garlic, chiles and ginger; stir-fry for 30 seconds. Add asparagus, snow peas and red pepper; stir-fry for 3 minutes. Transfer vegetables to a bowl.

3. Add beef and marinade to the wok and stir-fry over medium-high heat for 3 minutes or until beef is cooked to desired doneness.

4. Return vegetables to the wok. Stir in water and remove from heat.

Nutrition info per serving

Calories	118
Fat, total	4 g
Fat, saturated	1.0 g
Cholesterol	30 mg
Sodium	204 mg
Carbohydrate	8 g
Fiber	2 g
Protein	13 g

Food Choices

1	Meat & Alternatives
1	Extra

Make It a Meal

2 servings Sichuan Beef
Stir-Fry, topped with
1 tbsp (15 mL) toasted
sesame seeds (1 Fat)

⅔ cup (150 mL) unsalted
cooked white or
brown short-grain rice
(2 Carbohydrate)

2 cups (250 mL) unsalted
steamed vegetables,
such as Chinese
broccoli (1 Extra)

1 cup (250 mL)
fortified plain soy milk
(1 Carbohydrate)

½ medium mangosteen
(1 Carbohydrate)

Tips

One tablespoon (15 mL) of regular soy sauce contains 1000 mg
or more sodium. The reduced-sodium variety is a better
option, but even then, always measure the amount you use:
reduced-sodium soy sauce still has 580 mg or more sodium
per tablespoon.

Nonstick pans require good care to protect the nonstick
coating. Buy good-quality, heavy pans and never heat an
empty pan. And always use plastic, rubber, silicon or wood
utensils; metal tools or those with a sharp edge can cause
some of the nonstick coating to scrape off into your food.

Nutrition Tip

Bell peppers are a great source of vitamin C, and red bell
peppers also supply beta carotene, an antioxidant that may
help prevent cancer and heart disease.

Stir-Fried Lamb with Scallions

(Cong Bao Yang Rou)

Makes 4 servings

Lamb is not a common ingredient in Chinese cuisine. Dishes such as this one are thought to be influenced by the Turkic peoples living in northern and western China. I cut back on the amounts of high-sodium ingredients, such as dark and regular soy sauce and Chinese cooking wine. Serve with rice and steamed vegetables on the side.

Variation

Replace the lamb strips with beef or chicken breast strips.

Nutrition info per serving

Calories	225
Fat, total	10 g
Fat, saturated	3.0 g
Cholesterol	75 mg
Sodium	462 mg
Carbohydrate	7 g
Fiber	2 g
Protein	24 g

Food Choices

3	Meat & Alternatives
1/2	Fat

Preparation time: 30 minutes
Marinating time: 15 to 30 minutes
Cooking time: 5 to 10 minutes

2 tsp	crushed Sichuan peppercorns	10 mL
2 tsp	cumin seeds, divided	10 mL
1 tbsp	reduced-sodium soy sauce	15 mL
1 tbsp	dark soy sauce	15 mL
1 tbsp	Chinese cooking wine (see page 19)	15 mL
1 lb	lean boneless lamb shoulder, cut into very thin, 3-inch (7.5 cm) long strips	500 g
1 1/2 tsp	vegetable oil	7 mL
1 tbsp	minced gingerroot	15 mL
4	cloves garlic, minced	4
1/4 tsp	freshly ground black pepper	1 mL
9	green onions (scallions), cut into 3-inch (7.5 cm) lengths	9
1/2 tsp	toasted sesame oil	2 mL
1 tbsp	finely chopped fresh cilantro	15 mL

1. In a bowl, combine Sichuan peppercorns, 1 tsp (5 mL) cumin seeds, soy sauce, dark soy sauce and wine. Stir in lamb. Marinate for 15 to 30 minutes.

2. In a wok or large nonstick skillet, heat vegetable oil over medium heat. Add ginger and stir-fry for 10 seconds. Add garlic and the remaining cumin seeds; stir-fry for 10 seconds, reducing heat if ginger and garlic are burning.

3. Add lamb, marinade and black pepper; stir-fry on medium-high heat for 3 minutes. Add green onions and sesame oil; increase heat to high and stir-fry for 2 minutes or until lamb is browned and tender.

4. Serve garnished with cilantro.

Tips

The best cut of lamb for this dish is the shoulder, but if you prefer a leaner cut, you could use the loin. Do not use leg of lamb, as it would be too chewy.

Make sure to cut the lamb into very thin strips so it will cook faster. Be careful not to overcook it, or it will get tough.

If you like cilantro, add more with the green onions.

Steamed Egg with Ground Pork
(Zheng Dan)

Serve this dish right away, without letting it cool, as it does not taste as good when refrigerated or reheated. Watch the number of servings you have: it is high in dietary cholesterol thanks to the egg yolks.

Make It a Meal

1 serving Steamed Egg with Ground Pork

1 serving Crispy Tofu with Vegetables (page 118)

1/3 cup (75 mL) unsalted cooked white or brown short-grain rice (1 Carbohydrate)

1 cup (250 mL) fortified plain soy milk (1 Carbohydrate)

10 lychees (1 Carbohydrate)

Nutrition info per serving

Calories	115
Fat, total	8 g
Fat, saturated	2.7 g
Cholesterol	108 mg
Sodium	196 mg
Carbohydrate	2 g
Fiber	0 g
Protein	8 g

Food Choices

1	Meat & Alternatives
1	Fat

Preparation time: **10 minutes**
Cooking time: **25 minutes**

- **Stainless steel Chinese steamer**
- **Four 4-oz (175 mL) ramekins, preferably aluminum**

1 tsp	minced gingerroot (optional)	5 mL
1 cup	ready-to-use reduced-sodium chicken broth	250 mL
1 tbsp	reduced-sodium soy sauce	15 mL
1 tsp	Chinese cooking wine (see page 19)	5 mL
2 1/2 oz	lean ground pork	90 g
2	large eggs, well beaten	2

Dressing

1 tsp	toasted sesame oil	5 mL
1 tsp	reduced-sodium soy sauce	5 mL

1. In the bottom of the steamer, bring water to a boil over high heat.

2. Meanwhile, in a bowl, combine ginger, broth, soy sauce and wine. Stir in pork and eggs.

3. Divide pork mixture evenly among ramekins. Cover each ramekin with foil and poke several small holes in the top of each.

4. Place ramekins gently in a steamer basket. Steam for 25 minutes or until pork is no longer pink and eggs are set.

5. *Dressing:* Sprinkle with sesame oil and soy sauce. Serve hot.

Tips

Egg whites would not work well in this recipe, so do not try to substitute them. Instead, enjoy this dish in small portions, as the fat and cholesterol are high.

Stainless steel Chinese steamers are an easy way to cook without oil. They usually have three tiers. You bring water to a boil in the bottom tier, and it steams food placed in the two tiers above. You can purchase a Chinese steamer at any Asian grocery store or online.

To reduce the sodium in this recipe, use ready-to-use no-salt-added chicken broth or, for more flavor, make your own chicken stock at home (see recipe, page 246).

Ma-Po Tofu with Pork
(Rou Jiang Ma Po Dou Fu)

This popular Sichuan dish, served in Chinese restaurants all over the world, combines tofu with pork (or beef) in a thick sauce. It can also be made vegetarian (see page 120).

Make It a Meal

1 serving Ma-Po Tofu with Pork

1 cup (250 mL) unsalted cooked buckwheat or soba noodles (2 Carbohydrate)

2 cups (250 mL) unsalted steamed vegetables, such as Chinese broccoli (1 Extra)

2 tbsp (30 mL) toasted almonds (1 Fat)

1 cup (250 mL) fortified plain soy milk (1 Carbohydrate)

½ medium mangosteen (1 Carbohydrate)

Nutrition info per serving

Calories	156
Fat, total	5 g
Fat, saturated	0.7 g
Cholesterol	16 mg
Sodium	243 mg
Carbohydrate	4 g
Fiber	0 g
Protein	21 g

Food Choices

3	Meat & Alternatives
1	Extra

Preparation time: **15 minutes**
Cooking time: **15 minutes**

1½ tsp	vegetable oil	7 mL
4 oz	ground pork loin (see tip, below)	125 g
3	green onions, thinly sliced	3
1 tsp	ground Sichuan pepper	5 mL
1 tbsp	chile bean paste (see page 19)	15 mL
1 tsp	granulated sugar	5 mL
⅓ cup	water	75 mL
2 tbsp	Chinese cooking wine (see page 19)	30 mL
2 tbsp	reduced-sodium soy sauce	30 mL
1 tsp	dark soy sauce	5 mL
1 lb	low-fat firm tofu, cut into ½-inch (1 cm) cubes	500 g
1½ tsp	cornstarch	7 mL
1½ tsp	cold water	7 mL
1 tsp	finely chopped green onion (green part only)	5 mL

1. In a pot, heat oil over medium heat. Add pork, sliced green onions, Sichuan pepper and chile paste; cook, breaking pork up with a spoon, for about 2 minutes or until pork is starting to turn white. Add sugar, water, wine, soy sauce and dark soy sauce; cook, stirring, for 1 minute.

2. Add tofu, being careful not to stir, as tofu will break; cook, without stirring, for about 5 minutes or until tofu is heated through and slightly softened and sauce is thickened. Reduce heat and simmer for 1 minute.

3. In a small bowl, quickly stir together cornstarch and cold water to form a paste. Add to pot and cook, stirring gently, for 1 minute.

4. Serve garnished with chopped green onion.

Tips

Ask your butcher to grind pork loin meat if it's not readily available in the grocery store.

The traditional version of this dish is a bit saucier, but to keep the sodium level in check, I've reduced the amount of sauce while keeping all the flavor this dish is known for.

Tofu with Spicy Meat and Vegetables *(Ma Po Dou Fu)*

Makes 6 servings

This spicy dish, made all over China, is traditionally served with rice. For more flavor, use homemade chicken stock (see recipe, page 246).

Make It a Meal

1 serving Tofu with Spicy Meat and Vegetables, topped with 1 tbsp (15 mL) toasted sesame seeds (1 Fat)

²/₃ cup (150 mL) unsalted cooked white or brown short-grain rice (2 Carbohydrate)

1 cup (250 mL) fortified plain soy milk (1 Carbohydrate)

½ cup (125 mL) chopped jackfruit (1 Carbohydrate)

Nutrition info per serving

Calories	216
Fat, total	8 g
Fat, saturated	1.6 g
Cholesterol	22 mg
Sodium	289 mg
Carbohydrate	8 g
Fiber	1 g
Protein	26 g

Food Choices

3½	Meat & Alternatives
½	Fat

Preparation time: 20 minutes
Cooking time: 15 minutes

Sauce

1 tsp	cornstarch	5 mL
2 tbsp	ready-to-use reduced-sodium chicken broth	30 mL
½ tsp	freshly ground black pepper	2 mL
3 tbsp	water	45 mL
1 tbsp	oyster sauce	15 mL
1 tbsp	hoisin sauce	15 mL
1 tbsp	white wine	15 mL
¼ tsp	toasted sesame oil	1 mL

Stir-Fry

1½ tsp	peanut oil	7 mL
1 tbsp	minced gingerroot	15 mL
2 tsp	minced garlic	10 mL
2 tsp	hot pepper flakes	10 mL
3½ oz	lean ground chicken breast	100 g
4	green onions, finely chopped	4
1 cup	sliced stemmed shiitake mushrooms	250 mL
1	package (15 oz/454 g) medium-firm tofu, cut into 1-inch (2.5 cm) cubes	1

1. *Sauce:* In a small bowl, combine cornstarch and broth. Stir in pepper, water, oyster sauce, hoisin sauce, wine and sesame oil. Set aside.

2. *Stir-Fry:* In a wok or large nonstick skillet, heat peanut oil over low heat. Add ginger, garlic and hot pepper flakes; stir-fry for about 3 minutes or until fragrant.

3. Add chicken, increase heat to medium and stir-fry for about 5 minutes or until no longer pink. Add green onions and mushrooms; stir-fry for about 3 minutes or until mushrooms are softened.

4. Add tofu and stir-fry for 2 minutes. Stir in sauce and bring to boil over high heat, then immediately remove from heat.

Tips

Chinese tofu, sold at Asian grocery stores, tends to be moister and smoother than the tofu sold in regular grocery stores.

To reduce the total fat content of this dish, use low-fat tofu.

Sautéed Chicken with Onions and Balsam Pear *(Ku Gua Ji)*

Makes 4 servings

This simple dish is especially popular in the summer thanks to its cooling effect. In China, all foods and beverages are divided into two categories: "cold" (yin) and "hot" (yang). According to traditional Chinese medicine, it is best to balance the cold and hot foods we eat, to prevent disease. Balsam pear is considered very cold, while onion and chicken breast are right in the middle, so the overall dish is considered cold. Balsam pear is also believed to have many health properties, one of which is preventing diabetes.

Nutrition info per serving

Calories	165
Fat, total	4 g
Fat, saturated	0.7 g
Cholesterol	54 mg
Sodium	302 mg
Carbohydrate	12 g
Fiber	2 g
Protein	20 g

Food Choices

2	Meat & Alternatives
½	Fat
1	Extra

Preparation time: 15 minutes
Marinating time: 15 minutes
Cooking time: 20 to 25 minutes

Chicken and Marinade

1 ½ tsp	granulated sugar	7 mL
1 ½ tsp	cornstarch	7 mL
⅛ tsp	freshly ground white pepper	0.5 mL
1 tbsp	reduced-sodium soy sauce	15 mL
11 oz	boneless skinless chicken breasts, cut into ½-inch (1 cm) cubes	330 g

Sauté

1 ½ tsp	vegetable oil	7 mL
3	cloves garlic, minced	3
3 tbsp	minced gingerroot	45 mL
1	onion, cut into 1-inch (2.5 cm) slices	1
2 cups	thinly sliced peeled balsam pear	500 mL
3 tbsp	ready-to-use reduced-sodium chicken broth	45 mL
1 ½ tsp	cornstarch	7 mL
2 tbsp	cold water	30 mL
1 ½ tsp	granulated sugar	7 mL
1 tbsp	reduced-sodium soy sauce	15 mL
1 tsp	finely chopped green onion	5 mL

1. *Chicken and Marinade:* In a bowl, whisk together sugar, cornstarch, pepper and soy sauce. Stir in chicken. Marinate for 15 minutes. Remove chicken from marinade, reserving marinade.

2. In a pot of boiling water, cook chicken for about 3 minutes or until chicken is no longer pink inside. Drain and set aside.

3. *Sauté:* In a skillet, heat oil over medium heat. Add garlic and ginger; cook, stirring, for about 2 minutes or until fragrant. Add onion and balsam pear; cook, stirring, for 10 minutes or until onion is translucent.

4. Stir in chicken, broth and remaining marinade; cook, stirring, for about 5 minutes or until chicken is heated through.

Make It a Meal

1 serving Sautéed Chicken with Onions and Balsam Pear

1 serving Stir-Fried Mixed Vegetables (page 110)

$\frac{2}{3}$ cup (150 mL) unsalted cooked white or brown short-grain rice (2 Carbohydrate)

2 cups (500 mL) Red Date, Longan and Ginger Tea (page 147)

1 large Asian pear (1 Carbohydrate)

5. In a small bowl, quickly stir together cornstarch and cold water to form a paste. Add to pan, along with sugar and soy sauce; cook, stirring, for about 1 minute or until slightly thickened.

6. Serve garnished with green onions.

Tips

This recipe is often made with pork or beef, but as these options are high in fat, skinless chicken breast is a better choice. Poaching the chicken before pan-frying it reduces the amount of oil needed in the recipe, further reducing the fat.

To reduce the bitter flavor of the balsam pear, rub salt into the sliced pear, then soak it in water for 30 minutes or overnight. Squeeze out the liquid, then rinse well and drain before use.

One tablespoon (15 mL) of regular soy sauce contains 1000 mg or more sodium. The reduced-sodium variety is a better option, but even then, always measure the amount you use: reduced-sodium soy sauce still has 580 mg or more sodium per tablespoon.

To reduce the sodium in this recipe, use ready-to-use no-salt-added chicken broth or, for more flavor, make your own chicken stock at home (see recipe, page 246).

Balsam Pear

Balsam pear (*ku gua*), also known as Chinese bitter melon or bitter gourd, is in the same family as the bitter melon used in South Asian cuisine (see box, page 47), but is generally larger, greener, smoother and less bitter, and has more moisture. It can be boiled or salted before use to reduce its bitterness. Some preliminary research studies suggest that balsam pear may have blood glucose–lowering properties, but the evidence is not yet conclusive.

Hot-and-Spicy Chicken *(La Zi Ji)*

This spicy chicken dish, enjoyed all over China, is typically eaten with rice or rice noodles. If you want to add some vegetables, serve a side of steamed Chinese broccoli or cauliflower, or follow the suggested meal plan on page 133. Although I reduced the amount of dark soy sauce considerably, the sodium per serving is still high, so limit your portion to a single serving.

Nutrition info per serving

Calories	216
Fat, total	7 g
Fat, saturated	1.0 g
Cholesterol	73 mg
Sodium	*526 mg
Carbohydrate	10 g
Fiber	2 g
Protein	28 g

* This recipe is high in sodium. Balance it out by making lower-sodium choices for the rest of your meal and throughout the day.

Food Choices

3	Meat & Alternatives
1	Fat
1	Extra

Preparation time: **15 minutes**
Marinating time: **20 minutes**
Cooking time: **15 minutes**

Chicken and Marinade

1 tbsp	minced garlic	15 mL
1 tbsp	minced seeded red chile pepper	15 mL
1 tsp	cornstarch	5 mL
1½ tbsp	dark soy sauce	22 mL
1 tbsp	white wine	15 mL
1	large egg white	1
1 lb	boneless skinless chicken breasts, cut into 2-inch (5 cm) cubes	500 g

Stir-Fry

1 tbsp	vegetable oil	15 mL
2	red chile peppers, seeded and chopped	2
½ cup	chopped green onions (cut diagonally into 1-inch/2.5 cm pieces)	125 mL
1 tbsp	minced gingerroot	15 mL
1 tbsp	minced garlic	15 mL
1 tbsp	ground anise seeds	15 mL
1½ tsp	granulated sugar	7 mL
1 tsp	hot pepper flakes	5 mL
3 tbsp	ready-to-use no-salt-added chicken broth	45 mL
1 tbsp	white wine vinegar	15 mL
⅛ tsp	toasted sesame oil	0.5 mL

1. *Chicken and Marinade:* In a bowl, combine garlic, chile, cornstarch, soy sauce, wine and egg white. Stir in chicken. Cover and refrigerate for 20 minutes.

2. *Stir-Fry:* In a wok or large nonstick skillet, heat vegetable oil over medium heat. Add chiles, green onions, ginger and garlic; stir-fry for about 1 minute or until fragrant.

3. Add chicken and marinade; stir-fry for about 10 minutes or until chicken is no longer pink inside.

4. Add anise seeds, sugar, hot pepper flakes, broth and vinegar; stir-fry for 3 minutes. Remove from heat and stir in sesame oil.

1 serving Hot-and-Spicy Chicken

1 serving Bamboo Shoots with Mushrooms (page 108)

1½ cups (375 mL) unsalted cooked buckwheat or soba noodles (3 Carbohydrate)

1 cup (250 mL) Red Date, Longan and Ginger Tea (page 147)

½ large Asian pear (½ Carbohydrate)

Tips

Dark soy sauce is needed to create the traditional brown color of this dish. There is no reduced-sodium variety, so measure carefully and be sure not to use more than is called for.

To easily separate an egg, crack it gently at the middle and use your thumbs to gently pry the halves apart. Let the yolk settle in the lower half while the white runs off into a bowl.

Anise seeds have a mild flavor similar to licorice. If ground anise seeds are not available, you can substitute 1 tbsp (15 mL) ground fennel seeds, 1½ tsp (7 mL) ground star anise or a few drops of anise extract.

Nonstick pans require good care to protect the nonstick coating. Buy good-quality, heavy pans and never heat an empty pan. And always use plastic, rubber, silicon or wood utensils; metal tools or those with a sharp edge can cause some of the nonstick coating to scrape off into your food.

Nutrition Tip

Some studies have shown that eating garlic has health benefits that include reducing blood pressure and controlling blood cholesterol levels. If you can, add one clove of garlic to your diet daily — it's great for the heart!

Kung Pao Chicken *(Gong Bao Ji Din)*

Makes 6 servings

Most Chinese restaurants in North America serve a version of this dish, although it may not be as spicy as those prepared in the province of Sichuan. This recipe is also a milder one, and it has added vegetables and reduced amounts of high-sodium sauces and peanuts. But don't worry: it still has amazing flavor!

Preparation time: **25 minutes**
Marinating time: **10 minutes**
Cooking time: **20 minutes**

Chicken and Marinade

1	large egg white	1
2 tbsp	oyster sauce	30 mL
1 tbsp	water	15 mL
2 tsp	cornstarch	10 mL
1 lb	boneless skinless chicken breast, cut into 2-inch (5 cm) cubes	500 g

Sauce

2	green chile peppers, seeded and chopped	2
1 tsp	minced garlic	5 mL
1 tsp	granulated sugar	5 mL
1/4 cup	natural rice vinegar	60 mL
1/4 cup	ready-to-use reduced-sodium chicken broth	60 mL
1 tbsp	hoisin sauce	15 mL
1 tbsp	sherry	15 mL
1 1/2 tsp	reduced-sodium soy sauce	7 mL
1/8 tsp	toasted sesame oil	0.5 mL

Stir-Fry

2 tbsp	peanut oil	30 mL
10	small dried red chile peppers	10
2	stalks celery, diced	2
1/2	red bell pepper, cut into 1-inch (2.5 cm) pieces	1/2
1 1/2 cups	thinly sliced rinsed drained canned bamboo shoots (see box, page 108)	375 mL
4 tsp	minced garlic	20 mL
4 tsp	minced gingerroot	20 mL
1 tbsp	water (optional)	15 mL
1 tbsp	unsalted roasted peanuts	15 mL

1. *Chicken and Marinade:* In a bowl, combine egg white, oyster sauce, water and cornstarch. Stir in chicken. Marinate for 10 minutes.

2. *Sauce:* Meanwhile, in a bowl, combine green chiles, garlic, sugar, vinegar, broth, hoisin sauce, sherry, soy sauce and sesame oil. Set aside.

Nutrition info per serving

Calories	188
Fat, total	8 g
Fat, saturated	1.4 g
Cholesterol	45 mg
Sodium	329 mg
Carbohydrate	11 g
Fiber	2 g
Protein	19 g

Food Choices

2	Meat & Alternatives
1	Fat
1	Extra

Tips

To reduce the sodium in this recipe, use ready-to-use no-salt-added chicken broth or, for more flavor, make your own chicken stock at home (see recipe, page 246).

This recipe calls for natural rice vinegar. Be careful not to use seasoned rice vinegar, as it has added sugar and salt, and 1 tbsp (15 mL) can have as much as 250 mg of sodium.

3. *Stir-Fry:* In a wok or large nonstick skillet, heat peanut oil over medium heat. Add chicken and marinade; stir-fry for 6 to 8 minutes or until chicken is browned on all sides. Transfer chicken to a plate and set aside.

4. Add red chiles to the wok and cook for about 10 seconds or until fragrant. Add celery, red pepper, bamboo shoots, garlic and ginger; stir-fry, adding 1 tbsp (15 mL) water if vegetables are sticking, for about 5 minutes or until celery is tender. Stir in sauce.

5. Return chicken to the wok and cook for 2 to 3 minutes or until chicken is no longer pink inside. Remove from heat and stir in peanuts.

Tips

Oyster sauce, hoisin sauce and soy sauce all have a lot of sodium. Hoisin sauce also has a lot of added sugar and salt. Reduced-sodium soy sauce is used in this recipe, but it is still quite high in sodium, at over 1000 mg per 2 tbsp (30 mL). And there are no reduced-sodium versions of oysters sauce and hoisin sauce available. The bottom line? Use these sauces sparingly!

Nonstick pans require good care to protect the nonstick coating. Buy good-quality, heavy pans and never heat an empty pan. And always use plastic, rubber, silicon or wood utensils; metal tools or those with a sharp edge can cause some of the nonstick coating to scrape off into your food.

Hakka Chicken Curry *(Ga Li Ji)*

The Hakka people have migrated to many places around the world from Guangdong, China, including South and Southeast Asia. As a result, Hakka cuisine often intertwines Chinese and South or Southeast Asian influences. This is a very flavorful dish that goes wonderfully well with a side of long-grain brown rice.

Preparation time: 30 minutes
Cooking time: 40 minutes

5	dried red chile peppers	5
½ cup	cold water	125 mL
1	stalk lemongrass	1
1 tbsp	peanut oil, divided	30 mL
1 ½ tsp	annatto seeds	7 mL
10	dried curry leaves	10
2	shallots, minced	2
1 cup	red onion, coarsely chopped	250 mL
1 ½ tsp	minced garlic	7 mL
1 ½ tsp	minced gingerroot	7 mL
1 ½ tsp	Chinese curry powder	7 mL
¾ tsp	salt	3 mL
½ tsp	ground coriander	2 mL
½ tsp	paprika	2 mL
¼ tsp	freshly ground black pepper	1 mL
½ cup	chopped Chinese long beans (1-inch/2.5 cm pieces)	125 mL
¾ cup	water, divided	175 mL
1 ½ cups	cubed taro (1-inch/2.5 cm cubes)	375 mL
1 lb	boneless skinless chicken breasts, cut into 2-inch (5 cm) pieces	500 g
1 cup	ready-to-use reduced-sodium chicken broth	250 mL
1 cup	skim milk	250 mL
1 tbsp	cashew paste	15 mL
¼ cup	nonfat plain yogurt	60 mL
2	sprigs fresh cilantro leaves, chopped	2

1. Place red chiles in a bowl and cover with ½ cup (125 mL) cold water; let soak for about 10 minutes or until soft. Drain, mince and set aside.

2. Meanwhile, keeping lemongrass whole, hit it several times with the back of a knife to release the oils and flavor. Set aside.

3. In a large skillet, heat oil over medium heat. Add annatto seeds and cook, stirring, for 1 to 2 minutes or until color starts to seep into oil. Discard annatto seeds. Add soaked chiles, curry leaves, shallots, onion, garlic, ginger, curry powder, salt, coriander, paprika and pepper; cook, stirring, for about 4 minutes or until fragrant.

Nutrition info per serving	
Calories	193
Fat, total	6 g
Fat, saturated	1.2 g
Cholesterol	49 mg
Sodium	441 mg
Carbohydrate	15 g
Fiber	2 g
Protein	20 g
Food Choices	
½	Carbohydrate
2	Meat & Alternatives
½	Fat

Make It a Meal

1 serving Hakka Chicken Curry, topped with 1 tbsp (15 mL) toasted cashews (1 Fat)

⅔ cup (150 mL) unsalted cooked long-grain brown rice (2 Carbohydrate)

1 cup (250 mL) fortified plain soy milk (1 Carbohydrate)

5 whole lychees (½ Carbohydrate)

4. Stir in long beans and ¼ cup (60 mL) water; cook for 5 minutes. Stir in taro and another ¼ cup (60 mL) water; cook for 2 minutes. Stir in chicken and cook, stirring, for 3 minutes.

5. Stir in lemongrass, broth and the remaining water; bring to a boil. Reduce heat to low, cover and simmer for about 10 minutes or until chicken is no longer pink inside and taro and long beans are tender.

6. Stir in milk and cashew paste; cover, increase heat to medium and bring to a boil. If a thicker sauce is desired, uncover and cook on low heat for about 4 minutes. Remove from heat and stir in yogurt.

7. Serve garnished with cilantro.

Tips

Chinese curry powder contains ground turmeric, dried chiles, anise, fennel, cumin, cloves, cinnamon, coriander, bay leaves, garlic, black cardamom, annatto, Sichuan pepper, nutmeg and coriander. If Chinese curry powder is unavailable, Singapore or Malaysian curry powder can be used.

Taro root is the starchy edible root of the taro plant. Native to Southeast Asia, taro is used in curries, dim sum and even desserts. If you cannot find it, use sweet potato or Chinese or regular yam.

To reduce the sodium in this recipe, use ready-to-use no-salt-added chicken broth or, for more flavor, make your own chicken stock at home (see recipe, page 246).

Cashew paste adds flavor and texture, but is high in fat, so use it sparingly. If cashew paste is not available, substitute 1 tbsp (15 mL) ground whole cashews.

Lemongrass

Lemongrass (*ning meng cao*), popular in Thai cuisine, grows in tropical countries and looks like thick green onions or very skinny leeks. It has a very intense lemon flavor. When buying lemongrass, look for firm, pale yellow and green (not brown) stalks. If fresh lemongrass is not available, look for frozen stalks.

Hakka Chicken Bao *(Ke Jia Ji Bao)*

This recipe is a Hakka-style take on the steamed buns that are so popular at dim sum restaurants. Serve them at your next brunch, with sensible portions of congee, steamed vegetables and some roasted meat or another meat dish, as in the meal plan on page 139.

Preparation time: **90 minutes**
Cooking time: **1 hour and 10 minutes**

- **Bamboo steamer (see tip, page 103), lined with parchment paper**

1 cup	1% milk	250 mL
1 tbsp	granulated sugar	15 mL
2 ½ cups	bao instant flour (see tip, opposite)	625 mL
¼ tsp	vegetable oil	1 mL
1 ½ tsp	peanut oil	7 mL
¼ cup	finely chopped onion	60 mL
½ tsp	minced gingerroot	2 mL
½ tsp	minced garlic	2 mL
1 ½ cups	shredded napa cabbage	375 mL
1 tsp	natural rice vinegar	5 mL
2 tbsp	finely diced Chinese pork sausage	30 mL
8 oz	lean ground chicken	250 g
2	shiitake mushrooms, stems removed and caps finely chopped	2
½ tsp	salt	2 mL
¼ tsp	freshly ground white pepper	1 mL
1 tsp	oyster sauce	5 mL
¼ tsp	toasted sesame oil	1 mL
1	hard-cooked egg, finely chopped	1

1. In a saucepan, heat milk and sugar over low heat until sugar is dissolved. Remove from heat and let cool to room temperature. Gradually add flour and stir for 7 minutes, until a smooth dough forms.

2. Transfer dough to a flat surface, add vegetable oil and knead for 3 minutes or until smooth and elastic. Form into a ball. Cover with a wet towel and let rise for 30 to 40 minutes or until doubled in size.

3. In a skillet, heat peanut oil over medium-low heat. Add onion, ginger and garlic; cook, stirring, for 2 minutes. Add cabbage and vinegar; cook, stirring, for about 5 minutes or until cabbage is tender. Transfer cabbage mixture to a bowl and let cool.

4. Add sausage to the skillet and cook, stirring, for 5 minutes. Drain off fat. Add sausage to the cabbage mixture. Let cool completely.

Nutrition info per serving	
Calories	210
Fat, total	4 g
Fat, saturated	1.2 g
Cholesterol	44 mg
Sodium	196 mg
Carbohydrate	33 g
Fiber	1 g
Protein	10 g
Food Choices	
2	Carbohydrate
½	Meat & Alternatives

Tips

Only a small amount of Chinese sausage is used in this recipe because of its high fat content. If you cannot find Chinese pork sausage, choose another, lower-fat pork sausage to use in its place.

To store extra chicken bao, first let them cool completely, then wrap each bun individually in plastic wrap and freeze in an airtight container for up to 3 months. Reheat buns in the microwave for a great snack on the go!

5. In a separate bowl, combine chicken, mushrooms, salt, pepper, oyster sauce and sesame oil. Add to the sausage mixture, combining well. Slam the mixture against the bowl until firm and elastic.

6. Divide dough into 10 pieces and flatten each into a 4-inch (10 cm) circle. To the center of each circle, add about 3 tbsp (45 mL) chicken and sausage mixture. Sprinkle each with hard-cooked egg, dividing equally. Fold all the sides up and pinch at the top to seal. Pinch 6 folds into the sides for pleats.

7. In a large skillet, bring 2 to 3 inches (5 to 7.5 cm) of water to a boil. Add 5 buns to the bamboo steamer, leaving space between them. Cover the steamer and place it in the skillet, making sure the sides of the steamer do not touch the pan. Steam for 15 to 18 minutes or until buns have risen and are firm and shiny. Repeat with the remaining buns.

Tips

Bao instant flour has been bleached and has a lower gluten level so that the buns will maintain their white color after steaming.

Napa cabbage (*da bai cai*), also known as celery cabbage or Chinese cabbage, has a mild cabbage flavor. When cooked, it loses its own flavor and absorbs the flavors of the ingredients it is cooked with.

Chinese Sausages

There are two main types of Chinese sausage (*xiang chang*): one is made with a combination of fat and meat (pork, duck or beef); the other, darker variety is made from pork or duck liver. There are sweet and spicy varieties. They are about 6 inches (15 cm) long and ¾ inch (2 cm) wide. Look for them in Asian grocery stores. They are high in fat (9 g per 2 tbsp/30 mL) and have a strong flavor, so use sparingly. Where available, look for leaner brands of Chinese sausages.

Hakka Braised Duck with Lily Flower *(Jin Zhen Zheng Ya)*

Makes 5 servings

Braised duck is a popular Hakka dish with complex flavors from an array of ingredients that include daylilies, shiitake mushrooms, bamboo shoots and, of course, Chinese five-spice powder. (No Chinese pantry is complete without it!)

Nutrition info per serving

Calories	180
Fat, total	6 g
Fat, saturated	2.0 g
Cholesterol	68 mg
Sodium	216 mg
Carbohydrate	13 g
Fiber	2 g
Protein	19 g
Food Choices	
2	Meat & Alternatives

Soaking time: 30 minutes
Preparation time: 20 minutes
Cooking time: 50 minutes

½ cup	dried wood ear mushrooms (see box, page 105)	125 mL
3	dried shiitake mushrooms, stems removed	3
	Water	
½ cup	dried daylily flowers (see box, page 123)	125 mL
1 lb	skin-on duck breasts	500 g
½	shallot, minced	½
1 tsp	minced garlic	5 mL
½ tsp	minced gingerroot	2 mL
1 cup	ready-to-use reduced-sodium chicken broth	250 mL
½ cup	rinsed drained canned bamboo shoots (see box, page 108), cut into 2-inch (5 cm) slices	125 mL
1 tsp	Chinese five-spice powder	5 mL
¼ tsp	ground ginger	1 mL
¼ tsp	freshly ground black pepper	1 mL
3	sprigs fresh cilantro leaves, chopped	3
¾ cup	sliced peeled fresh water chestnuts (see tip, opposite)	175 mL
¼ tsp	granulated sugar	1 mL
1 tbsp	oyster sauce	15 mL
1 tsp	reduced-sodium soy sauce	5 mL
½ tsp	natural rice vinegar	2 mL
¼ tsp	toasted sesame oil	1 mL

1. Place wood ear and shiitake mushrooms in a bowl with enough cold water to cover; let soak for 30 minutes. Drain and rinse well. Cut wood ear mushrooms in half. Cut shiitake mushrooms into thick slices. Set aside.

2. Meanwhile, place daylilies in a separate bowl with enough water to cover; let soak for 30 minutes. Drain, tie each lily into a knot and set aside.

3. Heat a skillet over medium heat. Add duck, skin side down, and cook, turning once, until well browned on both sides; about 12 minutes. Transfer duck to a plate, remove the skin and discard; set meat aside. Drain fat from pan.

4. Add shallot, garlic and minced ginger to the skillet; cook, stirring and adding 1 tbsp (15 mL) of the broth if vegetables are sticking, for about 2 minutes or until softened. Add wood ear and shiitake mushrooms, bamboo shoots, daylilies, five-spice powder, ground ginger and pepper; cook, stirring, for 2 minutes or until mushrooms are slightly softened.

5. Stir in cilantro, water chestnuts, sugar, 1 cup (250 mL) water, the remaining broth, oyster sauce, soy sauce and vinegar; cook, stirring often, for 5 minutes. Return duck to the pan and bring to a boil. Reduce heat to low, cover and simmer for 15 minutes or until duck is tender. Remove from heat and stir in sesame oil. Cover and let stand for 10 minutes before serving.

Tips

Searing the duck breasts with the skin on keeps them nice and moist, but remember to remove the skin at the end of step 3, as it is very high in fat. Be careful not to let the duck cook too long in step 5, or it will dry out.

If fresh water chestnuts are not available, canned may be used. Canned water chestnuts are readily available in all local grocery stores and contain very little or no added salt.

To reduce the sodium in this recipe, use ready-to-use no-salt-added chicken broth or, for more flavor, make your own chicken stock at home (see recipe, page 246).

One tablespoon (15 mL) of regular soy sauce contains 1000 mg or more sodium. The reduced-sodium variety is a better option, but even then, always measure the amount you use: reduced-sodium soy sauce still has 580 mg or more sodium per tablespoon.

Cantonese Mushroom, Vegetable and Scallop Stir-Fry
(Xing Bao Gu Chao Dai Zi)

This saucy Cantonese-style dish from Hong Kong is delicious served over buckwheat or soba noodles.

Preparation time: 20 minutes
Cooking time: 15 minutes

2 tsp	cornstarch	10 mL
2 tbsp	cold water	30 mL
1/2 tsp	freshly ground black pepper	2 mL
1/2 tsp	salt, divided	2 mL
1 lb	sea scallops, side muscles trimmed off	500 g
1/2 tsp	granulated sugar	2 mL
1/4 cup	ready-to-use no-salt-added chicken broth	60 mL
1 tsp	reduced-sodium soy sauce	5 mL
1 tsp	vegetable oil	5 mL
1 cup	finely chopped red onion	250 mL
3	cloves garlic, minced	3
1 cup	diagonally and thinly sliced carrot	250 mL
1 cup	diagonally and thinly sliced celery	250 mL
1 cup	broccoli florets	250 mL
2 cups	sliced king oyster mushrooms (cut lengthwise into 4 pieces each)	500 mL
1 tsp	sherry	5 mL
1/2 tsp	toasted sesame oil	2 mL

1. In a small bowl, quickly stir together cornstarch and cold water to form a paste.

2. In another bowl, combine half the cornstarch mixture, black pepper and half the salt. Add scallops and toss to coat.

3. To the remaining cornstarch mixture, add sugar, the remaining salt, broth and soy sauce.

4. In a large nonstick skillet, heat vegetable oil over medium heat. Add onion and garlic; cook, stirring, for about 3 minutes or until fragrant. Add scallops and sauce; cook, turning scallops once, for about 2 minutes per side or until lightly browned on both sides. Transfer scallop mixture to a plate and set aside.

Nutrition info per serving

Calories	106
Fat, total	2 g
Fat, saturated	0.3 g
Cholesterol	18 mg
Sodium	*536 mg
Carbohydrate	12 g
Fiber	2 g
Protein	11 g

* This recipe is high in sodium. Balance it out by making lower-sodium choices for the rest of your meal and throughout the day.

Food Choices

1	Meat & Alternatives
1/2	Fat
1	Extra

5. In a pot of boiling water, cook carrots for 3 minutes. Add celery and cook for 2 minutes. Add broccoli and cook for 1 minute. Drain vegetables.

6. In the same skillet, cook mushrooms over medium-high heat, stirring, for 2 minutes. Stir in the drained vegetables. Return scallops to skillet and stir in sherry. Stir in broth mixture and bring to a boil over high heat. Remove from heat and stir in sesame oil.

Tips

The traditional version of this dish is light on vegetables, but this more diabetes-friendly version ups the ante with more vegetables for more nutrients and fiber.

Nonstick pans require good care to protect the nonstick coating. Buy good-quality, heavy pans and never heat an empty pan. And always use plastic, rubber, silicon or wood utensils; metal tools or those with a sharp edge can cause some of the nonstick coating to scrape off into your food.

King Oyster Mushrooms

King oyster mushrooms, also known as eringii or royal trumpet mushrooms, are widely used in Asian cuisines. They have thick white stems and blunt tan caps, and are packed with flavor. If they're not available, substitute shiitake or chanterelle mushrooms. White button mushrooms are another option, although they may take longer to cook and will not add as much flavor.

Cantonese Fried Shrimp with Cashews and Cucumber
(Yao Guo Xia Ren)

Preparation time: **20 minutes**
Cooking time: **20 minutes**

1/4 cup	unsalted raw cashews	60 mL
11 oz	frozen medium shrimp, peeled, deveined, rinsed and drained	330 g
1 tsp	vegetable oil	5 mL
2	cloves garlic, minced	2
1 tbsp	minced gingerroot	15 mL
2 cups	sliced English cucumber (unpeeled)	500 mL
1 1/2 tsp	granulated sugar	7 mL
1 tbsp	Chinese cooking wine (see page 19)	15 mL
6 tbsp	water, divided	90 mL
1/4 tsp	salt	1 mL
1/8 tsp	freshly ground white pepper	0.5 mL
2 tsp	cornstarch	10 mL
1 tbsp	finely chopped green onion	15 mL

1. Heat a skillet over medium heat. Toast cashews, stirring constantly, for 5 to 10 minutes or until lightly browned. Transfer to a plate and set aside.

2. In a pot of boiling water, cook shrimp for about 10 seconds or until they change color. Rinse under cold water and drain.

3. In the skillet, heat oil over medium heat. Add garlic and ginger; cook, stirring, for about 2 minutes or until fragrant. Add cucumber and cook, stirring, for 2 to 3 minutes or until just softened. Stir in sugar and wine; cook for 2 minutes. Stir in 1 tbsp (15 mL) water and cook, stirring, for 1 minute.

4. Return cashews to the pan, along with shrimp, salt and pepper.

5. In a small bowl, quickly stir together cornstarch and the remaining water to make a paste. Add to pan and cook, stirring, until sauce is thickened and shrimp are firm and opaque.

6. Serve garnished with green onions.

Make It a Meal

1 serving Cantonese Fried Shrimp with Cashews and Cucumber, topped with 1 tbsp (15 mL) toasted cashews (1 Fat)

1 serving Hakka Stir-Fried Soybean Sprouts (page 109)

2/3 cup (150 mL) unsalted cooked white or brown short-grain rice (2 Carbohydrate)

2 cups (500 mL) Red Date, Longan and Ginger Tea (page 147)

1 large Asian pear (1 Carbohydrate)

Nutrition info per serving

Calories	140
Fat, total	6 g
Fat, saturated	1.0 g
Cholesterol	101 mg
Sodium	453 mg
Carbohydrate	9 g
Fiber	1 g
Protein	13 g

Food Choices

1 1/2	Meat & Alternatives
1/2	Fat
1	Extra

Tip

Rinse shrimp thoroughly under cold water before cooking it, to remove as much salt as possible, especially if they're frozen.

Asian Pear Drink (*Li Tang*)

Makes about 7 cups (1.75 L)

One of my culinary students, Jiaqi, shared this recipe with me. I had to cut back on the sugar, but it still tastes great. There are many types of Asian pear, all of which are crisp and sweet, similar to apples. I used the Chinese white pear, also known as the *ya* or *ya li* pear, but any variety will work. This drink can be served hot or cold. Alternatively, you can skip the straining step and serve it as a soup.

Preparation time: **5 minutes**
Cooking time: **30 minutes**

2	Asian pears, peeled and cut into eighths	2
4	1-inch (2.5 cm) piece dried orange peel	4
2	1 1/2-inch (4 cm) rock sugar cubes (see tip, below)	2
8 cups	water	2 L

1. In a pot, combine pears, orange peel, rock sugar and water. Bring to a boil over high heat. Reduce heat to medium-low, cover and simmer for 25 minutes.

2. Strain the pear mixture into a large pitcher and discard the solids. Serve hot or let cool and refrigerate until cold.

Tips

If you cannot find Asian pears, you can use regular pears, but they will be more tart. You may need to add one more rock sugar cube, but limit it to that, to avoid raising the carbohydrate content too much.

Look for packages of dried orange peel at Asian grocery stores.

Rock sugar has larger sugar crystals than white sugar, is gold in color and is less sweet. But it is higher in calories than white sugar, so use it sparingly. In South Asian and East Asian cuisines, it is added to teas, sauces, soups and meat dishes.

If you leave the pear in and serve this as a soup, the available carbohydrate will be 9 g per serving (1/2 Carbohydrate Choice).

Nutrition info per 1 cup (250 mL)	
Calories	5
Fat, total	0 g
Fat, saturated	0.0 g
Cholesterol	0 mg
Sodium	9 mg
Carbohydrate	1 g
Fiber	0 g
Protein	0 g
Food Choices	
1	Extra

Hawthorn Drink *(Hong Guo Tang)*

**Makes about
9 cups (2.25 L)**

This drink can be served hot or cold, and can also be served as a soup, in which case it is called *shan zha cha*.

Preparation time: 5 minutes
Cooking time: 40 minutes

½ cup	sliced dried hawthorn berries	125 mL
2	2-inch (5 cm) rock sugar cubes (see tip, page 145)	2
10 cups	water	2.5 L

1. In a large pot, combine hawthorn berries, rock sugar and water. Bring to a boil over high heat. Reduce heat to medium-low, cover and simmer for 25 minutes. Turn off heat and let steep for 10 minutes.

2. Strain the hawthorn mixture and discard the solids.

Tips

Hawthorn berries are used alone here, but in traditional Chinese medicine, it is common to combine the berries with other ingredients, such as red dates, white fungus, goji berries, dried longan and/or lotus seeds. Look for these ingredients at Asian grocery stores. Alternatively, you can add cranberries or crabapples to this drink.

If you prefer a more sour drink, use only one rock sugar cube. That will also help to cut back on the carbohydrate content.

If you prefer to leave the hawthorn berries in the drink, you can skip step 2. This will increase the available carbohydrate to 5 g (still just 1 Extra Choice).

Hawthorn Berries

Hawthorn berries (*shan zha*) are bright red and tart, similar to crabapples. They are used in teas, desserts, jellies, jams and wine. In traditional Chinese medicine, they are believed to help with digestion, especially after a greasy meal, and to strengthen the heart. Modern researchers agree that hawthorn berries are a potent source of antioxidants, including some similar to those found in grapes. Some preliminary studies suggest that these berries may help control blood pressure and cholesterol levels, and may help protect against heart failure and angina. However, research is still ongoing and there is no conclusive evidence.

Nutrition info per 1 cup (250 mL)

Calories	9
Fat, total	0 g
Fat, saturated	0.0 g
Cholesterol	0 mg
Sodium	8 mg
Carbohydrate	2 g
Fiber	0 g
Protein	0 g
Food Choices	
1	Extra

Red Date, Longan and Ginger Tea
(Zhao Zi Cha)

**Makes about
14 cups (3.5 L)**

The Chinese believe dates, longan and ginger are all rejuvenating, so the combination makes the perfect tea for a hot summer day. I have reduced the sugar content, so go ahead and enjoy a drink to your good health!

Preparation time: 5 minutes
Cooking time: 55 minutes

¾ cup	small Chinese red dates, halved and pitted	175 mL
½ cup	dried longan	125 mL
2 tbsp	minced gingerroot	30 mL
2	2-inch (5 cm) rock sugar cubes (see tip, page 145)	2
16 cups	water	4 L

1. In a large pot, combine dates, longan, ginger, rock sugar and water. Bring to a boil over high heat. Reduce heat to medium-low, cover and simmer for 40 minutes. Let cool.

2. Pour into a large pitcher and refrigerate until cold.

Tips

Longan (*gui yuan*), also called dragon eye, is a sweet fruit native to southern Asia. It looks similar to the lychee but is smaller. It is sold fresh, dried or canned in most Asian grocery stores, and is used in soups, drinks, snacks and desserts.

If you prefer a sweeter tea, add sucralose sweetener rather than additional rock sugar.

Chinese Red Dates

Chinese red dates (*hong zao*) are native to Southeast Asia. They are seen as a superfood in China and play an important role in Chinese herbal medicine. They are sweeter than regular dates. They can be found in Chinese grocery stores. If Chinese red dates are unavailable, regular dates can be used.

Nutrition info per 1 cup
(250 mL)

Calories	36
Fat, total	0 g
Fat, saturated	0.0 g
Cholesterol	0 mg
Sodium	10 mg
Carbohydrate	10 g
Fiber	1 g
Protein	0.3 g
Food Choices	
½	Carbohydrate

Hispanic Cuisine

Recipes from Latin America and Spain

Soups, Salads and Snacks

Cold Melon Cucumber Soup
(Sopa Fría de Melón) 150

Peruvian Potato Cheese Soup
(Sopa de Papas) 151

Mexican Black Bean Soup
(Sopa de Frijoles) 152

Spanish Ham and Rice Soup
(Sopa de Arroz con Jamón) . . . 154

Spanish Sausage and Bean Soup
(Fabada Asturiana) 155

Cactus Salad (Ensalada de
Nopales) 156

Spanish Orange and Avocado
Salad (Ensalada de Naranja
y Aguacate) 158

Corn Tortillas (Tortillas de
Masa Fresca) 159

Peruvian Mushroom and Spinach
Empanadas (Empanadas de
Champiñones y Espinacas) . . . 160

Argentinean Meat Empanadas
(Empanadas Santiagueñas) . . . 162

Mushroom Pinchos
(Pintxos de Champiñones) 164

Vegetarian Dishes

Spanish Ratatouille
(Pisto Manchego) 165

Spanish Piquillo Peppers
Stuffed with Piperade
(Pimientos del Piquillo) 166

Mexican Vegetarian Stew
in a Pot (Vegetarian Mole
de Olla) 168

Lentil and Fruit Stew
(Lentejas con Frutas) 170

Mexican Pot Beans
(Frijoles de la Olla) 171

Spanish Potato Omelet
(Tortilla Española) 172

Colombian Rice with Coconut
(Arroz con Coco) 174

Meat, Poultry, Fish and Seafood Dishes

Beef and Potato Stir-Fry
(Lomo Saltado) 175

Catalan Beef Stew
(Cocido Catalán) 176

Andalusian Meatballs with
Spanish Saffron Sauce
*(Albóndigas con Salsa
al Azafrán)* 177

Segovia-Style Lamb
(Cordero a la Segoviana) 178

Spicy Moorish Pork Kebabs
(Pinchitos Morunos) 179

Mexican Green Chilaquiles
(Chilaquiles Verdes) 180

Pasta in Tomato Sauce with
Chorizo *(Pasta en Salsa Brava
con Chorizo)* 182

Peruvian Ceviche 183

Chilean Fish Escabeche
(Pescado en Escabeche) 184

Tuna with Onions
(Atún Encebollado) 185

Valencia Seafood Paella
(Paella de Mariscos) 186

Spanish Seafood Pasta
(Fideuá) 188

Sauces, Condiments and Beverages

Mexican Spicy Tomato Salsa
(Pico de Gallo) 190

Mexican Morita Chipotle Sauce
(Salsa de Chile Morita) 191

Mexican Spicy Green Sauce
(Salsa Verde) 192

Peruvian Hot Sauce *(Ají)* 193

Argentinean Chimichurri 194

Spanish Saffron Sauce
(Salsa al Azafrán) 195

Spanish Tomato Sauce
(Sofrito) 196

Spanish Brava Tomato Sauce
(Sofrito Brava) 197

Peruvian Purple Corn Drink
(Chicha Morada) 198

Mexican Sweet Rice Drink
(Horchata) 200

Cold Melon Cucumber Soup
(Sopa Fría de Melón)

If you have been to Spain, you have certainly tried gazpacho, a cold tomato soup. Here is another fantastic cold soup to enjoy on a hot summer day, with some tapas on the side. This soup is so easy to make you can't go wrong, even if you are a novice cook! The key is the sherry vinegar and a good Spanish extra virgin olive oil.

Preparation time: **20 minutes**
Chilling time: **2 to 8 hours**

- **Blender**

5 cups	honeydew melon, cut into large chunks	1.25 L
1	clove garlic, minced	1
1/2	large cucumber, peeled and cut into large chunks	1/2
1 cup	nonfat plain yogurt	250 mL
4 tsp	extra virgin olive oil (see box, below)	20 mL
2 tbsp	sherry vinegar	30 mL
1/2 tsp	salt	2 mL
1/4 tsp	freshly ground white pepper	1 mL

1. In blender, in batches as necessary, combine melon, garlic, cucumber, yogurt and oil; purée until smooth. Transfer to a pitcher and stir in vinegar, salt and pepper.

2. Refrigerate until chilled, for at least 2 hours or for up to 8 hours. Stir thoroughly before serving.

Tips

If you want to serve this cold soup immediately after making it, be sure to chill the melon, cucumber and yogurt well before blending.

This soup typically has a lot more olive oil added, but that means a lot of fat. I have reduced the amount of oil to create a lower-fat version.

Spanish Olive Oil

Spain is the largest producer of olive oil in the world. Its climate and high altitude provide an ideal environment for growing olive trees. Spanish olive oil tends to be more golden than green, and has a fainter but a more fruity and nutty aroma than other olive oils. It is worth investing in a good-quality extra virgin Spanish olive oil for the Spanish recipes in this chapter, as it really enhances the flavor of the dishes, but if it is difficult to find, any extra virgin olive oil can be used in its place.

Nutrition info per serving	
Calories	116
Fat, total	4 g
Fat, saturated	1.0 g
Cholesterol	1 mg
Sodium	329 mg
Carbohydrate	20 g
Fiber	2 g
Protein	4 g

Food Choices	
1	Carbohydrate
1	Fat

Peruvian Potato Cheese Soup
(Sopa de Papas)

Makes 6 servings

This nourishing soup is popular in Ecuador and Peru. Peru is the world's potato capital, with about 300 different varieties and colors, and Peruvians love to use potatoes any way they can! To make this soup more practical for someone with diabetes, though, I cut back on the amount of potatoes used in the traditional recipe, to reduce the carbohydrate content.

Variation

For a spicier soup, add 1 to 2 chopped yellow chile peppers (*ajís amarillos*) with the onion. They will add a beautiful yellow hue to the soup. They can be found fresh, canned or frozen at Latin American grocery stores.

Nutrition info per serving	
Calories	114
Fat, total	5 g
Fat, saturated	2.0 g
Cholesterol	44 mg
Sodium	495 mg
Carbohydrate	14 g
Fiber	2 g
Protein	5 g
Food Choices	
1	Carbohydrate
½	Fat

Preparation time: 15 minutes
Cooking time: 20 minutes

	Water	
3 cups	cubed peeled potatoes (1-inch/2.5 cm cubes)	750 mL
½ tsp	vegetable oil	2 mL
½ cup	finely diced white onion	125 mL
3	cloves garlic, minced	3
1 tsp	hot smoked Spanish paprika (see page 22)	5 mL
1 tsp	salt	5 mL
½ tsp	freshly ground black pepper	2 mL
1	large egg, well beaten	1
⅓ cup	cubed queso fresco (¼-inch/0.5 cm cubes)	75 mL
1 tbsp	finely chopped fresh cilantro	15 mL

1. In a deep pot, bring 4 cups (1 L) water to a boil over high heat. Add potatoes and boil for 3 to 4 minutes. Reduce heat to low, cover and let simmer.

2. Meanwhile, in a nonstick skillet, heat oil over medium heat. Add onion and garlic; cook, stirring, for 1 minute. Add paprika, salt and pepper; cook, stirring, for about 3 minutes or until onions are translucent. If ingredients are sticking to the pan, add ¼ cup (60 mL) water and stir well.

3. Stir onion mixture into potatoes and simmer for 5 minutes or until potatoes are fork-tender. Remove from heat and add egg, whisking for about 1 minute. Stir in cheese and cilantro. Serve immediately.

Tips

This recipe contains a lightly cooked egg. If you are concerned about the food safety of lightly cooked eggs, substitute a pasteurized egg in the shell or ¼ cup (60 mL) pasteurized liquid whole eggs.

Queso fresco is a mild-flavored fresh cheese that softens without melting when heated. Stick to the amount used in this recipe, because it is high in total fat and saturated fat.

In Ecuador, this soup is called *locro*. A dish with the same name is found in Argentina, but Argentine *locro* is a vegetable and meat stew.

Mexican Black Bean Soup
(Sopa de Frijoles)

Makes 4 servings

This super-healthy dish can be eaten on its own, with a dollop of salsa verde (page 192) or with brown rice on the side. Beans are a superfood, providing protein and a good source of fiber, especially soluble fiber, and they're fat-free! You couldn't ask for a better food for managing diabetes and heart disease.

Preparation time: **20 minutes**
Cooking time: **15 minutes**

• Blender

2	medium plum (Roma) tomatoes, roughly chopped	2
1	clove garlic	1
1/3 cup	roughly chopped onion	75 mL
3 cups	Mexican Pot Beans (page 171), made with black turtle beans	750 mL
1 1/2 cups	cooking liquid from Mexican Pot Beans	375 mL
1 1/2 tsp	vegetable oil	7 mL
1	sprig dried epazote (see page 22)	1
1/4 tsp	salt	1 mL
1 1/2 cups	ready-to-use reduced-sodium vegetable broth	375 mL

Garnish

1 tsp	vegetable oil	5 mL
2	Corn Tortillas (page 159), cut into thin strips	2
2 tsp	chopped fresh oregano (optional)	10 mL
2 tsp	fat-free sour cream	10 mL

1. In blender, combine tomatoes, garlic and onion; purée until smooth. Transfer to a bowl and set aside.

2. In blender, combine beans and cooking liquid; purée until thick and creamy. Set aside.

3. In a deep pot, heat oil over high heat. Add tomato mixture and cook, stirring, for 1 minute. Reduce heat to medium and cook, stirring, for 2 minutes.

4. Stir in bean purée, epazote, salt and broth; bring to a boil. Reduce heat and boil gently, stirring occasionally, for 5 minutes. Discard epazote.

Nutrition info per serving

Calories	198
Fat, total	3 g
Fat, saturated	0.2 g
Cholesterol	0 mg
Sodium	366 mg
Carbohydrate	34 g
Fiber	10 g
Protein	9 g

Food Choices

1 1/2	Carbohydrate
1	Meat & Alternatives
1/2	Fat

5. *Garnish:* Meanwhile, in a large skillet, heat oil over medium-low heat. Add tortilla strips and cook, turning at least once, until golden brown on both sides. Transfer to a plate lined with paper towels and let drain.

6. Ladle soup into bowls and garnish with oregano (if using), tortilla strips and sour cream.

Tips

To reduce the sodium in this recipe, use ready-to-use no-salt-added vegetable broth or, for more flavor, make your own vegetable stock at home (see recipe, page 245).

Homemade corn tortillas (page 159) are a great addition to this soup, but they do increase the amount of carbohydrate. Make sure not to use more than 2 tortillas in the garnish.

Traditionally, this soup is garnished with cheese or regular sour cream. To help reduce the fat content, fat-free sour cream was used here, but even it should be added sparingly, as it still contains added sodium.

Nutrition Tip

Study after study shows the benefits of legumes for disease prevention and management — especially for diabetes. Legumes include beans, peas, lentils, soybeans and peanuts. When dried, beans, peas and lentils are collectively known as pulses. Legumes are high in protein and fiber, low in fat and have a low glycemic index. They are high in soluble fiber, which helps lower blood glucose and blood cholesterol levels. Low-glycemic foods also help in the management of blood glucose and in weight management. In addition, eating $1/2$ to 2 cups (375 to 500 mL) of legumes per day can help lower blood pressure and triglycerides.

Spanish Ham and Rice Soup
(Sopa de Arroz con Jamón)

This warm soup, of northern Spanish origins, is typically made with leftover ham that was cooked for a special occasion.

Make It a Meal

1 serving Spanish Ham and Rice Soup

1 serving Segovia-Style Lamb (page 178)

1 cup (250 mL) unsalted steamed green beans (1 Extra)

²⁄₃ cup (150 mL) unsalted cooked long-grain brown rice (2 Carbohydrate)

1 medium Valencia orange (1 Carbohydrate)

Nutrition info per serving

Calories	139
Fat, total	3 g
Fat, saturated	0.1 g
Cholesterol	23 mg
Sodium	471 mg
Carbohydrate	18 g
Fiber	2 g
Protein	11 g

Food Choices

1	Carbohydrate
1	Meat & Alternatives

Preparation time: 15 minutes
Cooking time: 30 minutes

2 cups	ready-to-use reduced-sodium chicken broth	500 mL
2¹⁄₂ cups	water	625 mL
¹⁄₄ cup	dry white wine	60 mL
1 tsp	hot smoked Spanish paprika (see page 22)	5 mL
¹⁄₄ tsp	Spanish saffron threads (see page 22), crumbled	1 mL
¹⁄₄ tsp	freshly ground black pepper	1 mL
¹⁄₂ cup	medium-grain white rice	125 mL
1	medium green bell pepper, finely chopped	1
1	medium red bell pepper, finely chopped	1
2 cups	finely chopped cooked smoked lean ham	500 mL
¹⁄₄ cup	Spanish Tomato Sauce (page 196)	60 mL
¹⁄₄ cup	frozen green peas, thawed	60 mL

1. In a large pot, combine broth, water, wine, paprika, saffron and pepper. Bring to a boil over high heat. Stir in rice, reduce heat to low, cover and simmer for 5 minutes.

2. Stir in green pepper, red pepper, ham and tomato sauce; cover and simmer for about 15 minutes or until rice is tender. Stir in peas, cover and simmer for 1 to 2 minutes or until heated through.

Tips

To reduce the sodium in this recipe, use ready-to-use no-salt-added chicken broth or, for more flavor, make your own chicken stock at home (see recipe, page 246).

Traditionally, bomba rice (a short-grain white rice) is used in this dish, but I used medium-grain rice because bomba can be difficult to find. Either short- or medium-grain white rice will give the soup a nice thickness. Long-grain white rice is not a good choice for soup.

When choosing ham, read labels and select one with minimal added salt. The sodium content for hams can range from 400 to over 1000 mg per serving! For the best flavor, choose a smoked ham.

Spanish Sausage and Bean Soup
(Fabada Asturiana)

This tasty soup, made with a special smoked Spanish chorizo, is traditionally served as a meal on its own, perhaps with whole-grain baguette or bread on the side.

Make It a Meal

1 serving Spanish Sausage and Bean Soup

2 slices (each 1 oz/30 g) whole-grain baguette or 2 slices whole-grain bread (2 Carbohydrate)

4 Spanish Piquillo Peppers Stuffed with Piperade (page 166)

1 medium persimmon (1 Carbohydrate)

Nutrition info per serving

Calories	169
Fat, total	3 g
Fat, saturated	1.1 g
Cholesterol	6 mg
Sodium	*528 mg
Carbohydrate	25 g
Fiber	6 g
Protein	10 g

* This recipe is high in sodium. Balance it out by making lower-sodium choices for the rest of your meal and throughout the day.

Food Choices

1	Carbohydrate
1½	Meat & Alternatives

Preparation time: **20 minutes**
Cooking time: **15 minutes**

* **Blender**

3	medium plum (Roma) tomatoes, quartered	3
2	cloves garlic	2
¼	medium onion	¼
¼ cup	minced smoked cured chorizo	60 mL
1	can (19 oz/540 mL) navy beans, drained and rinsed well	1
1	bay leaf	1
½ tsp	hot smoked Spanish paprika (see page 22)	2 mL
½ cup	water	125 mL
¼ tsp	salt	1 mL

1. In blender, combine tomatoes, garlic and onion; purée until smooth. Press through a sieve, discarding solids, and set pulp aside.

2. Heat a large pot over medium heat. Add chorizo and cook, stirring, for 2 minutes. Add tomato mixture and cook for 6 minutes or until mixture turns dark orange.

3. Stir in beans, bay leaf, paprika and water; bring to a boil over high heat. Reduce heat and boil gently, stirring often, for 5 minutes or until thickened. Discard bay leaf. Stir in salt.

Tips

Spanish chorizo is made with pork, fat and paprika, which gives the sausage its characteristic color and smokiness. Because of its high fat and sodium content, the amount of chorizo in this recipe has been reduced. It's available as either fresh or cured sausage; use the cured type for this recipe.

Beans are a great substitution for meat, as they are low in fat and high in fiber. When using canned beans, make sure to rinse them well under running water to wash away the salted liquid they are preserved with or, better yet, look for canned beans with no salt or very little salt added.

This dish is an excellent source of fiber and is low on the glycemic index thanks to the beans.

Cactus Salad *(Ensalada de Nopales)*

Makes 4 servings

Nopales, the edible leaf pads of the prickly pear cactus (*nopal*), are very popular in Mexican cuisine. Many people believe *nopal* can prevent or manage diabetes. Scientific research is ongoing and has shown some promise, but in the meantime, there's no harm in enjoying *nopales* in delicious recipes, such as this one.

Preparation time: **25 minutes**
Cooking time: **20 minutes**

Salad

6	large cactus leaves (about 22 oz/660 g total)	6
1/8	red onion (left in one piece)	1/8
1 tsp	baking soda	5 mL
2 cups	water	500 mL
3	large plum (Roma) tomatoes, diced	3
1	serrano chile pepper, seeded and minced	1
1/2 cup	finely chopped red onion	125 mL
1/2 cup	finely chopped fresh cilantro	125 mL
1/4 cup	cubed panela cheese (1/8-inch/3 mm cubes)	60 mL

Dressing

1/4 cup	freshly squeezed lime juice	60 mL
1 tbsp	olive oil	15 mL
1/2 tsp	salt	2 mL

1. *Salad:* Holding a knife parallel to the cutting board and aiming the blade away from you, use the tip of the knife to remove the cactus spines. Cut around the perimeter of the cactus leaves to remove the spines on the edges. Wash leaves and cut into 1-inch (2.5 cm) squares. You should have about 3 1/2 cups (875 mL).

2. In a large pot, combine cactus, 1/8 onion, baking soda and water. Bring to a boil over high heat. Boil for 20 minutes or until cactus is tender. Discard onion. Drain and cool cactus under cold water.

3. In a medium bowl, combine cactus, tomatoes, chile, chopped onion, cilantro and cheese.

4. *Dressing:* In a small bowl, combine lime juice, oil and salt.

5. Add dressing to salad and toss to coat.

Nutrition info per serving

Calories	94
Fat, total	5 g
Fat, saturated	1.7 g
Cholesterol	7 mg
Sodium	354 mg
Carbohydrate	10 g
Fiber	4 g
Protein	5 g

Food Choices

1	Fat
1	Extra

Tip

If fresh serrano chiles are not available, jalapeño peppers can be substituted, but you'll need to add more, as they aren't as hot. Another option is canned serranos or jalapeños; make sure to rinse them well, as they have a lot of added salt.

Tips

Panela cheese, also known as *queso de canasta*, has a mild "fresh milk" flavor. Only a small amount is used in this dish, as it is high in fat and saturated fat.

If you cannot find panela cheese, substitute farmer's cheese or reduced-sodium feta.

When purchasing any cheese, read the Nutrition Facts table, as sodium and fat per serving can vary. Be sure to choose the lowest-sodium and lowest-fat brand you can find.

Cactus Leaves

Fresh cactus leaves are typically harvested between spring and the end of summer and come in different sizes, from small to large. They are usually boiled until tender-crisp or tender and served in salads or as a cooked vegetable. Baking soda is often added during the cooking process to remove the cactus's natural sliminess and enhance its color. Look for cactus leaves at Latin American grocery stores. They can be found canned, with the spines already removed, but these are very high in sodium (as much as 2000 mg per 1 cup/250 mL!) and should be avoided or consumed in very small amounts.

Spanish Orange and Avocado
Salad *(Ensalada de Naranja y Aguacate)*

In Spain, this delightfully refreshing salad is eaten during the winter months, when tomatoes are not at their prime, but I recommend serving it on a hot summer day. The use of avocado is a Mexican influence on Spanish cuisine.

Preparation time: **20 minutes**

Dressing

3 tbsp	extra virgin olive oil (see box, page 150)	45 mL
1 tbsp	sherry vinegar	15 mL
1 1/2 tsp	freshly squeezed lemon juice	7 mL
1 tsp	grainy Dijon mustard	5 mL
1/4 tsp	salt	1 mL

Salad

1/2	head romaine lettuce (green part only), finely chopped (about 4 cups/1 L)	1/2
4	large navel or Valencia oranges, cut into 1/2-inch (1 cm) thick slices	4
2	large avocados, thinly sliced	2
1	roasted red bell pepper (see tip, page 187), julienned	1
1 cup	thinly sliced red onion	250 mL
2 tbsp	finely chopped fresh mint	30 mL

1. *Dressing:* In a small bowl, whisk together oil, vinegar, lemon juice, mustard and salt.

2. *Salad:* Arrange lettuce on a large platter. Arrange oranges decoratively on top, then avocados, roasted peppers and onion.

3. Just before serving, drizzle dressing over salad and sprinkle with mint.

Tips

This salad is best eaten soon after it is made.

Grainy Dijon mustard (also called old-fashioned or whole Dijon mustard) is preferred in this recipe because it has a milder flavor. If it's not available, you can use regular Dijon, but use half as much, as the flavor is very strong.

It is important to buy seedless oranges, such as navel or Valencia oranges, for this salad. Navel and Valencia oranges are available almost year-round.

The fat in this salad is high, but it comes mostly from the avocado, which provides healthy monounsaturated fat.

Nutrition info per serving

Calories	175
Fat, total	10 g
Fat, saturated	1.4 g
Cholesterol	0 mg
Sodium	96 mg
Carbohydrate	23 g
Fiber	6 g
Protein	3 g

Food Choices

1	Carbohydrate
2	Fat

Corn Tortillas *(Tortillas de Masa Fresca)*

Makes 20 tortillas

Corn tortillas are worth making at home: they taste so much better fresh! Plus, you can control the amount of carbohydrate by making them a smaller size. Enjoy these in Chilaquiles (page 180) or as a topping on Mexican Black Bean Soup (page 152), or use them to make tacos or fajitas … the possibilities are endless!

Tips

Instant corn flour for tortillas (*masa*) has a high glycemic index, so it is important to divide the dough equally into 20 portions and make the specified size of tortillas.

Be sure to use instant corn flour, not regular corn flour, which is used to make breads.

Nutrition info per tortilla

Calories	47
Fat, total	1 g
Fat, saturated	0.0 g
Cholesterol	0 mg
Sodium	1 mg
Carbohydrate	9 g
Fiber	1 g
Protein	1 g

Food Choices

½	Carbohydrate

Preparation time: **20 to 30 minutes**
Cooking time: **40 minutes**

- **Tortilla press or rolling pin**
- **Plastic wrap**
- ***Comal* or small nonstick skillet**

2 cups	instant corn flour for tortillas (approx.)	500 mL
2 cups	warm water (approx.)	500 mL
1 ½ tsp	vegetable oil	7 mL

1. In a medium bowl, combine corn flour and water. Knead for 2 minutes to form a firm dough. If it is too moist or sticky, add a little more flour. If it is too dry, add a little more water.

2. Form dough into 20 equal balls. Cover tortilla press with a sheet of plastic wrap large enough to cover and place one dough ball in the center. Place another plastic circle on top of the ball. Lower the lid of the press to form a 5-inch (12.5 cm) tortilla. Repeat with the remaining dough balls. (Alternatively, if you don't have a tortilla press, use a rolling pin to roll each dough ball out to a 5-inch/12.5 cm diameter. Still place each ball between sheets of plastic wrap to prevent sticking.)

3. Brush the *comal* with a very thin layer of oil and heat over low heat. Removing the plastic wrap, add one tortilla, increase heat to medium and cook, turning once, for 1 minute per side or until light brown on both sides. Transfer the tortilla to a clean kitchen towel and cover it with the towel to prevent it from drying out. Repeat with the remaining tortillas, brushing pan with oil and adjusting heat as necessary between each to prevent sticking and burning. As you remove each tortilla from the pan, stack it on top of the previous tortilla and recover the stack with the towel.

Tips

A *comal* is a smooth, flat griddle used in Mexico to cook tortillas, toast spices and sear meat, among other uses. Similar cookware is called a *budare* in South America.

If you have an insulated container (hot case), you can use it in place of the kitchen towel to keep the cooked tortillas from drying out in step 3.

To save time, this recipe makes a large number of tortillas. Extras can be frozen for later use. Let the tortillas cool completely, then wrap each tortilla individually in plastic wrap and freeze in an airtight container for up to 3 months.

Peruvian Mushroom and Spinach Empanadas
(Empanadas de Champiñones y Espinacas)

An empanada is a stuffed bread or pastry, usually deep-fried. The name comes from the Spanish verb *empanar*, which means "to coat in bread." Empanadas come in all sizes and flavors, and are found all over Latin America, the Caribbean, Spain and Portugal. This version is a typically Peruvian take, except that it's baked instead of fried.

Preparation time: **45 minutes**
Cooking time: **50 minutes**

• **Large baking sheet, lined with parchment paper**

Dough

3 cups	whole wheat flour, divided	750 mL
1/4 cup	yellow pea flour	60 mL
1 1/2 tbsp	baking powder	22 mL
1	large egg, well beaten	1
3/4 cup	skim milk	175 mL
2 tbsp	light cream cheese	30 mL
1 1/2 tsp	vegetable oil	7 mL
1 1/2 tsp	water (optional)	7 mL

Filling

1/4 cup	water	60 mL
3 cups	finely chopped baby spinach (about 6 oz/175 g)	750 mL
1 tsp	vegetable oil	5 mL
1/2 cup	finely chopped onion	125 mL
4	cloves garlic, minced	4
3 cups	sliced mushrooms (1/8-inch/3 mm thick slices)	750 mL
1 tbsp	fresh thyme leaves	15 mL
1/2 tsp	freshly ground black pepper	2 mL
1/2 tsp	salt	2 mL
2 tbsp	light cream cheese	30 mL
2 tbsp	nonfat plain yogurt	30 mL
2	large egg yolks, well beaten	2

1. *Dough:* In a medium bowl, combine 2 1/2 cups (625 mL) whole wheat flour, yellow pea flour and baking powder. Make a well in the center and add egg, milk, cream cheese and oil. Using your hands, mix together until a soft dough forms. If dough is too dry, mix in water.

2. On a work surface sprinkled with 1/4 cup (60 mL) whole wheat flour, knead dough. Return dough to the bowl, cover with plastic wrap and refrigerate for 30 minutes.

Nutrition info per empanada

Calories	152
Fat, total	3 g
Fat, saturated	0.8 g
Cholesterol	43 mg
Sodium	148 mg
Carbohydrate	26 g
Fiber	5 g
Protein	7 g

Food Choices

1	Carbohydrate
1/2	Fat

Make It a Meal

1 serving Peruvian Potato Cheese Soup (page 151)

1 Peruvian Mushroom and Spinach Empanada

1 serving Peruvian Hot Sauce (page 193)

$1/2$ serving Peruvian Ceviche (page 183)

$1/4$ cup (60 mL) Peruvian Purple Corn Drink (page 198)

1 medium Valencia orange (1 Carbohydrate)

Tips

The dough should be light and fluffy. Baking powder is a key ingredient that helps to increase the volume of baked goods and lighten them, especially when whole wheat flour is used.

The traditional empanada dough for this recipe is prepared with white flour, butter and full-fat cream cheese, and is very high in fat and refined carbohydrate. Replacing these ingredients with whole wheat flour, yellow pea flour and lower-fat cream cheese creates a well-balanced snack that is high in fiber with a low glycemic index.

3. *Filling:* Meanwhile, in a saucepan, bring water to a boil over high heat. Add spinach and cook for 1 minute. Drain and let cool. Squeeze spinach to remove excess water.

4. In the same saucepan, heat oil over medium heat. Add onion and garlic; cook, stirring, for 1 minute. Add mushrooms, thyme, pepper, salt, cream cheese and yogurt; cook, stirring, for 10 minutes or until mixture is dry.

5. Transfer mushroom mixture to a bowl and refrigerate for 5 minutes. Stir in spinach and refrigerate for 10 minutes.

6. Preheat oven to 350°F (180°C).

7. Divide dough into 13 equal pieces. On a work surface sprinkled with the remaining whole wheat flour, roll out each piece into a 5-inch (12.5 cm) diameter circle (about $1/4$ inch/0.5 cm thick). Place 2 tbsp (30 mL) filling in the center of each circle. Lightly brush beaten egg yolks over half the edge and fold the other half over top. Using a fork, seal the edges. Place empanadas on prepared baking sheet, spaced an equal distance apart, and lightly brush the top of each empanada with egg.

8. Bake for 20 minutes. Turn empanadas over and bake for 5 minutes or until golden brown and filling is hot.

Nutrition Tip

Yellow pea flour is made by grinding dried yellow field peas, a great source of fiber and vegetable protein. It also has a low glycemic index, which may help lower blood glucose levels and low-density lipoprotein (LDL) blood cholesterol and help reduce the risk of getting heart disease!

Argentinean Meat Empanadas
(Empanadas Santiagueñas)

In Argentina, these empanadas are among the best street foods you can get, especially when you have some *ají* (page 193) on the side! Empanadas can be high in carbohydrate, so I have made these smaller, used whole wheat flour and reduced the amount of raisins. To make them even more healthy, I baked them instead of deep-frying.

Preparation time: **1 hour**
Cooking time: **1 hour**

• **Large baking sheet, lined with parchment paper**

Dough

5 cups	whole wheat flour	1.25 L
2 tbsp	baking powder	30 mL
1/4 tsp	salt	1 mL
1 tsp	freshly ground black pepper	5 mL
1	large egg, well beaten	1
3/4 cup	skim milk	175 mL
5 tsp	white wine vinegar	25 mL
1 tbsp	vegetable oil	15 mL
1 1/2 tsp	water (optional)	7 mL
2 tbsp	whole wheat flour	30 mL

Filling

1 1/2 tsp	olive oil	7 mL
2	cloves garlic, minced	2
2 cups	finely chopped onion	500 mL
1	medium green bell pepper, finely chopped	1
2 tsp	hot pepper flakes	10 mL
1 tsp	hot smoked Spanish paprika (see page 22)	5 mL
1 tsp	ground dried oregano	5 mL
1/2 tsp	salt	1 mL
1 lb	lean ground beef	500 g
1/4 cup	raisins	60 mL
1 tbsp	ground cumin	15 mL
1 cup	dry white wine	250 mL
1 tbsp	white wine vinegar	15 mL
1/3 cup	pitted olives, cut in half	75 mL
2	hard-cooked eggs, chopped	2
1	large egg yolk, well beaten	1

1. *Dough:* In a bowl, combine 5 cups (1.25 L) whole wheat flour, baking powder, salt and pepper. Make a well in the center and add egg, milk, vinegar and oil. Using your hands, mix together until a soft dough forms. If dough is too dry, add water. Cover bowl with plastic wrap and refrigerate for 30 minutes.

**Nutrition info
per empanada**

Calories	472
Fat, total	11 g
Fat, saturated	2.4 g
Cholesterol	124 mg
Sodium	389 mg
Carbohydrate	69 g
Fiber	10 g
Protein	26 g

Food Choices

3 1/2	Carbohydrate
1 1/2	Meat & Alternatives
1/2	Fat

Tips

Instead of greasing your baking sheets and pans, use parchment paper to prevent food from sticking.

Olives are very high in sodium and should be used sparingly.

The dough should be light and fluffy. Baking powder is a key ingredient that helps to increase the volume of baked goods and lighten them, especially when whole wheat flour is used.

2. *Filling:* In a large saucepan, heat oil over medium-high heat. Add garlic and cook, stirring, for 1 minute. Add onion and cook, stirring, for 1 minute. Add green pepper, hot pepper flakes, paprika, oregano and salt; cook, stirring, for 2 minutes.

3. Add beef, reduce heat to medium-low and cook, breaking beef up with a spoon, for 2 minutes. Add raisins and cumin; cook, stirring, for 2 minutes. Stir in wine and increase heat to medium and boil gently, stirring often, for 5 minutes or until liquid has reduced by half and beef is no longer pink. Add vinegar and cook, stirring, until liquid has evaporated. Remove from heat and let cool for 10 minutes.

4. Preheat oven to 350°F (180°C).

5. Divide dough into 8 equal pieces. On a work surface sprinkled with 2 tbsp (30 mL) whole wheat flour, roll out each piece into a 7-inch (18 cm) diameter circle. Place $\frac{1}{3}$ cup (75 mL) filling in the center of the circle. On top, add about 2 tsp (10 mL) olives and one-quarter of the hard-cooked egg. Lightly brush egg yolk over half the edge and fold the other half over top. Using a fork, seal the edges. Place empanadas at least 1 inch (2.5 cm) apart on prepared baking sheet and lightly brush the top of each empanada with egg yolk.

6. Bake for 40 minutes, turning halfway through, until golden brown and filling is hot.

Mushroom Pinchos
(Pintxos de Champiñones)

Pinchos (or pintxos) are finger foods or small snacks served in northern Spain that originated in Basque country. The term comes from the word *pinchar*, which means "to pierce," and most pinchos are served skewered on toothpicks. Enjoy them as a light snack, with a refreshing drink on the side, or with other tapas.

Preparation time: **25 minutes**
Marinating time: **30 to 60 minutes**
Cooking time: **20 minutes**

- **30 toothpicks**

1	medium eggplant, cut into 1-inch (2.5 cm) cubes	1
3 cups	skim milk (optional)	750 mL
4	cloves garlic, puréed (see tips, page 77)	4
¼ cup	finely chopped fresh parsley	60 mL
3 tbsp	sweet smoked Spanish paprika (see page 22)	45 mL
1½ tsp	ground cumin	7 mL
½ cup	unsweetened apple juice	125 mL
¼ cup	sherry vinegar	60 mL
1 tbsp	extra virgin olive oil (see box, page 150)	15 mL
30	mushrooms, stems removed	30
2	medium zucchini, cut crosswise into 1-inch (2.5 cm) thick slices	2

1. If desired (to remove bitterness and to soften eggplant), place eggplant in a large bowl, cover with milk and let soak for 20 minutes. Drain well.

2. In a small bowl, combine garlic, parsley, paprika, cumin, apple juice, vinegar and oil. Stir in eggplant, mushrooms and zucchini. Marinate at room temperature for 30 to 60 minutes.

3. Heat a large nonstick skillet over medium-high heat. Add mushrooms and zucchini; cook, turning once, for about 6 minutes per side or until tender-crisp. If vegetables are browning too quickly, reduce heat as necessary. Transfer vegetables to a plate.

4. Add eggplant to the pan and cook, stirring, for about 5 minutes or until tender-crisp. Remove from heat and let cool slightly.

5. When cool enough to handle, thread a mushroom, eggplant cube and zucchini slice onto each skewer. Let cool to room temperature before serving.

Tip

There is no real substitute for sherry vinegar, but for this recipe, cider vinegar is an acceptable replacement. If all you have on hand is red wine vinegar, use less, as it is tarter and more acidic.

Nutrition info per serving (5 pinchos)

Calories	89
Fat, total	3 g
Fat, saturated	0.5 g
Cholesterol	0 mg
Sodium	15 mg
Carbohydrate	14 g
Fiber	4 g
Protein	3 g

Food Choices

½	Fat
1	Extra

Spanish Ratatouille *(Pisto Manchego)*

Makes 14 servings

This simple dish, originally from the region of Murcia, is now served all over Spain, on its own or to accompany meats, eggs, fish or bread. Although the vegetables are usually fried in oil, they turn out just as delicious when baked. Serve as a tapa or side dish. If you serve it on whole-grain baguette or bread slices, be sure to count the added carbohydrate. Leftovers are great for lunch.

Preparation time: **30 minutes**
Cooking time: **30 minutes**

- **Preheat oven to 350°F (180°C), with racks positioned in top and bottom thirds of oven**
- **2 large rimmed baking sheets, lined with parchment paper**

1	medium eggplant, cut into $1/4$-inch (0.5 cm) cubes	1
2 cups	skim milk (optional)	500 mL
2	medium zucchini (unpeeled), cut into $1/4$-inch (0.5 cm) cubes	2
2	medium red bell peppers, cut into $1/4$-inch (0.5 cm) pieces	2
1	large butternut squash, cut into $1/2$-inch (1 cm) cubes	1
1	large red onion, cut into $1/4$-inch (0.5 cm) cubes	1
1	sprig fresh thyme leaves	1
1 tbsp	dried oregano	15 mL
1 tbsp	ground coriander	15 mL
1 tsp	salt	5 mL
$1/4$ tsp	freshly ground white pepper	1 mL
2 tsp	extra virgin olive oil (see box, page 150)	10 mL
$2 1/2$ cups	Spanish Brava Tomato Sauce (page 197)	625 mL

1. If desired (to remove bitterness and to soften), place eggplant in a large bowl, cover with milk and let soak for 20 minutes. Drain well.

2. In a large bowl, combine eggplant, zucchini, red peppers, squash and onion. Add thyme, oregano, coriander, salt, pepper and oil; toss to coat. Divide vegetables equally between prepared baking sheets and spread into a single layer.

3. Bake in upper and lower thirds of preheated oven for 30 minutes, switching sheets between racks and stirring vegetables halfway through, until vegetables are light golden brown and tender-crisp.

4. In a serving bowl, combine vegetables and tomato sauce.

Tip

Extra ratatouille can be refrigerated in an airtight container for up to 5 days.

Nutrition info per serving

Calories	73
Fat, total	2 g
Fat, saturated	0.3 g
Cholesterol	0 mg
Sodium	247 mg
Carbohydrate	14 g
Fiber	4 g
Protein	2 g
Food Choices	
1	Extra

Spanish Piquillo Peppers Stuffed with Piperade *(Pimientos del Piquillo)*

Piperade is a spicy, sweet and tangy sauce from the Basque region of France, though this recipe uses a Spanish version to stuff the piquillo peppers, typically served as a tapa. The peppers can be served on their own or on slices of whole-grain baguette or bread; if you serve them with bread, be sure to account for the added carbohydrate.

Preparation time: **30 minutes**
Cooking time: **35 to 40 minutes**

- **Preheat barbecue grill to high or preheat broiler**
- **Preheat oven to 350°F (180°C)**
- **Rimmed baking sheet**

Piperade

1	medium red bell pepper	1
1	medium green bell pepper	1
1 tsp	extra virgin olive oil (see box, page 150)	5 mL
1	medium onion, finely chopped	1
1	clove garlic, minced	1
1	medium zucchini, finely chopped	1
4	sprigs fresh thyme leaves	4
1/2 tsp	salt	2 mL
1/4 tsp	freshly ground black pepper	1 mL
1/4 tsp	sweet smoked Spanish paprika (see page 22)	1 mL
1/4 tsp	ground dried oregano	1 mL
3 tbsp	Spanish Tomato Sauce (page 196)	45 mL
20	canned water-packed piquillo peppers, drained	20
1/3 cup	light ricotta cheese, light goat cheese or queso fresco	75 mL

1. *Piperade:* Grill red and green peppers on preheated barbecue, or on a baking sheet under the broiler, turning often, until blackened and blistering on all sides. Transfer to a bowl and cover with plastic wrap (or transfer to a paper bag) and let cool. Peel off skins and remove core, ribs and seeds. Finely chop.

2. In a medium skillet, heat oil over medium heat. Add onion and garlic; cook, stirring, for 3 minutes. Stir in grilled peppers, zucchini, thyme, salt, pepper, paprika and oregano; cook, stirring, for 2 minutes. Stir in tomato sauce and remove from heat.

Nutrition info per 4 peppers

Calories	106
Fat, total	3 g
Fat, saturated	0.8 g
Cholesterol	4 mg
Sodium	381 mg
Carbohydrate	14 g
Fiber	2 g
Protein	5 g

Food Choices

1/2	Meat & Alternatives
1	Extra

Make It a Meal

4 Spanish Piquillo
Peppers Stuffed with
Piperade

1 serving Tuna with
Onions (page 185)

2 slices (each 1 oz/30 g)
whole-grain baguette
or 2 slices whole-grain
bread (2 Carbohydrate)

½ cup (125 mL) Mexican
Sweet Rice Drink
(page 200)

¾ cup (175 mL)
chopped pineapple
(1 Carbohydrate)

3. Stuff piquillo peppers with piperade and cheese, dividing evenly. Place peppers on baking sheet.

4. Bake in preheated oven for 10 minutes, turning halfway through, until cheese is slightly melted. Serve warm or let cool, refrigerate in an airtight container for up to 3 days and serve cold.

Tips

Queso fresco is the traditional choice for this recipe, but light ricotta cheese or goat cheese are better options because queso fresco is high in total fat and saturated fat.

The piperade can be used in a variety of dishes, such as stews, or as a garnish.

Piquillo Peppers

Piquillo peppers are small, sweet, mild red chile peppers, grown in northern Spain, that are hand-roasted, peeled and canned. They have a slightly smoky flavor and are traditionally either stuffed and baked, or puréed and added to sauces for meat and fish. They can be found in Spanish or Latin American specialty stores, in jars or cans, usually packed in oil or water. Choose peppers that are canned in water to avoid additional fat.

Mexican Vegetarian Stew in a Pot
(Vegetarian Mole de Olla)

Makes 8 servings

This vegetarian version of a traditionally beef-based recipe uses oyster mushrooms as a low-fat substitute for beef. Oyster mushrooms have a mild, delicate flavor and a velvety texture. Another great option would be chopped portobello mushrooms, for their naturally meaty texture. The ancho and pasilla peppers give this dish a distinctive flavor and deep, rich color. Serve with Mexican Pot Beans (page 171) or grilled meat and rice. Or see the suggested meal plan on page 169.

Preparation time: **45 minutes**
Cooking time: **1 hour**

* **Blender**

2	dried ancho chile peppers, stems and seeds removed	2
2	dried pasilla chile peppers, stems and seeds removed	2
1 cup	hot water	250 mL
4	medium plum (Roma) tomatoes	4
1 tbsp	olive oil	15 mL
1	small onion, chopped	1
3	cloves garlic, minced	3
2 cups	ready-to-use reduced-sodium vegetable broth	500 mL
3	sprigs dried epazote (see page 22)	3
2	ears corn, cut into 1-inch (2.5 cm) thick slices	2
2	chayotes, cut into 1-inch (2.5 cm) cubes	2
1 cup	halved trimmed green beans	250 mL
2½ cups	stemmed oyster mushrooms	625 mL
2	medium zucchini, cut in half lengthwise, then sliced crosswise	2
1 tsp	salt	5 mL
½ tsp	freshly ground black pepper	2 mL
2 tbsp	freshly squeezed lime juice (about 1 lime)	30 mL

1. In a small bowl, soak ancho and pasilla chiles in hot water for 30 minutes.

2. Meanwhile, heat a large saucepan over medium-low heat. Add tomatoes and cook, stirring, until softened. Let cool, then remove peels. Set aside.

3. Transfer chiles and soaking water to blender and purée until smooth.

4. In a large, deep pot, heat oil over medium heat. Add onion and garlic; cook, stirring, for 1 minute. Add chile purée, reduce heat to low and cook, stirring often, for 5 minutes.

Nutrition info per serving

Calories	114
Fat, total	3 g
Fat, saturated	0.5 g
Cholesterol	0 mg
Sodium	342 mg
Carbohydrate	21 g
Fiber	6 g
Protein	5 g

Food Choices

½	Carbohydrate
½	Fat

Make It a Meal

1 serving Mexican Vegetarian Stew in a Pot

1 serving Catalan Beef Stew (page 176)

2/3 cup (150 mL) unsalted cooked long-grain brown rice (2 Carbohydrate)

1/2 cup (125 mL) Mexican Sweet Rice Drink (page 200)

1/2 medium persimmon (1/2 Carbohydrate)

5. Stir in broth and bring to a boil over medium heat. Add peeled tomatoes, epazote, corn, chayotes and green beans. Cover and boil gently, stirring occasionally and breaking up tomatoes, for 20 minutes.

6. Stir in mushrooms and boil gently for 10 minutes. Add zucchini, salt and pepper; boil gently for about 5 minutes or until softened. Discard epazote. Stir in lime juice.

Tips

Ancho chile peppers are the most commonly used chiles in Mexico. They have a deep red color, wrinkled flesh and a sweet flavor similar to that of a bell pepper. In their fresh form, they're called poblano peppers.

Pasilla chiles — the dried version of chilaca chiles — are long, slender peppers with a mild and slightly "tobaccoish" flavor. Their seeds and veins are very hot. If you prefer more heat, do not seed them.

Plum tomatoes are the best choice for this recipe because they release less water than other tomatoes as they cook. To maintain the authenticity of this dish, use ripe, bright red tomatoes.

To reduce the sodium in this recipe, use ready-to-use no-salt-added vegetable broth or, for more flavor, make your own vegetable stock at home (see recipe, page 245).

Lentil and Fruit Stew
(Lentejas con Frutas)

Makes 6 servings

In Mexico, lentil stew is usually made with either chorizo or fruit. For its healthier fat and sodium profile, fruit is the better option. The stew is traditionally served for dinner, with a hard-cooked egg on the side. Although this is a Mexican dish, I used a Spanish brava sauce to contribute to the stew's characteristic sweet and spicy flavor.

Soaking time: **30 minutes**
Preparation time: **20 minutes**
Cooking time: **1 hour 15 minutes**

2 cups	dried green lentils, rinsed	500 mL
	Water	
2	bay leaves	2
2	cloves garlic (unpeeled)	2
1	small onion (unpeeled)	1
7 cups	ready-to-use no-salt-added vegetable broth, divided	1.75 L
2 cups	Spanish Brava Tomato Sauce (page 197)	500 mL
1 tsp	salt	5 mL
1 tsp	sweet smoked Spanish paprika (see page 22)	5 mL
2 cups	cubed pineapple (1/2-inch/1 cm cubes)	500 mL
1 cup	sliced yellow plantain (1/4-inch/0.5 cm thick slices)	250 mL
1 1/2 tsp	ground coriander	7 mL

1. Place lentils in a bowl with enough water to cover; let soak for 30 minutes. Drain.

2. In a large saucepan, combine bay leaves, garlic, onion, lentils and 6 cups (1.5 L) broth. Bring to a boil over medium heat. Reduce heat to low, cover and simmer for 45 minutes or until lentils are tender. Discard bay leaves, garlic and onion.

3. Stir in tomato sauce, salt and paprika; increase heat to medium and cook, stirring, for 1 minute. Stir in pineapple, plantain, coriander and the remaining broth; bring to a boil. Reduce heat to medium-low, cover and simmer, stirring occasionally, for 15 minutes.

Tips

This dish is high in carbohydrate, but it comes mostly from the lentils, which have a low glycemic index and are high in fiber, so they will not significantly increase blood glucose levels.

For more flavor, make your own vegetable stock at home (see recipe, page 245) and use it in place of some or all of the vegetable broth.

Nutrition info per serving	
Calories	326
Fat, total	2 g
Fat, saturated	0.1 g
Cholesterol	0 mg
Sodium	437 mg
Carbohydrate	69 g
Fiber	11 g
Protein	15 g

Food Choices	
3 1/2	Carbohydrate
2	Meat & Alternatives

Mexican Pot Beans *(Frijoles de la Olla)*

Makes 5 cups (1.25 L)

Frijoles de la olla is a popular dish of slow-cooked, creamy beans. In northern Mexico, red beans are the typical choice; in central Mexico, white beans; in southern Mexico (where this version is from), black turtle beans. Use pot beans to fill burritos, tacos or tostadas, or serve them on their own or with sides of brown rice and a mixed green salad.

Preparation time: **5 minutes**
Cooking time: **2 hours and 15 minutes**

⅓	white onion (left in one piece)	⅓
2 cups	dried black turtle beans (see tip, below)	500 mL
¼ tsp	salt	1 mL
5 cups	ready-to-use reduced-sodium vegetable broth	1.25 L
	Hot water (optional)	

1. In a large pot, combine onion, beans, salt and broth. Bring to a boil over high heat. Reduce heat and simmer, stirring occasionally, for 2 hours. Make sure there is always enough liquid to cover the beans; add hot water if needed. Discard onion.

Tips

Feel free to roam through the cuisines of Mexico and substitute dried red or white beans in this dish — or any other type of dried beans you fancy.

The beans are often cooked with lard or pork fat for flavor, but this adds a lot of fat.

To reduce the sodium in this recipe, use ready-to-use no-salt-added vegetable broth or, for more flavor, make your own vegetable stock at home (see recipe, page 245).

Variation

For extra flavor and spice, add Mexican ingredients such as whole jalapeño peppers, chipotle peppers or dried epazote sprigs, discarding them at the end of the cooking time. (For a real kick of spice, finely chop the peppers and leave them in.)

Nutrition info per 1 cup (250 mL)

Calories	211
Fat, total	0 g
Fat, saturated	0.0 g
Cholesterol	0 mg
Sodium	256 mg
Carbohydrate	40 g
Fiber	14 g
Protein	12 g

Food Choices

2	Carbohydrate
2	Meat & Alternatives

Spanish Potato Omelet
(Tortilla Española)

Makes 4 servings

Makes 4 servings

It took me a trip to Spain to realize that this dish, also called *tortillas de patatas*, is actually a tapa and not served for breakfast! It can be eaten warm or cold. To reduce the fat, I cut back on the number of eggs and the amount of oil, so using a nonstick skillet will really help you make a perfect omelet. For added flavor, I included parsley and green onions, but they can easily be omitted if you prefer the traditional simpler version.

Preparation time: **20 minutes**
Cooking time: **30 minutes**

• **Preheat barbecue grill to high or preheat broiler**

1	medium red bell pepper	1
1 ½ tbsp	extra virgin olive oil (see box, page 150), divided	22 mL
3	cloves garlic, minced	3
1 cup	finely chopped onion	250 mL
½ tsp	salt	2 mL
¼ tsp	freshly ground black pepper	1 mL
2 cups	finely grated potatoes	500 mL
1 tbsp	finely chopped fresh parsley	15 mL
1	green onion, finely chopped (optional)	1
3	large eggs, well beaten	3

1. Grill red pepper on preheated barbecue, or on a baking sheet under the broiler, turning often, until blackened and blistering on all sides. Transfer to a bowl and cover with plastic wrap (or transfer to a paper bag) and let cool. Peel off skins and remove core, ribs and seeds. Finely chop.

2. In a nonstick skillet, heat 1 tbsp (15 mL) oil over medium-low heat. Add garlic and cook, stirring, for 1 minute. Add onion, salt and pepper; cook, stirring, for 1 minute. Add grilled pepper and cook, stirring, for 1 minute. Add potatoes, parsley and green onion (if using); cook, stirring, for 3 minutes or until potatoes are almost tender.

3. Transfer potato mixture to a large bowl and whisk in eggs until combined.

Nutrition info per serving

Calories	186
Fat, total	9 g
Fat, saturated	1.9 g
Cholesterol	140 mg
Sodium	356 mg
Carbohydrate	20 g
Fiber	3 g
Protein	7 g

Food Choices

1	Carbohydrate
½	Meat & Alternatives
1	Fat

4. In the same skillet, heat the remaining oil over medium heat. Add egg mixture and cook for 2 minutes or until bottom is light brown. To flip omelet, place a plate the same size as the pan over the omelet. Gently turn skillet over so that the omelet sits on the plate. Return skillet to heat and slide omelet back into the pan. Cook for 2 minutes or until light brown. Serve warm or let cool, refrigerate in an airtight container for up to 1 day and serve cold.

Tips

This dish is usually made with a lot of oil and potatoes, and it can sometimes have added ham or chorizo. This is a more diabetes-friendly version, with a lower fat and carbohydrate content. Because the potatoes are grated, less oil is needed as they cook more quickly.

Because this recipe uses whole eggs, the cholesterol is high. To reduce it, you can replace the whole eggs with at least 6 egg whites (add more as necessary if the mixture seems dry in step 3; you need enough whites to make sure the omelet holds together).

Nonstick pans require good care to protect the nonstick coating. Buy good-quality, heavy pans and never heat an empty pan. And always use plastic, rubber, silicon or wood utensils; metal tools or those with a sharp edge can cause some of the nonstick coating to scrape off into your food.

Colombian Rice with Coconut
(Arroz con Coco)

With coconut, raisins and brown sugar, this popular Colombian dish is definitely comfort food. I kept it authentic by using long-grain white rice, but that meant I had to cut back on the raisins and sugar to keep the carbohydrate low. Watch your portions — you'll certainly want to eat more than one serving! This goes well with fish and other seafood.

Preparation time: 5 minutes
Cooking time: 25 minutes

1/3 cup	unsweetened shredded coconut	75 mL
1/4 cup	raisins	60 mL
1 1/2 cups	water	375 mL
1 cup	light coconut milk	250 mL
1 cup	long-grain white rice	250 mL
1/2 tsp	salt	2 mL
1/2 tsp	packed brown sugar	2 mL

1. Heat a small skillet over low heat. Toast coconut and raisins, stirring constantly, for about 2 minutes or until coconut is lightly browned. Immediately transfer to a bowl.

2. In a small saucepan, combine water and coconut milk; bring to a boil over high heat. Add rice and return to a boil. Stir in toasted coconut and raisins, salt and brown sugar; reduce heat to low, cover and simmer for about 15 minutes or until rice is tender and liquid is absorbed. Remove from heat and let stand, covered, for 5 minutes.

Tips

Regular coconut milk has three times as much fat as light coconut milk, so it's best to use the light version for all your cooking.

Raisins, brown sugar and white rice contribute to a high carbohydrate content. Omitting the raisins will reduce it to 40 grams of available carbohydrate per serving (2 1/2 Carbohydrate Choices).

To increase the coconut flavor of this recipe, add a few drops of coconut extract.

Nutrition info per serving

Calories	267
Fat, total	6 g
Fat, saturated	5.2 g
Cholesterol	5 mg
Sodium	304 mg
Carbohydrate	49 g
Fiber	2 g
Protein	4 g

Food Choices

3	Carbohydrate
1/2	Fat

Beef and Potato Stir-Fry
(Lomo Saltado)

Makes 4 servings

Lomo saltado is a popular Peruvian stir-fry that is traditionally served with white rice and french fries. Sometimes the fries are stir-fried in with the beef! This dish is heavily influenced by the Chinese culture in Peru, and sometimes soy sauce is added. I decided to omit it because the sodium is already high. For a tasty meal, serve it with low- or no-sodium sides, such as a small bowl of brown rice and a mixed green salad, steamed broccoli or more stir-fried onions and tomatoes.

Preparation time: 20 minutes
Cooking time: 50 minutes

● **Preheat oven to 350°F (180°C)**

1 ½ cups	sliced peeled potatoes (2- by ½-inch/ 5 by 1 cm slices)	375 mL
1 ½ tsp	vegetable oil, divided	7 mL
14 oz	lean boneless beef sirloin, cut into 2-inch (5 cm) thick strips	400 g
3	cloves garlic, minced	3
¾ tsp	salt, divided	3 mL
½ tsp	freshly ground black pepper	2 mL
1 cup	sliced onions (½-inch/1 cm thick slices)	250 mL
1	medium tomato, cut into ½-inch (1 cm) wedges	1
3 tbsp	finely chopped fresh cilantro	45 mL
1 ½ tsp	freshly squeezed lemon juice	7 mL

1. On a baking sheet, toss potatoes with half the oil, then spread out in a single layer. Roast in preheated oven for 40 minutes or until browned and tender.

2. In a large bowl, combine beef, garlic, ½ tsp (2 mL) salt and pepper.

3. In a large skillet, heat the remaining oil over high heat. Add beef mixture, cover and cook for 1 minute. Reduce heat to low and cook, uncovered and stirring, for 1 minute. Add onions and cook, stirring, for 3 minutes.

4. Add tomatoes, increase heat to high and cook for 2 minutes. Add cilantro and the remaining salt; cook, stirring, for 1 minute. Stir in lemon juice and cook for 1 minute. Stir in roasted potatoes and cook, stirring, for 1 minute.

Nutrition info per serving

Calories	219
Fat, total	6 g
Fat, saturated	1.5 g
Cholesterol	57 mg
Sodium	488 mg
Carbohydrate	18 g
Fiber	2 g
Protein	24 g

Food Choices

½	Carbohydrate
3	Meat & Alternatives
½	Fat

Catalan Beef Stew *(Cocido Catalán)*

Makes 5 servings

The region of Catalonia, best known for its capital, Barcelona, has some great cuisine! For this famous dish, many recipes use sofrito (page 196) as a base, but I decided to use fresh tomatoes. In place of mushrooms, I chose leeks and long beans.

Tip

Beef shoulder is a good stewing meat, but it's high in fat. An alternative, lower-fat cut of meat (bottom round) was used in this dish instead. When using lower-fat meats, it's important to watch the cooking time, as they can easily overcook and become tough.

Nutrition info per serving

Calories	212
Fat, total	8 g
Fat, saturated	2.3 g
Cholesterol	52 mg
Sodium	333 mg
Carbohydrate	10 g
Fiber	2 g
Protein	21 g

Food Choices

2	Meat & Alternatives

Preparation time: 20 minutes
Cooking time: 1 hour and 45 minutes

1 ½ tsp	extra virgin olive oil (see box, page 150)	7 mL
½ cup	chopped onion	125 mL
2	cloves garlic, minced	2
½	stalk celery, chopped	½
1 lb	boneless beef bottom round, visible fat removed, cut into 1-inch (2.5 cm) cubes	500 g
½ tsp	salt	2 mL
¼ tsp	freshly ground black pepper	1 mL
2	medium plum (Roma) tomatoes, chopped	2
1	medium leek (white and light green parts only), chopped	1
1 tbsp	finely chopped fresh oregano	15 mL
¼ tsp	ground cinnamon	1 mL
1	carrot, thinly sliced	1
1 cup	halved Chinese long beans	250 mL
2 cups	water	500 mL
1 ½ cups	ready-to-use reduced-sodium chicken broth	375 mL
½ cup	dry red wine	125 mL

1. In a large, deep pot, heat oil over medium heat. Add onion and cook, stirring, for about 2 minutes or until translucent. Add garlic and celery; cook, stirring, for 1 minute.

2. Stir in beef, salt and pepper; cook, stirring, for 10 minutes.

3. Stir in tomatoes, leek, oregano and cinnamon; cook, stirring, for 8 minutes.

4. Stir in carrot and cook, stirring, for 5 minutes.

5. Stir in green beans, water, broth and wine; reduce heat to medium-low, cover and simmer, stirring occasionally, for 1 hour and 20 minutes or until beef is tender.

Tips

Plum tomatoes are the best choice for this recipe because they release less water than other tomatoes as they cook. To maintain the authenticity of this dish, use ripe, bright red tomatoes.

Although this recipe is delicious just as it is, for true authenticity it requires an additional ingredient: chocolate. If you're feeling bold, add 1 oz (30 g) unsweetened chocolate with the chicken stock. Remember that this will increase the carbohydrate content by 1 g per serving.

Andalusian Meatballs with Spanish Saffron Sauce

(Albóndigas con Salsa al Azafrán)

Serve these yummy meatballs as a tapa, with saffron sauce to enhance their flavor. Or try another sauce, such as Spanish Brava Tomato Sauce (page 197), for a different taste combination.

Make It a Meal

1 serving Andalusian Meatballs with Spanish Saffron Sauce

1 cup (250 mL) unsalted roasted potatoes (2 Carbohydrate) with Spanish Brava Tomato Sauce (page 197)

1 serving Spanish Orange and Avocado Salad (page 158)

1 cup (250 mL) skim or 1% milk (1 Carbohydrate)

Nutrition info per serving

Calories	136
Fat, total	5 g
Fat, saturated	1.2 g
Cholesterol	68 mg
Sodium	430 mg
Carbohydrate	6 g
Fiber	1 g
Protein	16 g

Food Choices

2	Meat & Alternatives

Preparation time: **20 minutes**
Cooking time: **20 minutes**

- **Preheat oven to 350°F (180°C)**
- **Baking sheet, lined with parchment paper**

1 lb	lean ground beef	500 g
4	small shallots, finely chopped	4
2	cloves garlic, minced	2
1	medium red bell pepper, finely chopped	1
1/2 cup	pitted green olives, finely chopped	125 mL
1/4 cup	finely chopped fresh mint	60 mL
1 1/2 tsp	ground cumin	7 mL
1/2 tsp	salt	2 mL
1	large egg, well beaten	1
2 tsp	grated orange zest	10 mL
1/4 cup	freshly squeezed orange juice	60 mL
1/3 cup	Spanish Saffron Sauce (page 195)	75 mL

1. In a bowl, combine beef, shallots, garlic, red pepper, olives, mint, cumin, salt, egg, orange zest and orange juice. Shape into 2-inch (5 cm) balls and place on prepared baking sheet.

2. Bake in preheated oven for 20 minutes or until meatballs are well browned and no longer pink in the center. Serve with saffron sauce.

Tips

Pitted green olives may be difficult to find. If you strike out, buy regular olives and remove the pits yourself. Olives are very high in sodium and should be used sparingly.

As an alternative to the suggested meal, pair this dish with other tapas, such as roasted vegetables and potatoes, to make a complete meal.

Segovia-Style Lamb
(Cordero a la Segoviana)

The rocky, arid land around Segovia, Spain, is ideal for raising sheep and lamb, and their meats are traditionally roasted in Roman-style ovens, so it's no surprise that Segovia is known for its lamb dishes. This dish, usually eaten with bread, is simple but full of flavor. I used half lamb and half beef to reduce the fat content.

Preparation time: 20 minutes
Cooking time: 2 hours

1 tsp	extra virgin olive oil (see box, page 150)	5 mL
1	large onion, finely chopped	1
1	clove garlic, minced	1
1/4 cup	chopped fresh parsley	60 mL
8 oz	boneless lamb shoulder, visible fat removed, cut into 2-inch (5 cm) cubes	250 g
8 oz	boneless beef bottom round, visible fat removed, cut into 2-inch (5 cm) cubes	250 g
4	large portobello mushrooms, stems removed, caps cut into 1-inch (2.5 cm) slices	4
2	bay leaves	2
1/2 tsp	salt	2 mL
1/2 tsp	freshly ground black pepper	2 mL
1 tbsp	sherry vinegar	15 mL
1 cup	dry white wine	250 mL

1. In a small, deep pot, heat oil over medium heat. Add onion, garlic and parsley; cook, stirring, for 4 minutes or until onion is translucent.

2. Stir in lamb and beef; cook, stirring, for 15 minutes.

3. Stir in mushrooms, bay leaves, salt, pepper and vinegar; cook, stirring, for 5 minutes.

4. Stir in wine, reduce heat to low, cover and simmer, stirring occasionally, for 1 1/2 hours or until lamb and beef are tender. Discard bay leaves.

Tips

To keep the fat as low as possible in this dish, it's important to remove the visible fat from the meat. In this recipe, lamb shoulder and beef bottom round were used, as they are lower-fat cuts. When using lower-fat meats, it's important to watch the cooking time, as they can easily overcook and become tough.

In Spanish cuisine, sherry vinegar is often used to cook beef, duck or game. Look for it in specialty or gourmet food stores or well-stocked supermarkets. If you can't find it, substitute 1 1/2 tsp (7 mL) white wine vinegar.

Nutrition info per serving	
Calories	215
Fat, total	6 g
Fat, saturated	1.9 g
Cholesterol	63 mg
Sodium	309 mg
Carbohydrate	9 g
Fiber	2 g
Protein	23 g
Food Choices	
2 1/2	Meat & Alternatives

Spicy Moorish Pork Kebabs
(Pinchitos Morunos)

Makes 4 kebabs

Popular in southern Spain, this dish was influenced by the Moors who came to Andalusia, Spain, from North Africa in the sixth century, bringing with them their Muslim traditions and many new ingredients.

Make It a Meal

1 serving Spicy Moorish Pork Kebabs

1 serving Spanish Ratatouille (page 165), topped with 1 tsp (5 mL) olive oil (1 Fat)

1 cup (250 mL) unsalted roasted potatoes (2 Carbohydrate) with 1 serving Spanish Brava Tomato Sauce (page 197)

1 cup (250 mL) Mexican Sweet Rice Drink (page 200)

Nutrition info per kebab

Calories	163
Fat, total	4 g
Fat, saturated	1.0 g
Cholesterol	78 mg
Sodium	357 mg
Carbohydrate	6 g
Fiber	2 g
Protein	26 g

Food Choices

3	Meat & Alternatives

Preparation time: **20 minutes**
Marinating time: **4 hours or overnight**
Cooking time: **20 minutes**

- **Four 8- to 10-inch (20 to 25 cm) bamboo skewers**
- **Rimmed baking sheet**

3	cloves garlic, minced	3
1/4 cup	finely chopped fresh parsley	60 mL
2 tbsp	hot smoked Spanish paprika (see page 22)	30 mL
1 1/2 tbsp	ground cumin	22 mL
1 tsp	cayenne pepper	5 mL
1/2 tsp	salt	2 mL
1/4 tsp	freshly ground black pepper	1 mL
1/4 cup	unsweetened apple juice	60 mL
2 tbsp	freshly squeezed lemon juice	30 mL
1 lb	boneless pork tenderloin, cut into 1-inch (2.5 cm) cubes	500 g
	Lemon wedges (optional)	

1. In a bowl, combine garlic, parsley, paprika, cumin, cayenne, salt, black pepper, apple juice and lemon juice. Add pork and toss to coat. Cover and refrigerate for at least 4 hours or (preferably) overnight.

2. Let pork stand at room temperature for 15 minutes. Meanwhile, preheat oven to 350°F (180°C) and soak skewers in water.

3. Remove pork from marinade, discarding marinade, and thread about 5 pieces of pork onto each skewer. Place skewers on baking sheet.

4. Bake for about 20 minutes, giving skewers a quarter turn every 5 minutes, until just a hint of pink remains inside pork. Serve with lemon wedges, if desired.

Tips

Moorish spice blends are available, but use them with caution, as they can have added salt.

The marinade traditionally used for this pork has 3 to 4 tbsp (45 to 60 mL) of oil. This version uses apple juice instead, for a lower fat content.

Tenderloin is the leanest cut of pork. Be careful not to cook it for too long, or it will dry out and be tough.

Mexican Green Chilaquiles
(Chilaquiles Verdes)

This is not the Tex-Mex version of chilaquiles but the real deal, made with fresh, homemade tortillas. Chilaquiles is an easy Mexican dish originally created as a way to use up leftovers. It's low in carbs, so go ahead and enjoy!

Preparation time: **20 minutes**
Cooking time: **55 minutes**

- **Preheat oven to 350°F (180°C)**
- **Blender**
- **Baking sheet, lined with parchment paper**

8 oz	boneless skinless chicken breasts	250 g
2	cloves garlic, smashed	2
½	white onion (left in one piece)	½
¾ tsp	salt, divided	3 mL
4 cups	water, divided	1 L
5	tomatillos (8 oz/250 g total), husks removed	5
2	serrano chile peppers	2
1 cup	finely chopped fresh cilantro	250 mL
1 ½ tsp	vegetable oil	7 mL
2	sprigs dried epazote (see page 22)	2
10	Corn Tortillas (page 159), cut into quarters	10
2 tbsp	queso fresco or crumbled light feta cheese	30 mL
2 tbsp	fat-free sour cream (optional)	30 mL

1. Place chicken in a deep pot with garlic, onion, ½ tsp (2 mL) salt and 2 cups (500 mL) water. Bring to a boil over high heat. Reduce heat to low, cover and simmer for 20 minutes or until chicken is no longer pink inside. Remove and shred chicken, reserving ½ cup (125 mL) broth.

2. In the same pot, bring the remaining water to a boil over medium-high heat. Add tomatillos and chiles; cook for 15 minutes or until tomatillos lighten to light green. Drain.

3. In blender, combine tomatillos, chiles, cilantro and the remaining salt; purée until smooth.

4. In a skillet, heat oil over low heat. Add tomatillo purée and epazote; cook, stirring, for 10 minutes. If mixture is too thick, stir in the reserved broth. Discard epazote.

Nutrition info per serving

Calories	250
Fat, total	7 g
Fat, saturated	1.4 g
Cholesterol	44 mg
Sodium	322 mg
Carbohydrate	29 g
Fiber	3 g
Protein	19 g

Food Choices

1½	Carbohydrate
2	Meat & Alternatives

If you don't like the heat of serrano chiles, you can substitute jalapeños or small green chiles.

Queso fresco has a mild flavor and creamy texture. Thanks to its high fat content, it does not melt easily. To control the fat and saturated fat in this dish, use no more than 2 tbsp (30 mL). For even less fat, replace it with light feta.

To help reduce the fat content, fat-free sour cream was used here, but even it should be added sparingly, as it still contains added sodium.

5. Meanwhile, place tortilla pieces on prepared baking sheet. Bake in preheated oven for 10 minutes or until light golden brown and crispy.

6. Place baked tortilla pieces on a serving platter. Top with shredded chicken, then tomatillo purée and queso fresco. Dollop with sour cream, if desired.

Tomatillos

Tomatillos are small green fruits used as a vegetable in Mexican and Latin American cooking. They give a nice tart flavor to dishes. When cooked, their color changes from bright green to a lighter green; if cooked for too long, they turn a brownish color. Tomatillos are now more regularly available at supermarkets. If you can't find them, canned tomatillos can be used, but rinse them well, as they have a lot of added salt ($\frac{1}{2}$ cup/125 mL can have 560 mg of sodium or even more).

Pasta in Tomato Sauce with Chorizo *(Pasta en Salsa Brava con Chorizo)*

Makes 6 servings

Chorizo, a heavily seasoned pork sausage, is very popular in both Spain and Mexico. Spanish chorizos come in many different varieties and flavors. For this dish, you're looking for spicy smoked cured chorizo.

Make It a Meal

1 serving Pasta in Tomato Sauce with Chorizo

1 serving Andalusian Meatballs with Spanish Saffron Sauce (page 177)

½ serving Spanish Orange and Avocado Salad (page 158)

1 serving Cold Melon Cucumber Soup (page 150)

Nutrition info per serving

Calories	313
Fat, total	6 g
Fat, saturated	1.6 g
Cholesterol	10 mg
Sodium	383 mg
Carbohydrate	50 g
Fiber	11 g
Protein	14 g

Food Choices

2½	Carbohydrate
½	Meat & Alternatives

Preparation time: **10 minutes**
Cooking time: **25 minutes**

½ cup	chopped spicy smoked cured chorizo	125 mL
1 ½ tsp	extra virgin olive oil (see box, page 150)	7 mL
½	medium onion, minced	½
3	cloves garlic, minced	3
1	medium red bell pepper, minced	1
2	bay leaves	2
1 tsp	hot smoked Spanish paprika (see page 22)	5 mL
½ tsp	ground dried oregano	2 mL
½ tsp	salt	2 mL
1	can (28 oz/796 mL) no-salt-added crushed tomatoes, with juice	1
12 oz	whole-grain rotini pasta	375 g

1. Heat a large saucepan over medium heat. Add chorizo and cook, stirring occasionally, for about 5 minutes to release some of the fat and brown the sausage.

2. Meanwhile, in a medium saucepan, heat oil over medium heat. Add onion and garlic; cook, stirring, for about 5 minutes or until onion is translucent. Add red pepper and cook, stirring, for 2 minutes. Stir in bay leaves, paprika, oregano and salt. Add tomatoes and cook, stirring, for 8 minutes.

3. Meanwhile, in a pot of boiling water, cook pasta for 8 minutes or until al dente. Drain.

4. Stir the tomato mixture into the chorizo and cook over medium heat, stirring, for 3 minutes. Discard bay leaves. Stir in pasta.

Tips

Spanish chorizo is made with pork, fat and paprika, which gives the sausage its characteristic color and smokiness. If it's not available, Portuguese linguiça sausage, or any cured sausage, can be used instead.

Chorizo is very high in fat, so it should be used sparingly, as in this recipe.

In this recipe, whole-grain rotini replaces the traditional white pasta, for added fiber. Choose whole-grain pastas whenever possible.

Other types of pasta, such as penne or spaghetti, can be used.

Peruvian Ceviche

Makes 6 servings

Ceviche is a cooking method in which acid is used instead of heat to cook fish or seafood. The traditional acid choice is the juice of the *naranja agria* (bitter orange), but today, lemon, lime or orange juice is more commonly used. Peruvians prefer their ceviche spicy and serve it on lettuce leaves, along with rice, slices of cold sweet potato and corn on the cob or a bowl of toasted dried corn. That's a lot of carbohydrate for someone with diabetes, so I would advise choosing your favorite (rice, sweet potato or corn), then adding other types of non-starchy vegetables on the side.

Nutrition info per serving	
Calories	166
Fat, total	3 g
Fat, saturated	0.9 g
Cholesterol	76 mg
Sodium	385 mg
Carbohydrate	6 g
Fiber	1 g
Protein	31 g
Food Choices	
4	Meat & Alternatives

Preparation time: **25 to 40 minutes**

2	cloves garlic, minced	2
3/4 tsp	salt	3 mL
1/2 tsp	freshly ground black pepper	2 mL
1 cup	freshly squeezed lime juice	250 mL
2 lbs	skinless tilapia fillets, rinsed and cut into 1/2-inch (1 cm) cubes	1 kg
1/4 cup	very finely diced celery leaves and stalk (from the thin top part of the stalk only)	1
1/2	red onion, thinly sliced	1/2
3 tbsp	finely chopped fresh cilantro	45 mL
1 1/2 tsp	finely minced gingerroot (approx.)	7 mL
3 tbsp	skim milk (approx.)	45 mL

1. In a large bowl, combine garlic, salt, pepper and lime juice. Add fish and toss to coat. Cover and let "cook" in the refrigerator for 15 to 30 minutes or until fish has turned white.

2. In another bowl, combine celery, onion and cilantro. Remove fish from marinade, discarding marinade, and add fish to celery mixture. Stir in ginger and milk. Taste and, if too sour, add more ginger or milk.

Tips

Very fresh fish is the key to this dish. The thickness of the fish will dictate how long it needs to "cook."

Any white fish can be used in place of the tilapia.

Shark is another popular choice for this dish in Peru, but it is high in mercury and certain species are endangered. Women of childbearing age, pregnant women and children should not eat shark.

The ginger and milk are added to counteract the sourness of the lime juice. Traditionally, condensed milk is used, but this adds a lot of fat and sugar; skim milk is a better choice.

Chilean Fish Escabeche
(Pescado en Escabeche)

The Spanish word *escabeche*, meaning "pickled," refers to fresh fish that is either cooked in oil and vinegar, or cooked and then pickled in a vinegar-based marinade. This dish has countless variations and is popular in many countries around the world, especially those with a Spanish influence, such as Latin America, Mexico and the Philippines. It is traditionally served cold on a hot day.

Preparation time: **15 minutes**
Cooking time: **15 minutes**
Chilling time: **2 hours or overnight (optional)**

1 1/2 tsp	extra virgin olive oil (see box, page 150)	7 mL
3	bay leaves	3
2 cups	sliced onion rings (1/8-inch/3 mm thick rings)	500 mL
1/2	medium red bell pepper, julienned	1/2
1/2	medium green bell pepper, julienned	1/2
1 tbsp	chopped fresh parsley, divided	15 mL
1/2 tsp	salt	2 mL
1/2 tsp	whole black peppercorns	2 mL
2 lbs	skinless tilapia fillets, cut in half lengthwise	1 kg
2	cloves garlic, minced	2
1 cup	Chilean Chardonnay wine (see tip, below)	250 mL
1/2 cup	white wine vinegar	125 mL

1. In a large, deep skillet, heat oil over high heat. Add bay leaves, onion rings, red pepper, green pepper, half the parsley, salt and peppercorns; cook, stirring, for 3 minutes or until onions are translucent.

2. Place fish on top of onion mixture and spread garlic on top of fish. Cook for 2 minutes. Reduce heat to low, cover and simmer for about 6 minutes or until fish is opaque and flakes easily when tested with a fork.

3. Stir in wine and vinegar; cover and simmer until sauce is thickened. (Do not stir, to avoid breaking the fish.) Discard bay leaves.

4. Remove from heat and let cool completely, then serve garnished with the remaining parsley. Alternatively, refrigerate for 2 hours or overnight and serve chilled, garnished with the remaining parsley.

Tips

Rinse fish thoroughly under cold water before cooking it, to remove as much salt as possible, especially if it is frozen.

Chilean Chardonnays pair perfectly with a light white fish such as tilapia, but you can substitute another fruity, unoaked Chardonnay.

Nutrition info per serving

Calories	172
Fat, total	3 g
Fat, saturated	0.8 g
Cholesterol	51 mg
Sodium	236 mg
Carbohydrate	9 g
Fiber	2 g
Protein	22 g

Food Choices

3	Meat & Alternatives

Tuna with Onions *(Atún Encebollado)*

This simple dish, from the south of Spain, is served mostly in the summer. It is also prepared in northern Spain, where they add other ingredients, such as red and green bell peppers, diced tomatoes and hot Spanish paprika. This dish can be paired with any whole-grain or high-fiber pasta; try to find one with at least 4 g of fiber per serving.

Preparation time: 10 minutes
Cooking time: 10 minutes

1 tbsp	extra virgin olive oil (see box, page 150)	15 mL
1 cup	thinly sliced onion	250 mL
1 tsp	minced garlic	5 mL
1/2 tsp	salt	2 mL
1/4 tsp	freshly ground black pepper	1 mL
1 cup	dry white wine	250 mL
1 lb	tuna steak, cut into 3- by 1/2-inch (7.5 by 1 cm) strips	500 g
1 tbsp	finely chopped fresh parsley (optional)	15 mL

1. In a large pan or skillet, heat oil over high heat. Add onion, garlic, salt and pepper; cook, stirring, for 2 minutes. Stir in wine.
2. Add fish, reduce heat and simmer, without stirring, for about 5 minutes or until liquid is thickened and tuna is opaque and flakes easily when tested with a fork.
3. Serve garnished with parsley, if desired.

Tips

Shark and swordfish are often used in this dish, but because they are predatory fish (they eat other fish), they accumulate high levels of mercury in their meat, so they should be eaten only on occasion. Other substitutions include salmon or trout, which typically have lower levels of mercury. Women of childbearing age, pregnant women and children should not eat shark or swordfish.

Certain types of tuna, such as albacore, are also high in mercury. Smaller tuna, such as skipjack or blackfin, are better choices. North American health authorities recommend eating no more than 5 oz (150 g) of tuna steak per week. One serving of this recipe is 4 oz (125 g).

If you try to stir the fish in step 2, it will break apart. Instead, just shake the pan occasionally.

Nutrition Tip

Fish is a good source of omega-3 fatty acids, which have been shown to help maintain healthy heart function.

Nutrition info per serving

Calories	176
Fat, total	3 g
Fat, saturated	0.5 g
Cholesterol	35 mg
Sodium	275 mg
Carbohydrate	4 g
Fiber	1 g
Protein	23 g

Food Choices

2 1/2	Meat & Alternatives
1/2	Fat

Valencia Seafood Paella
(Paella de Mariscos)

Versions of paella can be found all over Spain and Portugal, but the best-known recipe is from Valencia, Spain. Most restaurants in Spain serve paella at lunch, when the heavier meal is traditionally eaten. The key to this dish is the Spanish saffron, which gives paella its characteristic color and flavor.

Nutrition info per serving

Calories	309
Fat, total	11 g
Fat, saturated	1.7 g
Cholesterol	94 mg
Sodium	*585 mg
Carbohydrate	34 g
Fiber	2 g
Protein	17 g

* This recipe is high in sodium. Balance it out by making lower-sodium choices for the rest of your meal and throughout the day.

Food Choices

1½	Carbohydrate
1½	Meat & Alternatives
2	Fat

Preparation time: **20 minutes**
Marinating time: **30 minutes or overnight**
Cooking time: **45 minutes**

- **12- to 13-inch (30 to 33 cm) skillet or paella pan**

1 tsp	minced garlic	5 mL
4 tbsp	extra virgin olive oil (see box, page 150), divided	60 mL
3½ oz	calamari, cut lengthwise into strips	100 g
½ cup	Spanish Tomato Sauce (page 196)	125 mL
1 cup	long-grain white rice	250 mL
3 cups	ready-to-use no-salt-added chicken broth	750 mL
½ tsp	Spanish saffron threads (see page 22)	2 mL
½ tsp	salt	2 mL
6½ oz	large tiger shrimp (unpeeled), rinsed	200 g
6½ oz	small mussels, scrubbed and debearded (see tips, opposite)	200 g
¼ cup	fresh or frozen green peas	60 mL
¼	roasted red bell pepper (see tip, opposite), cut into ⅛-inch (3 mm) thick slices	¼
¼	roasted green bell pepper, cut into ⅛-inch (3 mm) thick slices	¼
2 tsp	freshly squeezed lemon juice (or 4 lemon wedges)	10 mL
2 tbsp	finely chopped fresh parsley	30 mL

1. In a shallow bowl, combine garlic and 3 tbsp (45 mL) oil. Add calamari and toss to coat. Cover and refrigerate for at least 30 minutes or overnight.

2. Remove calamari from marinade, discarding marinade. Heat the skillet over medium-low heat. Add calamari and cook for 2 minutes. Add tomato sauce and the remaining oil; increase heat to medium and cook, stirring, for 3 to 4 minutes to combine the flavors.

3. Stir in rice and cook, stirring occasionally, for about 3 minutes. Stir in broth and bring to a boil. Stir in saffron and salt.

4. Gently stir in shrimp, one at a time. Reduce heat to low and simmer for 2 minutes.

5. Add mussels, one at a time. Gently stir in peas. Place roasted red and green pepper on top, and drizzle with lemon juice. Cover with foil and simmer for 20 minutes or until rice is tender and liquid is absorbed. Remove from heat, remove foil and let stand for 10 minutes. Discard any mussels that have not opened.

6. Serve garnished with parsley.

Tips

Paella is often made with a short-grain white rice called bomba, which is similar to risotto but not as starchy. It can be difficult to find, however, and long-grain white rice is just as authentic and works just as well.

Short-grain and long-grain white rice are both high on the glycemic index (long-grain is slightly lower), so limit portion sizes.

When purchasing mussels, tap each one to make sure it snaps shut. Tap again just before cooking. Discard any mussels that don't close, as they are no longer alive. After cooking, discard any mussels that have not opened.

Store mussels in the coolest part of the refrigerator, wrapped loosely in a damp cloth (allowing them to breathe), but not in water. Clean them just before use so as to not disturb them. To do so, hold them under cool running water and scrub them with a firm brush to ensure that all the sand is removed. Remove the "beards" by firmly tugging them toward the hinge of the shell.

To roast bell peppers, preheat the barbecue grill to high or preheat the broiler. Grill peppers on barbecue, or on a baking sheet under the broiler, turning often, until blackened and blistering on all sides. Transfer to a bowl and cover with plastic wrap (or transfer to a paper bag) and let cool. Peel off skins and remove core, ribs and seeds.

Spanish Seafood Pasta *(Fideuá)*

Makes 5 servings

Fideuá is an authentic Valencian dish that is very similar to paella, but uses pasta instead of rice. It is usually served for lunch in Spain. This recipe, along with the paella (page 186), is a must-try! Chef Mali Fernandez generously contributed both recipes.

Preparation time: 20 minutes
Marinating time: 30 minutes or overnight
Cooking time: 35 to 40 minutes

1 tsp	minced garlic	5 mL
3 tbsp	extra virgin olive oil (see box, page 150)	45 mL
5 oz	calamari, cut lengthwise into strips	150 g
½ cup	Spanish Tomato Sauce (page 196)	125 mL
2 tsp	extra virgin olive oil	10 mL
1 cup	durum wheat fedelini tagliati pasta (see tip, opposite)	250 mL
2 cups	ready-to-use no-salt-added chicken broth	500 mL
½ tsp	Spanish saffron threads (see page 22)	2 mL
½ tsp	salt	2 mL
¼ tsp	freshly ground black pepper	1 mL
7 oz	large tiger shrimp (unpeeled), rinsed	210 g
3½ oz	skinless cod fillet, rinsed and cut into 1-inch (2.5 cm) cubes	100 g
6½ oz	small mussels, scrubbed and debearded (see tips, opposite)	200 g
¼	roasted red bell pepper (see tip, opposite), thinly sliced	¼
¼	roasted green bell pepper, thinly sliced	¼
1	small lemon, cut into 4 wedges	1

1. In a shallow bowl, combine garlic and 3 tbsp (45 mL) oil. Add calamari and toss to coat. Cover and refrigerate for at least 30 minutes or overnight.

2. Remove calamari from marinade, discarding marinade. Heat a large skillet over medium-low heat. Add calamari and cook for 2 minutes. Add tomato sauce and 2 tsp (10 mL) oil; increase heat to medium and cook, stirring, for 3 to 4 minutes to combine the flavors

3. Stir in pasta and broth; bring to a boil over high heat. Reduce heat to low and stir in saffron, salt and pepper.

4. Place shrimp and cod on top of the pasta. Cook, without stirring, for 2 minutes.

5. Place mussels gently on top, cover and cook for 12 minutes. Uncover and cook for about 1 minute or until sauce is thickened, shrimp are pink and opaque, and mussels have opened.

6. Place roasted red and green peppers and lemon wedges on top. Turn off heat and let stand for about 10 minutes or until liquid is absorbed.

Tips

The pasta used in fideuá needs to be very fine in order to cook. Fedelini tagliati are thin noodles about 1 inch (2.5 cm) long. If you can't find them, cut regular spaghettini into 1-inch (2.5 cm) lengths.

If at all possible, use fresh seafood in this dish for the best flavor. If buying frozen, look for seafood with the least amount of added salt, and rinse it thoroughly under cold water before cooking it, to remove as much salt as possible.

When purchasing mussels, tap each one to make sure it snaps shut. Tap again just before cooking. Discard any mussels that don't close, as they are no longer alive. After cooking, discard any mussels that have not opened.

Store mussels in the coolest part of the refrigerator, wrapped loosely in a damp cloth (allowing them to breathe), but not in water. Clean them just before use so as to not disturb them. To do so, hold them under cool running water and scrub them with a firm brush to ensure that all the sand is removed. Remove the "beards" by firmly tugging them toward the hinge of the shell.

To roast bell peppers, preheat the barbecue grill to high or preheat the broiler. Grill peppers on barbecue, or on a baking sheet under the broiler, turning often, until blackened and blistering on all sides. Transfer to a bowl and cover with plastic wrap (or transfer to a paper bag) and let cool. Peel off skins and remove core, ribs and seeds.

Mexican Spicy Tomato Salsa
(Pico de Gallo)

Makes 8 servings

Pico de gallo, also known as salsa fresca, is a beautiful and aromatic Mexican condiment that is served with fajitas, tacos, nachos, tortillas and even salads. It has less liquid than a regular salsa.

Preparation time: 10 minutes

3	large plum (Roma) tomatoes, finely diced	3
1	serrano chile pepper, minced	1
1/2 cup	finely chopped red onion	125 mL
1/4 cup	finely chopped fresh cilantro	60 mL
2 tbsp	freshly squeezed lime juice	30 mL
1 1/2 tsp	olive oil	7 mL
1/4 tsp	salt	1 mL

1. In a bowl, combine tomatoes, chile, onion and cilantro.
2. In a small bowl, combine lime juice, oil and salt. Add to tomato mixture and toss to coat.

Tips

If you like heat, feel free to add more serrano chiles.

To tame the heat, seed the serrano chiles or substitute jalapeños or small green chiles.

Serrano Chile Peppers

Serrano chiles are very spicy — five times hotter than jalapeños — with a sharp flavor. They start out green, then ripen to red, brown, orange or yellow. Serranos are too meaty to dry well, so it's best to use fresh. They are used a lot in Mexican cuisine to make sauces, salsas and guacamole.

Nutrition info per serving	
Calories	17
Fat, total	1 g
Fat, saturated	0.1 g
Cholesterol	0 mg
Sodium	75 mg
Carbohydrate	2 g
Fiber	1 g
Protein	0 g
Food Choices	
1	Extra

Mexican Morita Chipotle Sauce
(Salsa de Chile Morita)

Makes 15 servings

This spicy, smoky sauce goes with pretty much anything! Just a word of caution: it packs a lot of heat. Serve it with enchiladas, tamales, beans or empanadas (page 160 or 162), or use it to replace your usual barbecue sauce.

Preparation time: **15 minutes**
Cooking time: **15 minutes**

- **Blender**

25	small dried morita chipotle peppers (see page 21 and tip, below)	25
	Water	
4	cloves garlic, mashed	4
½ tsp	olive oil	2 mL
½ tsp	salt	2 mL
1 tsp	cider vinegar	5 mL

1. Remove the stems and most of the seeds from the chipotle peppers. (You will not be able to remove all of the seeds.)

2. In a small pot, bring 2 cups (500 mL) water to a boil over high heat. Add chipotles, reduce heat to low, cover and simmer for 15 minutes or until softened.

3. Transfer chipotles and cooking water to blender. Add garlic and oil; blend into a paste. With the motor running, through the feed tube, gradually add more water as needed until the sauce is smooth and thick, with a chutney-like texture.

4. Transfer sauce to a bowl and stir in salt and vinegar.

Tips

Morita chipotle peppers have a distinct flavor, so there is no true substitute, but if you are just looking to make a spicy sauce, then any dried red chile pepper can be used.

If you want more heat, leave all of the seeds in the peppers.

The amount of oil in this sauce was significantly reduced to improve the fat profile.

This sauce can be stored in an airtight container in the refrigerator for up to 3 days or in the freezer for up to 3 months.

Nutrition info per serving	
Calories	2
Fat, total	0 g
Fat, saturated	0.0 g
Cholesterol	0 mg
Sodium	78 mg
Carbohydrate	1 g
Fiber	0 g
Protein	0 g
Food Choices	
1	Extra

Mexican Spicy Green Sauce
(Salsa Verde)

Makes 8 servings

If you have ever been to a Mexican restaurant, you've probably tried salsa verde, which owes its green hue to tomatillos (see box, page 181). It's wonderful with chilaquiles (page 180), empanadas (pages 160 and 162), tortillas (page 159), tacos and even corn chips!

Preparation time: **15 minutes**
Cooking time: **15 minutes**

- **Blender**

	Water	
5	tomatillos (8 oz/250 g total), husks removed	5
2	serrano chile peppers (whole, with stems)	2
1 cup	finely chopped fresh cilantro	250 mL
1/2 tsp	salt	2 mL

1. In a saucepan, bring 2 cups (500 mL) water to a boil over medium-high heat. Add tomatillos and chiles; cook for 15 minutes or until tomatillos lighten to light green. Drain and remove stems of chile peppers.

2. In blender, combine tomatillos, chiles, cilantro and salt; purée until smooth. With the machine running, through the feed tube, gradually add up to 1/2 cup (125 mL) water until the desired consistency is reached. Be careful not to add too much water; the sauce should be thick.

Tips

For a spicier salsa, add one more serrano chile.

This sauce can be stored in an airtight container in the refrigerator for up to 2 weeks or in the freezer for up to 3 months.

Nutrition info per serving	
Calories	7
Fat, total	0 g
Fat, saturated	0.0 g
Cholesterol	0 mg
Sodium	140 mg
Carbohydrate	2 g
Fiber	0 g
Protein	0 g
Food Choices	
1	Extra

Mexican Black Bean Soup (page 152)

Spanish Orange and Avocado Salad (page 158)

Spicy Moorish Pork Kebabs (page 179)
and Spanish Ratatouille (page 165)

Caribbean Pumpkin Soup (page 202)

Bora Beans (page 211)

Jamaican Fricassee Chicken (page 230)
and Ginger Beer (page 243)

Peruvian Hot Sauce *(Ají)*

There are different versions of this spicy Peruvian sauce, and I've given you three options here: a red sauce (*ají rojo*) and a yellow sauce (*ají amarillo*), plus a bonus green sauce (*ají verde*) as a variation.

Variation

To make *ají verde*, add 2 finely chopped green onions, ⅓ cup (75 mL) finely chopped fresh cilantro, 2 tbsp (30 mL) finely chopped fresh Peruvian herbs (such as huacatay) and 1 tsp (5 mL) freshly squeezed lemon juice to the red sauce in place of the mayo and mustard.

Preparation time: **15 minutes**

• **Blender**

For Ají Rojo

4	frozen rocoto peppers, thawed, seeded and chopped	4
⅔ cup	water	150 mL
2	cloves garlic	2
½ tsp	freshly ground black pepper	2 mL
¼ tsp	salt	1 mL

For Ají Amarillo

2 tbsp	light mayonnaise	30 mL
½ tsp	mustard	2 mL

For Ají Rojo

1. In blender, combine rocoto peppers and water; purée until smooth.

2. Transfer to a bowl and stir in garlic, pepper and salt.

For Ají Amarillo

3. In a small bowl, combine mayonnaise and mustard. Stir into the red sauce.

Tips

If you like more heat, leave the seeds in the peppers.

Ají amarillo has a milder, less spicy flavor than *ají rojo*, thanks to the mayonnaise and mustard. It traditionally contains a lot of oil and more mayo. This version is lower in fat.

Rocoto Peppers

Rocoto peppers have a thick flesh and resemble a small bell pepper. They are grown in the Andes, as well as in Central America and Mexico. They are difficult to find fresh in North America, but are typically available frozen at Spanish or Latin American grocery stores.

Nutrition info per serving of *ají amarillo*

Calories	30
Fat, total	1 g
Fat, saturated	0.2 g
Cholesterol	1 mg
Sodium	92 mg
Carbohydrate	4 g
Fiber	2 g
Protein	1 g

Food Choices

1	Extra

Argentinean Chimichurri

Makes 4 servings

Chimichurri is a spicy green oil-and-vinegar sauce. In South America, and especially Argentina, chimichurri is traditionally used as a marinade or served as a condiment for grilled meat. Trust me when I say that it makes everything taste good. It is easy and inexpensive to make at home and will keep for up to 3 days in the fridge.

Preparation time: 10 minutes
Chilling time: 2 hours

6 tbsp	finely chopped fresh parsley (with stems)	90 mL
4 tsp	minced onion	20 mL
1 tbsp	puréed garlic (see tips, page 195)	15 mL
1 tsp	dried oregano	5 mL
1 tsp	hot pepper flakes	5 mL
1 tsp	freshly ground black pepper	5 mL
½ tsp	salt	2 mL
3 tbsp	olive oil	45 mL
1 tbsp	freshly squeezed lime juice	15 mL

1. In a small bowl, combine parsley, onion, garlic, oregano, hot pepper flakes, black pepper, salt, oil and lime juice.

2. Cover and refrigerate for at least 2 hours or for up to 3 days before serving.

Tips

Parsley is traditionally used as the base herb for chimichurri, but other aromatic herbs, such as cilantro, can be substituted.

The amount of oil in this sauce was significantly reduced to improve the fat profile. As a result, it may be thicker than the chimichurris you are used to. If you prefer a thinner consistency, add up to 3 tbsp (45 mL) more lime juice.

Premade chimichurri sauces are available, but they can be expensive and are usually high in fat and sodium. Most importantly, they just don't taste as good as homemade!

Nutrition info per serving	
Calories	101
Fat, total	10 g
Fat, saturated	1.4 g
Cholesterol	0 mg
Sodium	295 mg
Carbohydrate	2 g
Fiber	1 g
Protein	1 g
Food Choices	
2	Fat

Spanish Saffron Sauce
(Salsa al Azafrán)

Makes 5 servings

This sauce is the traditional accompaniment to Andalusian meatballs (page 177) and can also be served with other meat dishes, such as Spicy Moorish Pork Kebabs (page 179), lamb or chicken. It is usually made with mayonnaise, but even with light mayo the fat content is very high. An easy substitution of fat-free sour cream means the fat in this version is negligible.

Preparation time: **10 minutes**

¹⁄₄ tsp	Spanish saffron threads (see page 22)	1 mL
1 tbsp	hot water	15 mL
1	clove garlic, puréed	1
¹⁄₂ tsp	hot smoked Spanish paprika (see page 22)	2 mL
¹⁄₄ tsp	cayenne pepper	1 mL
²⁄₃ cup	fat-free sour cream	150 mL

1. In a small bowl, combine saffron and hot water. Let stand for about 5 minutes or until water turns bright yellow.
2. Stir in garlic, paprika, cayenne and sour cream until well combined.

Tips

Purée the garlic in a mini food processor. You can do a small amount and refrigerate in a jar for up to 2 days. If you prefer to purée a large amount, store it in an airtight container or jar in the freezer for up to 3 months.

Premade garlic purées can have a lot of added sodium, so avoid them in favor of homemade.

Nutrition info per serving	
Calories	24
Fat, total	0 g
Fat, saturated	0.0 g
Cholesterol	3 mg
Sodium	43 mg
Carbohydrate	5 g
Fiber	0 g
Protein	1 g
Food Choices	
1	Extra

Spanish Tomato Sauce *(Sofrito)*

**Makes 2 cups
(500 mL)**

Sofrito is a simple tomato sauce used in countless Mediterranean and Latin American dishes, including soups, stews, bean dishes and meat dishes. It is commonly used as a base sauce, as for Valencia Seafood Paella (page 186) and Spanish Seafood Pasta (page 188), but is sometimes added at the end of a recipe, as with Spanish Ham and Rice Soup (page 154).

Preparation time: **15 minutes**
Cooking time: **35 minutes**

• **Food processor**

3	cloves garlic	3
4 cups	diced plum (Roma) tomatoes (about 8 medium)	1 L
1 cup	finely chopped onion	250 mL
1 cup	finely chopped red bell pepper	250 mL
½ cup	packed fresh parsley leaves	125 mL
1 ½ tsp	extra virgin olive oil (see box, page 150)	7 mL

1. In food processor, combine garlic, tomatoes, onion, red pepper and parsley; purée until smooth.

2. In a medium saucepan, heat oil over medium heat. Add purée and bring to a boil, stirring often. Boil gently, stirring occasionally, for 12 minutes. Reduce heat and simmer, stirring often, for about 15 minutes or until thickened.

Tips

The key to this sauce is to make it thick. Plum tomatoes are the best choice, as they do not release as much liquid.

This sauce is easy to make at home. It is best not to use premade sofrito sauces, as they can be high in sodium. (I have seen brands with 115 mg of sodium per 1 tbsp/15 mL!)

It is handy to make a double or triple batch of this recipe and freeze it for later use; use a large saucepan if increasing the batch size. Individual portions of this sauce can be stored in airtight containers in the freezer for up to 6 months.

Nutrition info per ½ cup (125 mL)	
Calories	67
Fat, total	2 g
Fat, saturated	0.3 g
Cholesterol	0 mg
Sodium	13 mg
Carbohydrate	11 g
Fiber	3 g
Protein	2 g
Food Choices	
½	Fat
1	Extra

Nutrition Tip

Studies have shown that eating garlic has health benefits that may include reducing blood pressure. If you can, add one clove of garlic to your diet daily — it's great for the heart!

Spanish Brava Tomato Sauce
(Sofrito Brava)

Makes 5½ cups (1.375 L)

This spicy sauce is served throughout Spain on top of potato wedges as an appetizer (*patatas bravas*), and is used in many other dishes, such as *pisto manchego* (page 165) and *lentejas con frutas* (page 170). Chef Mali Fernandez, who created this recipe, serves it to her kids on top of omelets, vegetables, pasta or potatoes… almost anything!

Nutrition info per ½ cup (125 mL)

Calories	72
Fat, total	2 g
Fat, saturated	0.3 g
Cholesterol	0 mg
Sodium	234 mg
Carbohydrate	11 g
Fiber	2 g
Protein	2 g

Food Choices

½	Fat
1	Extra

Preparation time: **15 minutes**
Cooking time: **1 hour**

• **Blender (optional)**

1½ tbsp	extra virgin olive oil (see box, page 150)	22 mL
1	large red bell pepper, finely chopped	1
¾ cup	chopped onion	175 mL
8	cloves garlic, minced	8
2	cans (each 28 oz/796 mL) no-salt-added diced tomatoes, with juice	2
2	bay leaves	2
2 tsp	dried oregano	10 mL
2 tsp	hot smoked Spanish paprika (see page 22)	10 mL
1 tsp	salt	5 mL
1 tsp	hot pepper flakes	5 mL

1. In a large pot, heat oil over medium heat. Add red pepper and onion; cook, stirring, for about 5 minutes or until onion is translucent. Reduce heat to low and cook, stirring occasionally, for 8 minutes.

2. Add garlic and cook, stirring, for 10 minutes or until pepper and onion are very soft and mixture is dry.

3. Stir in tomatoes, increase heat to medium-low and cook, stirring often, for 15 minutes.

4. Stir in bay leaves, oregano, paprika, salt and hot pepper flakes; increase heat to medium and cook, stirring often, for about 15 minutes or until tomatoes are very soft but sauce is still moist (see tip, below). Discard bay leaves.

5. Leave sauce chunky or, if desired, working in batches, transfer sauce to blender and purée until smooth.

Tips

As written, this sauce is intended to be used as a base for other recipes, so be careful not to cook the sauce for too long in step 4, or all the liquid will evaporate. However, if you plan to use it more like a pasta sauce, you will want to cook it for longer in step 4, until the liquid from the tomatoes evaporates and the sauce thickens.

Canned tomatoes can be high in sodium, so be sure to choose no-salt-added tomatoes.

Individual portions of this sauce can be stored in airtight containers in the freezer for up to 6 months.

Peruvian Purple Corn Drink
(Chicha Morada)

Chicha morada is a sweet and spicy drink popular in South America. This version is authentic to Peru, dating back to before the Inca civilization. Powdered *chicha morada* mix is available, but the resulting drink will not be as nutritious and will have more added sugar. Most of the carbohydrate in this drink comes from natural sugars in the fruit or corn. If you prefer a lower-carbohydrate beverage, omit the pineapple or apple.

Nutrition info per ½ cup (125 mL)

Calories	104
Fat, total	2 g
Fat, saturated	0.2 g
Cholesterol	0 mg
Sodium	12 mg
Carbohydrate	31 g
Fiber	1 g
Protein	0 g
Food Choices	
2	Carbohydrate

Preparation time: 10 minutes
Cooking time: 1 hour and 15 minutes
Chilling time: 4 hours

4	whole cloves	4
1	4-inch (10 cm) cinnamon stick	1
1	pineapple, cut into 2-inch (5 cm) slices with rind	1
2 cups	dried purple corn	500 mL
4½ cups	water	1.125 L
1	Royal Gala, Golden Delicious, Pink Lady or other sweet apple, peeled and cut into ½-inch (1 cm) cubes	1
¼ cup	granulated sugar	60 mL
3 tbsp	freshly squeezed lime juice	45 mL
	Ice	

1. In a large, deep pot, combine cloves, cinnamon, pineapple, corn and water. Bring to a boil over high heat. Reduce heat to medium, cover and boil gently for 1 hour. The water will turn deep purple.

2. Place the hot pot in a sink full of ice water to chill quickly to room temperature, refreshing ice as necessary. Transfer to a freezer-safe container and freeze for 2 hours or until cool. Foam will form on top of the mixture as it cools.

3. Skim off the foam and strain the liquid into a pitcher. Discard the cloves, cinnamon and corn. Remove rind from pineapple and cut enough flesh into ½-inch (1 cm) cubes to make 1 cup (250 mL); reserve extra pineapple for another use.

4. Add 1 cup (250 mL) pineapple, apple, sugar and lime juice to the pitcher. Refrigerate and serve cold.

Tips

Dried purple corn on the cob (*maiz morado*) is available at Latin American grocery stores. Fresh purple corn cannot be used for this drink as it will be too bitter.

Strained corn cobs from this recipe can be frozen and reused to make another batch of *chicha morada*, although the flavor may not be as strong the second time.

Traditionally, this recipe calls for twice as much added sugar. This version gets its sweetness from the apple and pineapple.

After straining, leftover portions of this drink (without the fruit) can be stored in the refrigerator for up to 5 days or in an airtight container in the freezer for up to 1 month.

Mexican Sweet Rice Drink *(Horchata)*

The birthplace of this sweet drink is Valencia, Spain, where it is made with *chufa* (a tiger nut). In Mexico, tiger nuts are not readily available, so rice is used instead. There are many versions of horchata, and all of them use lots of sugar. I have created a more diabetes-friendly drink. Enjoy!

Soaking time: **3 hours or overnight**
Preparation time: **15 minutes**
Chilling time: **2 hours**

- **Blender**

³⁄₄ cup	long-grain white rice	175 mL
2 cups	water	500 mL
1	7-inch (18 cm) canela cinnamon stick (see tip, below)	1
3¹⁄₂ cups	cubed honeydew melon (1-inch/2.5 cm cubes)	875 mL
¹⁄₃ cup	blanched almonds (see tip, below)	75 mL
2 tbsp	granulated sugar	30 mL
¹⁄₂ cup	skim milk	125 mL
1 tsp	vanilla extract (optional)	5 mL

1. In a bowl, combine rice and water; let soak for 3 hours or overnight.

2. Transfer rice and soaking water to blender. Add cinnamon, melon, almonds, sugar, milk and vanilla (if using); blend until smooth.

3. Strain to remove bits of cinnamon and almonds if a smoother texture is preferred. Refrigerate and serve cold.

Tips

Canela is a spicy Mexican cinnamon stick that is softer and easier to blend than other varieties. If you cannot find it, use ¹⁄₂ tsp (2 mL) ground cinnamon instead.

The natural sugar of the honeydew maintains the traditional sweetness of this drink with little added sugar.

If blanched almonds are hard to find, soak regular almonds in hot water for 15 to 20 minutes and remove the skin with your fingers.

Horchata is traditionally made with sweetened condensed milk. Because this recipe uses skim milk, the consistency is less creamy. For a creamier drink, use ¹⁄₂ cup (125 mL) evaporated fat-free milk. This will increase the carbohydrate to 34 g and the sodium to 40 mg per serving.

Nutrition info per 1 cup (250 mL)

Calories	185
Fat, total	3 g
Fat, saturated	0.3 g
Cholesterol	0 mg
Sodium	32 mg
Carbohydrate	36 g
Fiber	2 g
Protein	4 g

Food Choices

2	Carbohydrate
¹⁄₂	Fat

Caribbean Cuisine

Recipes from Antigua, Barbados, Guyana, Jamaica and Trinidad

Soups and Snacks

Caribbean Pumpkin Soup 202
Guyanese Barley Soup 203
Callaloo 204
Jamaican Stewed Peas 206
Jamaican Callaloo Fritters 208
Jamaican Cocktail Bammy. 209
Fried Okra *(Ochroes)*. 210

Vegetarian Dishes

Bora Beans 211
Guyanese Roti. 212
Cou Cou. 214
Trinidadian Stewed
    Black-Eyed Peas 216
Trinidadian Curried Chickpeas. . . 217
Trinidadian Curried
    Pigeon Peas. 218
Guyanese Cook-Up Rice 219
Caribbean Peas and Rice. 220
Guyanese Roasted Eggplant
    Curry *(Baigan Choka)* 222

Meat, Poultry, Fish and Seafood Dishes

Guyanese Pepperpot. 224
Jamaican Curried Goat 226
Jerk Pork 228
Jerk Chicken 229
Jamaican Fricassee Chicken . . . 230
Guyanese Chicken
    Chow Mein 232
Guyanese Chicken Curry. 234
Trinidadian Shrimp Curry 235
Trinidadian Stewed Fish. 236
Jamaican Stuffed
    Steamed Fish. 238

Sauces, Condiments and Beverages

Caribbean Mango Chutney 240
Trinidadian Green Seasoning . . . 241
Sorrel Drink 242
Ginger Beer 243
Soursop Juice 244

Caribbean Pumpkin Soup

Makes 7 servings

I love pumpkin soup and have tried many variations during my travels in the Caribbean. This version is based on a traditional recipe given to me by a lady from Antigua. I removed the potatoes to reduce the carbohydrate and the seasoning salt to reduce the sodium. The soup is meant to have a kick, so add more cayenne pepper if you wish.

Tip

Caribbean pumpkin, also known as calabaza or Jamaican pumpkin, is a variety of tropical squash used widely in Caribbean and Latin American cuisine. It is a dense, bright orange pumpkin with a smooth texture and intense, sweet flavor. Pumpkin is an excellent source of beta carotene.

Nutrition info per serving

Calories	73
Fat, total	2 g
Fat, saturated	0.0 g
Cholesterol	0 mg
Sodium	348 mg
Carbohydrate	13 g
Fiber	2 g
Protein	2 g
Food Choices	
1/2	Fat
1	Extra

Preparation time: **30 minutes**
Cooking time: **50 minutes**

* **Blender, food processor or immersion blender**

1 tbsp	vegetable oil	15 mL
1 cup	chopped onion	250 mL
1 cup	finely chopped green cabbage	250 mL
1/2 cup	finely chopped celery	125 mL
2	bay leaves	2
2 lbs	Caribbean pumpkin, cut into 1-inch (2.5 cm) cubes	1 kg
4	cloves garlic, minced	4
1 tsp	finely chopped fresh thyme (see tip, page 205)	5 mL
1/8 tsp	cayenne pepper	0.5 mL
1 tbsp	chopped fresh parsley	15 mL
1 tsp	salt	5 mL
1/4 tsp	freshly ground black pepper	1 mL
5 cups	water	1.25 L

1. In a large pot, heat oil over medium heat. Add onion, cabbage, celery and bay leaves; cook, stirring, for about 5 minutes or until vegetables are softened. Add pumpkin, garlic, thyme and cayenne; cook, stirring, for 3 minutes.

2. Stir in parsley, salt, black pepper and water; bring to boil over high heat. Reduce heat to low, cover and simmer for 30 minutes. Discard bay leaves.

3. Working in batches, transfer soup to blender (or use immersion blender in pot) and purée to desired consistency (see tip, below). Return to pot, if necessary, and reheat over medium heat, stirring often, until steaming.

Tips

If you cannot find Caribbean pumpkin, substitute butternut squash.

When blending hot liquids in an upright blender, fill the blender no more than half full, leave the center hole in the lid open and cover the hole with a towel. Hold down the towel and the lid while the blender is running, allowing steam to be released.

Guyanese Barley Soup

Traditionally this recipe calls for potatoes, but I've replaced them with spinach to decrease the carbohydrate and add fiber. I also removed the seasoned salt typically used in this dish, to reduce the sodium. This version of the soup is vegetarian to keep the fat low, but for more flavor you can add some beef bones while the soup is simmering.

Variation

Replace the spinach with 2 chopped green onions (a more traditional inclusion).

Preparation time: **20 minutes**
Cooking time: **1 hour**

1 ½ tsp	vegetable oil	7 mL
5	cloves garlic, minced	5
2	stalks celery, finely chopped	2
1	medium onion, finely chopped	1
½	Scotch bonnet chile pepper (or 2 small green chile peppers), minced	½
½ cup	pot barley, rinsed	125 mL
1 tsp	salt	5 mL
½ tsp	freshly ground black pepper	2 mL
7 cups	water	1.75 L
1 cup	ready-to-use reduced-sodium vegetable broth	250 mL
8 oz	baby spinach, finely chopped	250 g

1. In a large pot, heat oil over medium heat. Add garlic, celery, onion and Scotch bonnet; cook, stirring, for 4 minutes or until onion is golden. Add barley and toast for 1 minute.

2. Stir in salt, pepper, water and broth; bring to a boil over high heat. Reduce heat to medium-low, cover and simmer for 45 minutes or until barley is tender.

3. Stir in spinach, cover and simmer for 5 minutes.

Tips

Pot barley takes longer to cook than pearl barley, as it is less processed. Pot barley has the bran layers intact and maintains more vitamins and minerals. The cooking time of this recipe would be shorter if you used pearl barley, but the dish would have less fiber.

For the best flavor and lower sodium, use homemade vegetable stock (see recipe, page 245) in place of the ready-to-use vegetable broth.

Nutrition Tip

Barley is a whole grain and a source of soluble fiber, which has been shown to lower low-density lipoprotein (LDL) blood cholesterol and blood glucose levels.

Nutrition info per serving

Calories	86
Fat, total	1 g
Fat, saturated	0.1 g
Cholesterol	0 mg
Sodium	399 mg
Carbohydrate	18 g
Fiber	4 g
Protein	3 g

Food Choices

½	Carbohydrate

Callaloo

Makes 6 servings

Callaloo is a popular Caribbean dish served in Guyana, Trinidad and Tobago and Jamaica. It can be served alone as a soup, or as a side dish with rice, chicken, corn or beans. There are many ways to make this dish. Here's a traditional version from Trinidad that tastes out of this world!

Preparation time: **15 minutes**
Cooking time: **45 minutes**

• **Blender, food processor or immersion blender**

1 1/2 tsp	vegetable oil	7 mL
2	cloves garlic, minced	2
1	medium onion, chopped	1
1	medium carrot, chopped	1
1	stalk celery, chopped	1
1	bay leaf	1
8 oz	callaloo (dasheen) or spinach leaves, stems removed	250 g
1 1/4 cups	sliced okra	300 mL
1 1/2	medium potatoes, peeled and chopped	1 1/2
3 cups	water	750 mL
1/3 cup	light coconut milk	75 mL
1 tbsp	chopped fresh thyme (see tip, opposite)	15 mL
1 tbsp	chopped fresh chives	15 mL
1/2 tsp	salt	2 mL
1/2 tsp	freshly ground black pepper	2 mL
1/4 tsp	cayenne pepper	1 mL
1	can (6 1/2 oz/185 g) lump crabmeat, drained and rinsed	1

1. In a large pot, heat oil over medium heat. Add garlic, onion, carrot, celery and bay leaf; cook, stirring, for about 5 minutes or until slightly softened and fragrant.

2. Stir in callaloo, okra, potatoes, water and coconut milk; bring to a boil over high heat. Reduce heat to low, cover and simmer for 20 to 30 minutes or until vegetables are tender. Stir in thyme, chives, salt, black pepper and cayenne; cover and simmer for 5 minutes to blend the flavors. Discard bay leaf.

3. Working in batches, transfer soup to blender (or use immersion blender in pot) and purée until smooth (see tip, opposite). Return to pot (if necessary) and stir in crabmeat. Heat over low heat for 2 minutes.

Nutrition info per serving

Calories	110
Fat, total	2 g
Fat, saturated	1.0 g
Cholesterol	31 mg
Sodium	359 mg
Carbohydrate	15 g
Fiber	3 g
Protein	8 g

Food Choices

1/2	Carbohydrate
1/2	Meat & Alternatives

Make It a Meal

1 serving Callaloo

½ serving Jerk Pork
(page 228) or Jerk
Chicken (page 229)

1 serving Caribbean Peas
and Rice (page 220)

⅙ large avocado (1 Fat)

½ cup (125 mL) Soursop
Juice (page 244)

½ medium mango
(1 Carbohydrate)

Tips

Chill onions in the freezer before cutting them. This reduces the amount of gas the onions release into the air — and it's the gas that makes your eyes tear up.

This recipe uses the type of callaloo from the taro root plant. Look for it at Caribbean grocery stores. If you cannot find callaloo, spinach makes a good substitute.

For a more authentic flavor, look for Caribbean thyme at a Caribbean grocery store. Every variety of thyme has a slightly different flavor. Jamaican thyme in particular tends to be more pungent than North American thyme, so add a bit less of it to your recipes.

When blending hot liquids in an upright blender, fill the blender no more than half full, leave the center hole in the lid open and cover the hole with a towel. Hold down the towel and the lid while the blender is running, allowing steam to be released.

Callaloo

Callaloo is a bit of a confusing ingredient, as there are two entirely different leafy green vegetables that go by this name. The one used across most of the Caribbean comes from the taro root (dasheen) plant and has heart-shaped leaves. It is also sometimes called dasheen. The type of callaloo used in Jamaica comes from the amaranth plant (*Amaranthus viridis*) and is also called Chinese spinach, Indian kale and, in Jamaica, callaloo bush leaves.

Jamaican Stewed Peas

Makes 8 servings

Stewed peas is a very popular Jamaican dish, eaten as a regular staple. The recipe typically includes a lot of spinners – a type of dumpling – but I trimmed them back to reduce the carbohydrate and added whole wheat flour to increase the fiber. Red kidney beans (the "peas" in this stew) are an integral part of the dish, adding dark color and thickness.

Preparation time: **30 minutes**
Cooking time: **2 hours and 15 minutes**

Stew

1 tbsp	vegetable oil	15 mL
1/4 cup	finely chopped onion	60 mL
4	green onions, chopped, divided	4
4	cloves garlic, minced	4
2	sprigs fresh thyme (see tip, opposite)	2
1 lb	lean stewing beef (chuck or shoulder), trimmed and cut into 1-inch (2.5 cm) cubes	500 g
1	Scotch bonnet chile pepper	1
1/2 tsp	salt	2 mL
6 cups	water	1.5 L
1	can (19 oz/540 mL) dark red kidney beans, with liquid	1

Spinners

1/2 cup	whole wheat flour	125 mL
1/2 cup	all-purpose flour	125 mL
1/2 cup	water	125 mL

1. *Stew:* In a large pot, heat oil over high heat. Add onion, three-quarters of the green onions, garlic and thyme; reduce heat to medium and cook, stirring, for 2 minutes or until onion is golden. Add beef and cook, stirring, for 2 minutes.

2. Stir in Scotch bonnet, salt and water; bring to a boil. Reduce heat to low, cover and simmer for 1 hour.

3. *Spinners:* Meanwhile, in a medium bowl, combine whole wheat flour and all-purpose flour. Gradually add water, 1 tbsp (15 mL) at a time, stirring until a smooth dough forms. Pinch off marble-sized pieces of dough and form into balls. Using the palm of your hand, roll each ball into a cylinder about 1 inch (2.5 cm) long and 1/4 inch (0.5 cm) thick.

Nutrition info per serving	
Calories	207
Fat, total	6 g
Fat, saturated	1.0 g
Cholesterol	34 mg
Sodium	212 mg
Carbohydrate	23 g
Fiber	4 g
Protein	17 g

Food Choices	
1	Carbohydrate
1 1/2	Meat & Alternatives
1	Fat

Make It a Meal

2 servings Callaloo
(page 204)

1 serving Jamaican
Stewed Peas

⅓ cup (75 mL) unsalted
cooked long-grain brown
rice (1 Carbohydrate)

1 small papaya
(1 Carbohydrate)

4. Add beans with liquid to the stew; stir and bring to a boil over high heat. Add spinners, reduce heat to medium-high and boil for about 45 minutes or until spinners are cooked through and sauce is thickened. Discard thyme.

5. Serve garnished with the remaining green onions.

Tips

Recipes for stewed peas often include a variety of meats, such as salted beef and/or pig's tail. However, these meats are very high in fat and sodium. Kidney beans have no fat, are high in fiber, and are a source of iron and an excellent source of folate. They also have a low glycemic index and do not raise blood glucose as much as meat, so to make this dish healthier, I have used more beans and less meat.

For a more authentic flavor, look for Jamaican or Guyanese thyme at a Caribbean grocery store. Every variety of thyme has a slightly different flavor, and Jamaican thyme in particular tends to be more pungent than North American thyme, so add a bit less of it to your recipes.

If you can only find 14- or 15-oz (398 or 425 mL) cans of beans, buy two. You'll need about 2¼ cups (550 mL) beans for this recipe.

Nutrition Tip

Kidney beans have no fat, are high in fiber and are a good source of protein. They do not increase blood glucose levels and can lower low-density lipoprotein (LDL) blood cholesterol, so they are a great choice for people with prediabetes or diabetes.

Jamaican Callaloo Fritters

Here, the stems and leaves of Jamaican callaloo (see box, page 205) are turned into fritters, with delicious results. Traditionally, fritters are deep-fried, but these are pan-fried instead, to reduce the fat.

Tips

Nonstick pans require good care to protect the nonstick coating. Buy good-quality, heavy pans and never heat an empty pan. And always use plastic, rubber, silicon, or wood utensils; metal tools or those with a sharp edge can cause some of the nonstick coating to scrape off into your food.

Nutrition info per 2 fritters	
Calories	114
Fat, total	7 g
Fat, saturated	1.0 g
Cholesterol	60 mg
Sodium	181 mg
Carbohydrate	11 g
Fiber	1 g
Protein	4 g
Food Choices	
½	Carbohydrate
1	Fat

Preparation time: **20 minutes**
Cooking time: **15 minutes**

4 tsp	vegetable oil, divided	20 mL
½ cup	finely chopped onion	125 mL
1	clove garlic, minced	1
4	sprigs fresh thyme leaves (see tip, page 207), finely chopped	4
½	plum (Roma) tomato, finely chopped	½
2½ cups	finely chopped seeded callaloo leaves and peeled stems	625 mL
1 tbsp	water	15 mL
¼ cup	all-purpose flour	60 mL
¼ tsp	baking powder	1 mL
¼ tsp	salt	1 mL
¼ tsp	freshly ground black pepper	1 mL
1	large egg, well beaten	1

1. In a large nonstick skillet, heat 1 tsp (5 mL) oil over medium heat. Add onion and garlic; cook, stirring, for 1 minute. Add thyme and tomato; cook, stirring, for 2 minutes.

2. Stir in callaloo and water; reduce heat to low, cover and steam, stirring occasionally, for 10 minutes or until callaloo is softened. Transfer to a bowl and let cool, then squeeze out any extra water. Wipe out skillet and set aside.

3. In a medium bowl, combine flour, baking powder, salt and pepper.

4. Stir egg into cooled callaloo mixture. Stir into flour mixture.

5. In the same skillet, heat 1½ tsp (7 mL) oil over medium heat for 1 minute. For each of 4 fritters, spoon 1 tbsp (15 mL) batter into pan and, using a wooden or plastic spoon, flatten into a 2-inch (5 cm) circle. Cook for about 30 seconds or until fritters are light golden on the bottom. Flip the fritters over and cook for about 30 seconds or until light golden. Transfer fritters to a serving platter and keep warm. Repeat with the remaining oil and batter, adjusting heat as necessary between batches to prevent burning.

Tips

Mature callaloo plants (*Amaranthus viridus*) may have seeds between the leaves. Be sure to remove them before chopping, as they will add a bitter flavor.

Jamaican Cocktail Bammy

Makes 8 bammies

Cocktail bammies are now readily available premade, but these packaged bammies are high in salt and carbohydrate. (One cocktail bammy can have up to 35 g of carbohydrate and 1100 mg of salt!) It is best — and much more nutritious — to make bammies at home in large batches and freeze them to snack on at your leisure.

Preparation time: **10 minutes**
Cooking time: **30 minutes**

- **Preheat oven to 350°F (180°C)**
- **Baking sheet, lined with parchment paper**

1	package (16 oz/454 g) frozen grated cassava, thawed	1
½ tsp	salt	2 mL
¼ cup	light coconut milk	60 mL
1 tbsp	vegetable oil, divided	15 mL

1. In a medium bowl, using your hands, combine cassava and salt. Divide cassava mixture into 8 equal portions. Form each portion into a 2-inch (5 cm) diameter round.

2. In a shallow dish, soak 4 bammies at a time in coconut milk for 3 minutes on each side or until bammies have absorbed some liquid and are moist.

3. In a large nonstick skillet, heat 1½ tsp (7 mL) oil over medium heat for 1 minute. Add 4 bammies and cook, turning once, for 2 minutes per side or until golden on both sides. Transfer bammies to prepared baking sheet. Repeat with the remaining oil and bammies, adjusting heat as necessary between batches to prevent burning.

4. Bake in preheated oven for 15 minutes or until the tip of a knife inserted in the center of the bammies comes out dry. Transfer bammies to a paper towel to drain off excess oil. Serve warm.

Tips

Cassava (also known as manioc and yuca) is naturally high in carbohydrate, so make sure your bammies are no larger than 2 inches (5 cm) and limit yourself to 2 per snack. Otherwise, the overall carbohydrate and fat content of your snack will be high.

If frozen cassava is not available, you can use fresh, but, after grating it, drain it well, then wring it out using clean cheesecloth, a lint-free linen tea towel or a heavy-duty paper towel, as the cassava needs to be dry for this recipe.

The fat in this recipe is much lower than in traditional bammy recipes because I've used just a small amount of light coconut milk to keep them moist, pan-fried and baked the bammies rather than deep-frying them, and drained off excess oil after baking.

Nutrition info per 2 bammies

Calories	251
Fat, total	5 g
Fat, saturated	1.0 g
Cholesterol	0 mg
Sodium	352 mg
Carbohydrate	50 g
Fiber	2 g
Protein	2 g

Food Choices

3	Carbohydrate
1	Fat

Fried Okra *(Ochroes)*

Makes 6 servings

For this recipe, the okra (or *ochro*, as it is called in Trinidad) is traditionally deep-fried in a lot of oil and served sprinkled with salt. Using a nonstick skillet makes it possible to cook with less oil, and the results still taste great! Instead of adding salt, serve the okra with a low-sodium salsa or chutney (see recipe, page 240).

Preparation time: **10 minutes**
Cooking time: **15 minutes**

1/4 cup	cornmeal	60 mL
1/4 cup	whole wheat flour	60 mL
3/4 tsp	salt	3 mL
1/2 tsp	freshly ground black pepper	2 mL
1/2 tsp	cayenne pepper	2 mL
3	large egg yolks	3
8 oz	small okra pods (about 24), stems and ends removed	250 g
2 tbsp	vegetable oil, divided	30 mL

1. In a medium bowl, combine cornmeal, whole wheat flour, salt, black pepper and cayenne.

2. In another bowl, beat egg yolks. Dip okra in egg yolk, then in cornmeal mixture, coating evenly. Discard any excess egg and cornmeal mixture.

3. In a nonstick skillet, heat 1 tbsp (15 mL) oil over medium-low heat for 1 minute. Add half the okra and cook, stirring, until light golden on all sides but still firm and crunchy. Transfer okra to a paper towel to drain off excess oil. Repeat with the remaining oil and okra, adjusting heat as necessary to prevent burning.

Tips

Frozen okra is available in many grocery stores, but for this recipe, it is important to use fresh, as frozen has too high a water content.

For nice crunchy okra, be sure not to overcook it.

To keep the fat in this dish as low as possible, make sure to drain off the excess oil after pan-frying the okra.

Nutrition info per serving

Calories	118
Fat, total	7 g
Fat, saturated	1.0 g
Cholesterol	92 mg
Sodium	299 mg
Carbohydrate	11 g
Fiber	2 g
Protein	3 g

Food Choices

1/2	Carbohydrate
1 1/2	Fat

Okra

Okra pods can grow from 2 to 12 inches (5 to 30 cm) or more in length. Larger pods are used often in the Caribbean, but can be fibrous and woody in texture. Smaller okra pods are more tender and have a pleasant flavor. Okra's aliases include ladyfinger, gumbo and bhindi.

Bora Beans

Known as bora beans in Guyana, these long, thin beans are also called bodi beans, Chinese long beans, yard-long beans or asparagus beans in various parts of the world. They take longer to cook than the green beans most North Americans are familiar with, but they are worth it for their unique taste!

Preparation time: 15 minutes
Cooking time: 40 minutes

2 tsp	vegetable oil	10 mL
1 cup	chopped onion	250 mL
2	cloves garlic, minced	2
5 cups	sliced bora beans (2-inch/5 cm pieces)	1.25 L
2 cups	chopped tomatoes	500 mL
1 1/2 cups	cubed peeled potatoes (1/2-inch/1 cm cubes)	375 mL
2/3 cup	water	150 mL
3/4 tsp	salt	3 mL
1/8 tsp	freshly ground black pepper	0.5 mL

1. In a large skillet, heat oil over medium heat. Add onion and garlic; cook, stirring, for about 5 minutes or until onion is translucent.

2. Stir in bora beans, tomatoes, potatoes and water; bring to a boil over high heat. Reduce heat to low, cover and simmer, stirring occasionally, for about 30 minutes or until beans and potatoes are tender. Stir in salt and pepper.

Tips

If bora beans are not available at your local grocery store, try a Caribbean or Asian grocery store.

This recipe contains a smaller amount of potatoes than the traditional recipe, to reduce the carbohydrate content and glycemic index of the dish.

Only a small amount of oil is used in this dish, so adjust the heat as needed to ensure the onion and garlic do not stick. If necessary, add a bit of water to the pan, but no extra oil.

Nutrition info per serving	
Calories	128
Fat, total	2 g
Fat, saturated	0.0 g
Cholesterol	0 mg
Sodium	362 mg
Carbohydrate	23 g
Fiber	2 g
Protein	5 g
Food Choices	
1/2	Carbohydrate
1/2	Fat

Guyanese Roti

Makes 6 roti

Roti is generally seen as an Indian bread, but it is also common in the Caribbean. Traditionally, Guyanese rotis are larger, are made with more oil and butter, and are unleavened. That is why they turn out nice and flaky. I've cut back on a huge amount of oil, but each roti still has a generous amount of fat and carbohydrate, so limit yourself to just one and enjoy it with a meal that is otherwise low in fat and carbohydrate.

Preparation time: **60 to 75 minutes**
Cooking time: **45 minutes**

- **Nonstick griddle or *tawa***

2 cups	all-purpose flour	500 mL
1 cup	whole wheat flour	250 mL
2 tsp	baking powder	10 mL
1/2 tsp	salt	2 mL
3 tbsp	olive oil	45 mL
1 1/2 cups	lukewarm water	325 mL
3 tbsp	whole wheat flour, divided	45 mL
6 1/2 tsp	olive oil, divided	32 mL

1. In a bowl, combine all-purpose flour, 1 cup (250 mL) whole wheat flour, baking powder and salt. Add 3 tbsp (45 mL) oil. Add lukewarm water and knead gently until combined, being careful to not overwork the dough. The dough should be sticky. Cover with a damp towel or plastic wrap and let rest for 15 to 30 minutes or until dough is soft and stretchy.

2. On a work surface floured with 1 1/2 tbsp (22 mL) whole wheat flour, using a rolling pin or your hands, spread dough into a large, thin circle (similar to a tortilla). Brush one side with 1/2 tsp (2 mL) oil.

3. Using a knife, slit the dough from the center to one edge and roll the dough into a cone. Press cone down from both ends to form a ball. Cover with a damp towel or plastic wrap and let rest for 30 minutes.

4. Using your hands, roll dough into a long cylinder and divide into 6 equal pieces. On a work surface floured with the remaining whole wheat flour, use a rolling pin to roll out each ball into a 9-inch (23 cm) circle.

5. Heat griddle over medium-high heat. Working with one roti at a time, brush one side with 1/2 tsp (2 mL) oil and place greased side down on griddle. Cook for 3 minutes or until bottom is golden brown. Brush top with another 1/2 tsp (2 mL) oil, flip roti over and cook for 3 minutes or until golden brown.

Nutrition info per roti	
Calories	340
Fat, total	13 g
Fat, saturated	1.8 g
Cholesterol	0 mg
Sodium	198 mg
Carbohydrate	50 g
Fiber	4 g
Protein	7 g
Food Choices	
3	Carbohydrate
2 1/2	Fat

Make It a Meal

1 serving Guyanese
Chicken Curry (page 234)

1 serving Guyanese
Roasted Eggplant Curry
(page 222) or 1 cup
(250 mL) vegetable curry
(no potatoes) (1 Extra)

1 serving Guyanese Roti

½ cup (125 mL) Sorrel
Drink (page 242)

½ small papaya
(½ Carbohydrate)

6. Remove roti from the pan and, while still hot, "clap" it between your hands, back and forth, about four times or until soft and flaky (see tip, below).

7. Repeat steps 5 and 6 with the remaining roti, adjusting heat as necessary between roti to prevent burning. Serve warm.

Tips

Roti is traditionally made using a large, flat pan called a *tawa*, usually made of iron. They are inexpensive and can be purchased at either Caribbean or South Asian grocery stores.

The "clapping" technique described in step 6 is the traditional Guyanese method used to make roti. This step removes the air in the roti so it does not dry out. Be very careful, as the roti is hot. For safety, you can put the roti between two clean tea towels before clapping it. Or, if you prefer, you can skip step 6 altogether, but the roti will not be as flaky.

Store the cooled roti wrapped in foil or a towel to prevent it from drying out. If it does dry out, just reheat it on the griddle or *tawa*, over low heat.

Because this recipe was modified to reduce the fat significantly and whole wheat flour was added, it is important to let the dough rest as indicated in order to get soft and flaky roti.

Cou Cou

Makes 4 servings

Cou cou is the national dish of Barbados, but it can be found across the Caribbean in different variations. It can be eaten on its own or as a side dish with meat and fish dishes, such as the popular flying fish of Barbados. It is similar to Italian polenta or Middle Eastern couscous, but the key to cou cou is the okra. Be careful about the portion you eat, as cornmeal is high in carbohydrate.

Preparation time: **10 minutes**
Cooking time: **40 minutes**

• Large circular pan

1 tbsp	vegetable oil, divided	15 mL
$1/2$ cup	finely chopped onion	125 mL
2 tbsp	minced fresh thyme (see tip, opposite)	30 mL
1 tbsp	minced garlic	15 mL
1 cup	sliced okra ($1/2$-inch/1 cm slices)	250 mL
4 cups	ready-to-use reduced-sodium vegetable broth	1 L
2 cups	cornmeal	500 mL
$1^3/4$ cups	water	425 mL
$1/2$ tsp	salt	2 mL
$1/4$ tsp	freshly ground black pepper	1 mL

1. In a large pot, heat half the oil over medium heat. Add onion, thyme and garlic; cook, stirring, for 3 minutes or until onions are golden. Add okra and cook, stirring, for 3 minutes or until slightly softened.

2. Stir in broth and bring to a boil. Reduce heat and simmer for 10 minutes.

3. Meanwhile, in a bowl, combine cornmeal and water; let soak until all of the water is absorbed.

4. Using a slotted spoon, transfer vegetables to a plate and set aside. Pour half of the broth out of the pot and set aside.

5. Bring the remaining broth to a boil over high heat, then add salt and pepper. Reduce heat to medium, stir in cornmeal and cook, stirring constantly, for 2 minutes. Return $1/4$ cup (60 mL) of the reserved broth to the pot. As cornmeal dries out, gradually add the remaining reserved broth, cooking until cornmeal breaks away from the pot and is firm but not stiff. Stir in the reserved vegetables.

Nutrition info per serving

Calories	251
Fat, total	5 g
Fat, saturated	0.2 g
Cholesterol	0
Sodium	459 mg
Carbohydrate	47 g
Fiber	11 g
Protein	4 g

Food Choices

$2^1/2$	Carbohydrate
1	Fat

1 serving Trinidadian
Stewed Fish (page 236)
or 2 oz (60 g) unsalted
steamed or baked fish
(2 Meat & Alternatives)

1 serving Callaloo
(page 204) or 1 cup
(250 mL) unsalted grilled
vegetables (1 Extra)

1 serving Cou Cou

½ cup (125 mL) Soursop
Juice (page 244)

1 medium tangerine
(½ Carbohydrate)

6. Grease circular pan with the remaining oil. With the help of a spoon, pour cornmeal mixture into the pan and shape while still hot. Let cool until firm to the touch and cornmeal is pulling away from edges of pan. Invert the pan onto a serving platter and cut cou cou into 4 wedges.

Tips

For a more authentic flavor, look for Jamaican or Guyanese thyme at a Caribbean grocery store. Every variety of thyme has a slightly different flavor, and Jamaican thyme in particular tends to be more pungent than North American thyme, so add a bit less of it to your recipes.

To easily peel a clove of garlic, place the clove on a flat side in the center of a cutting board. Place the widest part of the flat side of your blade on top of the clove and smash down on the middle of it with the palm of your hand. This will crack the papery skin of the garlic, helping you peel it off.

To reduce the sodium in this recipe, use ready-to-use no-salt-added vegetable broth or, for more flavor, make your own vegetable stock at home (see recipe, page 245).

Trinidadian Stewed Black-Eyed Peas

I first tried this dish at a family friend's place and had to ask for the recipe. It is easy to make and tastes great. The key is a great green seasoning, which makes everything taste fantastic!

Make It a Meal

1 serving Trinidadian Stewed Black-Eyed Peas

1 serving Caribbean Peas and Rice (page 220)

1 serving Guyanese Roasted Eggplant Curry (page 222) or 1 cup (250 mL) vegetable curry (no potatoes) (1 Extra)

$\frac{1}{6}$ large avocado (1 Fat)

1 medium tangerine ($\frac{1}{2}$ Carbohydrate)

Nutrition info per serving

Calories	190
Fat, total	2 g
Fat, saturated	0.3 g
Cholesterol	0 mg
Sodium	432 mg
Carbohydrate	33 g
Fiber	6 g
Protein	11 g

Food Choices

$1\frac{1}{2}$	Carbohydrate
$1\frac{1}{2}$	Meat & Alternatives
$\frac{1}{2}$	Fat

Preparation time: **15 minutes**
Cooking time: **35 minutes**

$1\frac{1}{2}$ tsp	vegetable oil	7 mL
$1\frac{1}{2}$ tsp	packed brown sugar	7 mL
$\frac{1}{4}$	Scotch bonnet chile pepper, seeded and chopped	$\frac{1}{4}$
$\frac{1}{2}$ cup	chopped onion	125 mL
1 tsp	minced garlic	5 mL
2	medium tomatoes, chopped	2
1	can (19 oz/540 mL) black-eyed peas, drained and rinsed well	1
$\frac{1}{4}$ cup	chopped celery	60 mL
2 tbsp	Trinidadian Green Seasoning (page 241)	30 mL
$\frac{1}{2}$ tsp	salt	2 mL
$\frac{1}{4}$ tsp	freshly ground black pepper	1 mL
$1\frac{1}{4}$ cups	water	300 mL

1. In a medium pot, heat oil over medium heat. Stir in brown sugar and cook, stirring, until sugar is melted, brown and bubbling, about 1 minute.

2. Add Scotch bonnet, onion and garlic; cook, stirring, for 1 minute. Add tomatoes, black-eyed peas, celery and green seasoning; cook, stirring, for 5 minutes or until vegetables are softened.

3. Stir in salt, pepper and water; bring to a boil over high heat. Reduce heat to medium, cover and cook for about 20 minutes or until sauce is thickened.

Tips

If you like heat, use a full Scotch bonnet pepper and leave the seeds in. If you are not able to find a Scotch bonnet pepper, any hot chile pepper will work, but you may need to use more to achieve the same heat level.

If you can only find 14- or 15-oz (398 or 425 mL) cans of black-eyed peas, buy two. You'll need about 2 cups (500 mL) well-rinsed drained peas for this recipe.

For a fresh, authentic flavor, I recommend making your own green seasoning, but if you use store-bought, choose a brand with as little sodium as possible. Some brands have as much as 240 mg of sodium per 1 tbsp (15 mL).

Trinidadian Curried Chickpeas

Makes 6 servings

This favorite dish can be made with or without potatoes; this recipe uses just a small amount to keep the carbohydrate low.

Make It a Meal

½ serving Jerk Chicken (page 229) or Jerk Pork (page 228)

1 serving Trinidadian Curried Chickpeas

1 cup (250 mL) vegetable curry (no potatoes) (1 Extra)

⅙ large avocado (1 Fat)

1 serving Caribbean Mango Chutney (page 240)

Two 6-inch (15 cm) plain whole wheat roti (2 Carbohydrate)

1 cup (250 mL) 1% or skim milk (1 Carbohydrate)

Nutrition info per serving

Calories	126
Fat, total	4 g
Fat, saturated	0.2 g
Cholesterol	0 mg
Sodium	215 mg
Carbohydrate	20 g
Fiber	6 g
Protein	6 g

Food Choices

1	Carbohydrate
½	Meat & Alternatives
½	Fat
1	Extra

Preparation time: 15 minutes
Cooking time: 25 minutes

1½ tsp	vegetable oil	7 mL
½ cup	chopped onion	125 mL
2 tsp	minced garlic	10 mL
¼	Scotch bonnet chile pepper (see tip, below), seeded and chopped	¼
2 tbsp	Caribbean curry powder (see page 23)	30 mL
1 tbsp	ground cumin	15 mL
⅔ cup	diced peeled potato (¼-inch/0.5 cm cubes)	150 mL
2 tbsp	Trinidadian Green Seasoning (page 241)	30 mL
1	can (19 oz/540 mL) chickpeas, drained and rinsed well	1
¼ tsp	salt	1 mL
¼ tsp	freshly ground black pepper	1 mL
1½ cups	water	375 mL

1. In a medium pot, heat oil over medium heat. Add onion and garlic; cook, stirring, for 3 minutes or until onions are golden. Add Scotch bonnet, curry powder and cumin; cook, stirring, for 4 minutes. Add potato and green seasoning; cook, stirring, for 2 minutes.

2. Stir in chickpeas, salt, pepper and water; bring to a boil over high heat. Reduce heat to low, cover and simmer for 10 minutes or until potato is tender.

Tips

If you are using a hot curry powder and prefer to otherwise keep the heat level down, you can omit the Scotch bonnet pepper. Or, if you like heat, you can add more Scotch bonnet.

If you can only find 14- or 15-oz (398 or 425 mL) cans of chickpeas, buy two. You'll need about 2 cups (500 mL) well-rinsed drained chickpeas for this recipe.

This dish is traditionally eaten with roti (page 212) or flatbread. Be sure to account for the carbohydrate and be sensible about how many rotis you eat.

Curried chickpeas are also featured in South Asian cuisine, but the flavors of Caribbean curry powder, green seasoning and Scotch bonnet pepper make this version distinct and delicious.

Trinidadian Curried Pigeon Peas

Makes 4 servings

Caribbean cooking is full of a variety of legumes. This popular Trinidadian-style dish uses pigeon peas, also known as gungo peas, gandules or just peas. Other versions of this recipe abound across the Caribbean. The dish is meant to be saucy, so be careful not to overcook it.

Preparation time: **20 minutes**
Cooking time: **35 minutes**

1 ½ tsp	vegetable oil	7 mL
½ cup	chopped onion	125 mL
2 tsp	minced garlic	10 mL
2	green onions, finely chopped	2
1	medium tomato, finely chopped	1
¼	Scotch bonnet chile pepper, seeded and chopped	¼
1 tbsp	Caribbean curry powder (see page 23)	15 mL
2 tsp	ground cumin	10 mL
1	can (14 oz/398 mL) green pigeon peas, drained and rinsed well	1
½ tsp	salt	2 mL
¼ tsp	freshly ground black pepper	1 mL
1 ¼ cups	water	300 mL

1. In a medium pot, heat oil over medium heat. Add onion and garlic; cook, stirring, for 1 minute. Add green onions, tomato and Scotch bonnet; cook, stirring, for 3 minutes. Add curry powder and cumin; cook, stirring, for 3 minutes. Add pigeon peas and cook, stirring, for 1 minute.

2. Stir in salt, pepper and water; bring to a boil over high heat. Reduce heat to low, cover and simmer for about 20 minutes or until sauce is thickened.

Tips

Chill onions in the freezer before cutting them. This reduces the amount of gas the onions release into the air — and it's the gas that makes your eyes tear up.

If you can only find a 15- or 19-oz (425 or 540 mL) can of pigeon peas, use about 1 ½ cups (375 mL) drained and rinsed.

Nutrition Tip

Pigeon peas are a very good source of folate and a source of iron. They are also a very good source of fiber, especially soluble fiber, which helps lower low-density lipoprotein (LDL) blood cholesterol and blood glucose levels.

Nutrition info per serving	
Calories	165
Fat, total	3 g
Fat, saturated	0.5 g
Cholesterol	0 mg
Sodium	277 g
Carbohydrate	26 g
Fiber	6 g
Protein	7 g

Food Choices	
1	Carbohydrate
1	Meat & Alternatives
½	Fat
1	Extra

Guyanese Cook-Up Rice

Makes 5 servings

Traditionally, beef or salted beef is used in this dish, but to keep the saturated fat low, I added spinach instead and made this dish vegetarian. A further reduction in saturated fat was gained by using light coconut milk instead of regular.

Make It a Meal

1 serving Guyanese Chicken Curry (page 234)

1 serving Guyanese Roasted Eggplant Curry (page 222)

1 serving Guyanese Cook-Up Rice

1 cup (250 mL) Sorrel Drink (page 242)

½ small papaya (½ Carbohydrate)

Nutrition info per serving

Calories	299
Fat, total	5 g
Fat, saturated	1.0 g
Cholesterol	0 mg
Sodium	461 mg
Carbohydrate	55 g
Fiber	8 g
Protein	11 g

Food Choices

2½	Carbohydrate
½	Meat & Alternatives
½	Fat

Preparation time: 15 minutes
Cooking time: 40 minutes

1 tbsp	vegetable oil	15 mL
8	cloves garlic, minced	8
3	sprigs fresh thyme (see tip, page 207)	3
2	green onions, thinly sliced	2
2	small green chile peppers, minced	2
1	large onion, chopped	1
1	tomato, finely diced	1
1 cup	parboiled (Converted) brown rice	250 mL
¾ tsp	salt	3 mL
¼ tsp	freshly ground black pepper	1 mL
1½ cups	water	375 mL
⅓ cup	light coconut milk	75 mL
2 cups	well-rinsed drained canned black-eyed peas	500 mL
8 oz	baby spinach, finely chopped	250 g

1. In a large skillet, heat oil over medium heat. Add garlic, thyme, green onions, chiles and onion; cook, stirring, for 2 minutes or until onions are golden. Add tomato and cook, stirring, for 2 minutes.

2. Stir in rice, salt, pepper, water and coconut milk; bring to a boil over high heat. Reduce heat to low, cover, leaving lid ajar, and simmer, without stirring, for 20 minutes.

3. Gently stir in black-eyed peas and spinach; simmer for about 10 minutes or until liquid is absorbed. Discard thyme.

Nutrition Tip

Parboiled (Converted) brown rice is lower on the glycemic index and higher in fiber than white rice. Parboiled rice is not processed like white rice, but is soaked, steamed and dried with the husk and bran intact, to make the grain less sticky. Because the husk and bran are intact, so are the nutrients, such as B vitamins. Choosing parboiled brown rice can help lower blood glucose levels.

Caribbean Peas and Rice

Makes 6 servings

Peas and rice is a frequent side dish at Caribbean meals and has many variations. This recipe is typical of a version made in Trinidad. Pigeon peas and brown rice add a boost of fiber, and the combination also creates a complete protein, with all essential amino acids.

Soaking time: **Overnight**
Preparation time: **10 minutes**
Cooking time: **1 hour and 45 minutes**

³⁄₄ cup	dried pigeon peas	175 mL
	Water	
1¹⁄₂ tsp	vegetable oil	7 mL
1	medium onion, finely chopped	1
1	clove garlic, minced	1
1	bay leaf	1
¹⁄₈ tsp	cayenne pepper	0.5 mL
1 cup	long-grain brown rice	250 mL
2	sprigs fresh thyme leaves (see tip, opposite), chopped	2
¹⁄₂ tsp	salt	2 mL
¹⁄₄ tsp	freshly ground black pepper	1 mL
¹⁄₂	can (14 oz/400 mL) light coconut milk	¹⁄₂

1. Place pigeon peas in a medium bowl with enough water to cover. Cover bowl and soak overnight in the refrigerator.

2. Drain soaking water from peas and transfer peas to a large, heavy pot. Add fresh water to cover and bring to a boil over high heat. Reduce heat to low, cover and simmer for 45 minutes. Remove from heat, drain and set aside.

3. In the same pot, heat oil over medium heat. Add onion, garlic, bay leaf and cayenne; cook, stirring, for 1 to 2 minutes or until fragrant and onion is starting to soften. Add peas, rice and thyme; cook, stirring, for 1 minute.

4. Stir in salt, pepper, coconut milk and 1¹⁄₂ cups (375 mL) water; bring to a boil over high heat. Reduce heat to low, cover and simmer for 30 to 40 minutes or until rice and peas are tender and liquid is absorbed. Discard bay leaf.

Nutrition info per serving

Calories	240
Fat, total	4 g
Fat, saturated	2.0 g
Cholesterol	0 mg
Sodium	208 mg
Carbohydrate	43 g
Fiber	5 g
Protein	9 g

Food Choices

2	Carbohydrate
1	Meat & Alternatives

½ serving Jerk Pork
(page 228) or Jerk
Chicken (page 229)

1 serving Bora Beans
(page 211)

1 serving Caribbean Peas
and Rice

⅙ large avocado (1 Fat)

¾ cup (175 mL) 1%
or nonfat plain yogurt
(1 Carbohydrate)
with 1 cup (250 mL)
strawberries
(½ Carbohydrate)

Tips

Despite the name of this dish, it's not always made with peas; indeed, a variety of legumes are used. If you cannot find dried pigeon peas, substitute any dried bean or other pulse.

For a more authentic flavor, look for Caribbean thyme at a Caribbean grocery store. Every variety of thyme has a slightly different flavor. Jamaican thyme in particular tends to be more pungent than North American thyme, so add a bit less of it to your recipes.

Although coconut milk has various vitamins, minerals and antioxidants, it is high in saturated fat and should be consumed in moderation. This recipe, for example, uses less coconut milk than the traditional version. Use light coconut milk whenever possible. There is some evidence to suggest that coconut and coconut products may have health benefits, but this research is not yet conclusive.

When cooking with a small amount of oil, be sure to heat it well before adding the other ingredients; otherwise, they may simply absorb the oil, which can cause sticking and burning.

Nutrition Tip

Beans, peas and lentils are low in fat, are very high in fiber and protein, have a low glycemic index and can help lower blood glucose levels, so be creative in adding them to your dishes.

Guyanese Roasted Eggplant Curry
(Baigan Choka)

Makes 6 servings

Although Guyana is in South America, it is also considered part of the Caribbean, and certainly in terms of its cuisine. Other cultures also influence its food and style of cooking, and this dish is similar to a South Asian eggplant curry. This dish does take some time to make, but it is worth the effort for its health benefits and incredible flavor.

Preparation time: **15 minutes**
Cooking time: **1 hour and 20 minutes**

- **Preheat oven to 375°F (190°C)**
- **Large rimmed baking sheet**

2	large dark-skinned eggplants	2
8	cloves garlic, sliced	8
1 1/2 tsp	vegetable oil	7 mL
2	medium onions, finely chopped	2
4	cloves garlic, minced	4
2	large tomatoes, finely chopped	2
1/2	Scotch bonnet chile pepper, seeded and minced	1/2
1 tsp	salt	5 mL
1 tsp	freshly ground black pepper	5 mL
2	green onions (green part only), finely chopped	2

1. Using a paring knife, make 4 deep slits in each eggplant. Place 1 clove's worth of sliced garlic inside each slit. Place eggplant on baking sheet. Bake in preheated oven for 1 hour or until mushy inside. Let cool, then cut in half and scoop out the eggplant flesh and garlic; discard skins. Set aside.

2. In a medium skillet, heat oil over medium heat. Add onions and cook, stirring, until golden. Add minced garlic, tomatoes, Scotch bonnet, salt and pepper; cook, stirring, for 5 minutes or until onions are well cooked. Add eggplant mixture, breaking it up with a wooden spoon, and cook for 2 minutes.

3. Serve garnished with green onions.

Nutrition info per serving	
Calories	95
Fat, total	2 g
Fat, saturated	0.2 g
Cholesterol	0 mg
Sodium	398 mg
Carbohydrate	20 g
Fiber	7 g
Protein	3 g
Food Choices	
1	Extra

Make It a Meal

1 serving Guyanese
Chicken Curry (page 234)

1 serving Guyanese
Roasted Eggplant Curry
or 1 cup (250 mL)
vegetable curry (no
potatoes) (1 Extra),
drizzled with 1 tsp
(5 mL) olive oil (1 Fat)

1 serving Guyanese
Cook-Up Rice (page 219)

$\frac{1}{6}$ avocado (1 Fat)

1 cup (250 mL) 1% or skim
milk (1 Carbohydrate)

$\frac{1}{2}$ small papaya
($\frac{1}{2}$ Carbohydrate)

Tips

For more heat, use a full Scotch bonnet pepper and leave the seeds in. If you are not able to find a Scotch bonnet pepper, any hot chili pepper will work, but you may need to use more to achieve the same heat level.

The key to this dish is to finely chop or mince everything; it is not meant to be chunky.

This recipe uses less oil than the traditional version, for a lower fat content.

Nutrition Tip

Eggplant is high in fiber, especially soluble fiber, which has been shown to lower low-density lipoprotein (LDL) blood cholesterol and blood glucose levels.

Guyanese Pepperpot

Makes 8 servings

This popular dish is served on special occasions, such as Christmas. The traditional version contains an astonishing amount of sugar, salt and fat. This healthier adaptation replaces the cow's feet with lean beef shoulder, reduces the amount of oxtail and uses much less added sugar and salt, but it should still be reserved as a special-occasion treat.

Preparation time: **20 minutes**
Marinating time: **Overnight**
Cooking time: **1 hour**

Meat and Marinade

12	cloves garlic, minced	12
4	green onions, finely chopped	4
2	Scotch bonnet chile peppers, seeded and minced	2
2 tbsp	chopped fresh thyme (see tip, opposite)	30 mL
2 tsp	freshly ground black pepper	10 mL
1/2 tsp	salt	2 mL
2 lbs	lean beef shoulder, with bone, cut into equal-size chunks (see tip, opposite)	1 kg
1 lb	oxtail, with bone, cut into equal-size chunks and visible fat removed	500 g

Stew

1 1/2 tsp	vegetable oil	7 mL
2	medium onions, finely chopped	2
2	stalks celery, chopped	2
1/3 cup	cassareep (see page 23 and tip, opposite)	75 mL
3	whole cloves	3
2	3-inch (7.5 cm) cinnamon sticks	2
2 tsp	packed brown sugar	10 mL
4 cups	water	1 L
2	green onions (green part only), finely chopped (optional)	2

1. *Meat and Marinade:* In a large bowl, combine garlic, green onions, Scotch bonnets, thyme, pepper and salt. Transfer one-third of the mixture to a medium bowl.

2. Add the beef to the large bowl and the oxtail to the medium bowl, tossing to coat. Cover both bowls and refrigerate overnight.

3. *Stew:* Transfer the oxtail to a pot and transfer any remaining marinade to the beef mixture. Add enough water to the pot to cover the oxtail. Bring to a boil over high heat. Cover, leaving lid ajar, and boil for 45 minutes, adding more water as needed to keep oxtail covered. Drain off water.

Nutrition info per serving	
Calories	265
Fat, total	10 g
Fat, saturated	3.0 g
Cholesterol	82 mg
Sodium	274 mg
Carbohydrate	13 g
Fiber	2 g
Protein	29 g
Food Choices	
3 1/2	Meat & Alternatives
1	Extra

4. Meanwhile, in a large pot, heat oil over medium heat. Add beef mixture, onions and celery; cover and cook for 15 to 20 minutes, adjusting the heat as needed, until beef is well browned.

5. Add oxtail and cassareep and cook, stirring, for 5 minutes. Stir in cloves, cinnamon, brown sugar and water; bring to a boil over high heat. Reduce heat to medium-low, cover, leaving lid ajar, and simmer for 20 minutes or until beef and oxtail are fork-tender. Discard cinnamon sticks.

6. Serve garnished with green onions, if desired.

Tips

For a more authentic flavor, look for Jamaican or Guyanese thyme at a Caribbean grocery store. Every variety of thyme has a slightly different flavor, and Jamaican thyme in particular tends to be more pungent than North American thyme, so add a bit less of it to your recipes.

For ease of preparation, ask your local butcher to cut the beef and oxtail into chunks for you if precut meat is not available. Ask for any visible fat to be trimmed as well.

The cooking time in step 3 will depend on the size of the chunks of meat. Check the tenderness of the meat after 1 hour, then continue cooking as needed, checking periodically, until the meat is fork-tender.

Cassareep, a syrup made from the juice of the cassava root, gives this dish a sweet flavor and dark color. Traditional pepperpot recipes call for up to 1 cup (250 mL) to be added, but that also adds a lot of carbohydrate and sodium, so this version uses a smaller amount. When choosing cassareep, look at the Nutrition Facts table and choose brands with lower carbohydrate and sodium.

Pepperpot is meant to be both sweet and spicy. If you want more heat, leave some or all of the seeds in the Scotch bonnet peppers.

Jamaican Curried Goat

Makes 6 servings

I was not a fan of goat meat until I tasted this dish, and now I can't get enough! The curry can be made with or without potatoes; I added a small amount to thicken the gravy. This dish is usually served with rice or roti. Watch your portions so your carbohydrates are not too high per meal.

Preparation time: **20 minutes**
Marinating time: **2 hours or overnight**
Cooking time: **1 ½ hours**

½	Scotch bonnet chile pepper, seeded and minced (optional)	½
2 tbsp	Caribbean curry powder (see page 23)	30 mL
1 tbsp	chili powder	15 mL
1 tbsp	ground cumin	15 mL
1 ½ tsp	ground allspice	7 mL
½ tsp	salt	2 mL
1 ¼ cups	water, divided	300 mL
1 tsp	tomato paste	5 mL
2 lbs	lean goat shoulder, with bone, visible fat removed, cut into 1-inch (2.5 cm) cubes	1 kg
1 tbsp	vegetable oil, divided	15 mL
3	green onions, chopped	3
2	cloves garlic, minced	2
1 cup	chopped onion	250 mL
1 tsp	minced gingerroot	5 mL
1 cup	ready-to-use reduced-sodium vegetable broth	250 mL
1 cup	cubed peeled potato (1-inch/2.5 cm cubes)	250 mL

1. In a large bowl, combine Scotch bonnet, curry powder, chili powder, cumin, allspice, salt, ¼ cup (60 mL) water and tomato paste to make a paste. Add goat meat and stir to coat. Cover and refrigerate for at least 2 hours or preferably overnight.

2. In a large skillet, heat half the oil over medium heat. Add the goat meat mixture and cook, stirring, for about 3 minutes or until meat is browned on all sides. Add the remaining water, scraping up any browned bits from the bottom of the pan. Remove from heat and set aside.

Nutrition info per serving	
Calories	247
Fat, total	6 g
Fat, saturated	1.3 g
Cholesterol	86 mg
Sodium	376 mg
Carbohydrate	13 g
Fiber	3 g
Protein	33 g

Food Choices

½	Carbohydrate
3 ½	Meat & Alternatives
½	Fat

Make It a Meal

1 serving Guyanese
Barley Soup (page 203)

1 serving Jamaican
Curried Goat

$\frac{2}{3}$ cup (150 mL) unsalted
cooked long-grain brown
rice (2 Carbohydrate)

$\frac{1}{6}$ large avocado (1 Fat)

$\frac{1}{2}$ cup (125 mL) Ginger
Beer (page 243)

$\frac{1}{2}$ small papaya
($\frac{1}{2}$ Carbohydrate)

3. In a large stockpot, heat the remaining oil over medium heat. Add green onions, garlic, onion and ginger; cook, stirring, for about 2 minutes or until tender. Add meat mixture, reduce heat to low, cover and simmer for 15 minutes.

4. Add broth and bring to a boil over high heat. Reduce heat to low, cover and simmer, stirring occasionally, for 50 minutes. Add potato and cook for about 10 minutes or until meat and potatoes are tender.

Tips

For ease of preparation, ask your local butcher or Caribbean or South Asian grocery store to cut the goat meat into 1-inch (2.5 cm) cubes for you, as finding precut goat meat with the bone in may be a challenge.

The addition of tomato paste is not traditional in this dish, but it does help to thicken the gravy, boost the flavor and compensate for the reduction in salt.

To reduce the sodium in this recipe, use ready-to-use no-salt-added vegetable broth or, for more flavor, make your own vegetable stock at home (see recipe, page 245).

Jerk Pork

Jerk seasoning is a spicy blend of chile peppers, herbs and spices such as thyme, allspice, cinnamon and nutmeg. It is used in Jamaican cooking to flavor meat such as pork or chicken. For best results, marinate the pork tenderloin pieces overnight.

Tips

It is best to make your own jerk marinade, as store-bought versions can have up to 920 mg of sodium per 2 tbsp (30 mL).

Some cuts of pork are high in saturated fat. This recipe calls for the tenderloin, which is the leanest cut. Be careful not to overcook it, as it dries out easily.

This recipe makes a large batch of jerk pork. Store the extras in an airtight container in the refrigerator for up to 3 days or in the freezer for up to 3 months.

Nutrition info per serving	
Calories	147
Fat, total	3 g
Fat, saturated	0.9 g
Cholesterol	74 mg
Sodium	277 mg
Carbohydrate	5 g
Fiber	1 g
Protein	25 g
Food Choices	
3	Meat & Alternatives
1	Extra

Preparation time: **20 minutes**
Marinating time: **2 hours or overnight**
Cooking time: **40 minutes**

- **Large rimmed baking sheet**

6	cloves garlic, puréed (see tips, page 195)	6
1 1/2 cups	chopped green onions (about 10)	375 mL
1 tbsp	onion powder	15 mL
1 tbsp	garlic powder	15 mL
2 tsp	dried thyme	10 mL
2 tsp	chili powder	10 mL
1 1/2 tsp	freshly ground black pepper	7 mL
1 tsp	ground ginger	5 mL
1 tsp	ground allspice	5 mL
1/2 tsp	ground nutmeg	2 mL
1/3 cup	reduced-sodium soy sauce	75 mL
3 tbsp	tomato paste	45 mL
3 lbs	boneless pork tenderloin (4 tenderloins), cut into 1-inch (2.5 cm) cubes	1.5 kg

1. In a bowl, combine garlic, green onions, onion powder, garlic powder, thyme, chili powder, pepper, ginger, allspice, nutmeg, soy sauce and tomato paste.

2. Place meat in a non-metallic container or bowl. Pour in marinade and stir well to coat meat evenly with marinade. Cover and refrigerate for at least 2 hours or preferably overnight.

3. Preheat oven to 350°F (180°C).

4. Arrange pork in a single layer on baking sheet and drizzle any remaining marinade on top. Bake for 20 minutes. Flip pieces over and bake for about 20 minutes or until just a hint of pink remains inside pork.

Nutrition Tip

One tablespoon (15 mL) of regular soy sauce contains 1000 mg or more sodium. The reduced-sodium variety is a better option, but even then, always measure the amount you use: reduced-sodium soy sauce still has 580 mg or more sodium per tablespoon.

Jerk Chicken

Makes 4 servings

Traditionally, jerk chicken is made with the skin on, which keeps it tender and gives it a dark color, but skin also contributes a lot of fat. To reduce the saturated fat in this recipe, use skinless chicken and remove any excess fat before preparing the dish.

Make It a Meal

1 serving Guyanese Barley Soup (page 203)

1 serving Jerk Chicken

2/3 cup (150 mL) unsalted cooked long-grain brown rice (2 Carbohydrate)

1/6 large avocado (1 Fat)

1 cup (250 mL) Ginger Beer (page 243)

1 medium tangerine (1/2 Carbohydrate)

Nutrition info per serving

Calories	152
Fat, total	5 g
Fat, saturated	1.2 g
Cholesterol	108 mg
Sodium	397 mg
Carbohydrate	4 g
Fiber	1 g
Protein	23 g

Food Choices

3	Meat & Alternatives

Preparation time: **15 minutes**
Marinating time: **1 hour or overnight**
Cooking time: **45 minutes**

- **Small food processor or mini chopper**
- **8-inch (20 cm) square shallow glass baking dish**

3	green onions, chopped	3
1/2	Scotch bonnet chile pepper, seeded	1/2
3	cloves garlic	3
1 1/2 tsp	minced gingerroot	7 mL
1 1/2 tsp	ground allspice	7 mL
1 tsp	chopped fresh thyme (see tip, page 231)	5 mL
1/2 tsp	salt	2 mL
1/2 tsp	freshly ground black pepper	2 mL
1/2 tsp	ground cinnamon	2 mL
1/4 tsp	ground nutmeg	1 mL
1 1/2 tbsp	water	22 mL
1 tbsp	freshly squeezed lime juice	15 mL
1 lb	boneless skinless chicken thighs (about 6)	500 g

1. In food processor, combine green onions, Scotch bonnet, garlic, ginger, allspice, thyme, salt, pepper, cinnamon, nutmeg, water and lime juice; process until a thick paste forms.

2. Score meaty side of chicken thighs with 1-inch (2.5 cm) slits and place in baking dish. Rub paste over chicken and into slits. Cover and refrigerate for at least 1 hour or preferably overnight.

3. Preheat oven to 375°F (190°C).

4. Uncover dish. Bake chicken for 30 minutes or until golden. Increase oven temperature to 400°F (200°C) and bake for 15 minutes or until juices run clear when chicken is pierced and a meat thermometer inserted in the thickest part of a thigh registers 165°F (74°C).

Tips

It is best to make your own jerk marinade, as store-bought versions can have more than 900 mg of sodium per 2 tbsp (30 mL).

You can increase the amount of Scotch bonnet pepper in the marinade or leave the seeds in if you like your jerk chicken spicier.

Jamaican Fricassee Chicken

Makes 6 servings

Fricassee chicken is another recipe that is typically cooked with the skin on, and the whole chicken is usually used. Avery Chin, a great Jamaican chef, shared this fantastic recipe with me, and I've reduced the fat by using skinless chicken thighs and drumsticks and by draining off the oil after pan-frying.

Preparation time: **20 minutes**
Marinating time: **20 minutes or overnight**
Cooking time: **1 hour**

¹⁄₂	Scotch bonnet chile pepper, seeded and chopped	¹⁄₂
1 tbsp	paprika	15 mL
1 tbsp	garlic powder	15 mL
1 tbsp	onion powder	15 mL
1 ¹⁄₂ tsp	ground allspice	7 mL
³⁄₄ tsp	ground ginger	3 mL
1 tsp	freshly ground black pepper	5 mL
¹⁄₂ tsp	salt	2 mL
3 tbsp	water	45 mL
1 tbsp	reduced-sodium soy sauce	15 mL
2 lbs	bone-in skinless chicken thighs and drumsticks	1 kg
3 tbsp	vegetable oil, divided	45 mL
1	large onion, chopped	1
2	cloves garlic, minced	2
2	large tomatoes, diced	2
1 cup	water	250 mL
3	sprigs fresh thyme leaves (see tip, opposite), chopped	3

1. In a large bowl or sealable plastic bag, combine Scotch bonnet, paprika, garlic powder, onion powder, allspice, ginger, pepper, salt, 3 tbsp (45 mL) water and soy sauce. Add chicken and toss to coat. Cover or seal, and refrigerate for at least 20 minutes or preferably overnight.

2. In a large skillet, heat 2 tbsp (30 mL) oil over medium heat. Working in batches, remove chicken from marinade, reserving marinade, and add chicken to pan. Cook chicken for about 5 minutes per side or until well browned on both sides. Transfer chicken to a plate. When all of the chicken is browned, drain the oil from the skillet.

Nutrition info per serving	
Calories	213
Fat, total	10 g
Fat, saturated	2.0 g
Cholesterol	104 mg
Sodium	311 mg
Carbohydrate	7 g
Fiber	2 g
Protein	23 g

Food Choices

3	Meat & Alternatives
1	Fat
1	Extra

Make It a Meal

1 serving Caribbean
Pumpkin Soup
(page 202)

1 serving Jamaican
Fricassee Chicken

1 cup (250 mL) unsalted
grilled vegetables or
vegetable curry (no
potatoes) (1 Extra)

⅔ cup (150 mL) unsalted
cooked long-grain brown
rice (2 Carbohydrate)

1 cup (250 mL) Soursop
Juice (page 244)

½ medium mango
(1 Carbohydrate)

3. Reduce heat to low and add the remaining oil to the pan. Add onion and cook, stirring, for about 5 minutes or until softened. Add garlic and cook, stirring, for 5 minutes. Add tomatoes and cook, stirring, for 3 minutes. Stir in 1 cup (250 mL) water, scraping up any browned bits from the bottom of the pan.

4. Return the chicken to the pan, along with any accumulated juices and the reserved marinade; bring to a boil over high heat. Reduce heat to medium-low, cover and simmer for 12 minutes, turning chicken once. If liquid is evaporating quickly, reduce heat to low. Stir in thyme and simmer for 5 minutes or until juices run clear when chicken is pierced and a meat thermometer inserted in the thickest part of a thigh registers 165°F (74°C).

Tips

This recipe is usually made spicy. For more heat, use a full Scotch bonnet pepper and leave the seeds in.

Always check the labels for ground spices such as allspice and ginger to make sure there is no added sodium.

Chill onions in the freezer before cutting them. This reduces the amount of gas the onions release into the air — and it's the gas that makes your eyes tear up.

For a more authentic flavor, look for Jamaican or Guyanese thyme at a Caribbean grocery store. Every variety of thyme has a slightly different flavor, and Jamaican thyme in particular tends to be more pungent than North American thyme, so add a bit less of it to your recipes.

Guyanese Chicken Chow Mein

Chinese cooking has an influence around the world — even on Caribbean cuisine. Guyanese chow mein noodles have their own distinct flavor, and the completed dish tends to be spicier than its Asian counterpart.

Nutrition info per serving

Calories	294
Fat, total	5 g
Fat, saturated	0.7 g
Cholesterol	44 mg
Sodium	467 mg
Carbohydrate	47 g
Fiber	3 g
Protein	18 g

Food Choices

2½	Carbohydrate
1	Meat & Alternatives
½	Fat

Preparation time: **15 minutes**
Marinating time: **1 hour or overnight**
Cooking time: **40 minutes**

7	cloves garlic, minced	7
1	small green chile pepper, finely chopped (see tip, opposite)	1
½ tsp	salt	2 mL
½ tsp	freshly ground black pepper	2 mL
½ tsp	paprika	2 mL
¼ tsp	cayenne pepper	1 mL
3 tbsp	reduced-sodium soy sauce	45 mL
8 oz	boneless skinless chicken thighs (4 small thighs)	250 g
1 tbsp	vegetable oil	15 mL
½ tsp	browning sauce (optional)	2 mL
½	package (12 oz/340 g) Guyanese chow mein noodles	½
8 oz	frozen mixed vegetables (corn, beans, carrots, peas)	250 g
4	green onions (green part only), chopped	4

1. In a large bowl, combine garlic, chile, salt, black pepper, paprika, cayenne and soy sauce. Add chicken and toss to coat. Cover and refrigerate for at least 1 hour or overnight.

2. In a large pot, heat oil over medium heat. Add chicken and marinade; cook for 1 to 2 minutes per side or until chicken is lightly browned on both sides and liquid has evaporated.

3. Stir in 1 cup (250 mL) water and bring to a boil over high heat. Reduce heat to low, cover and simmer for 20 minutes or until juices run clear when chicken is pierced. Check after 10 minutes and add more water if needed (there should always be a bit of gravy at the bottom of the pot). When chicken is nearly done, stir in browning sauce (if using). Remove from heat.

4. Transfer chicken thighs to a cutting board and cut into ¼-inch (0.5 cm) thick strips. Return to the pot and place over low heat to keep warm.

5. Meanwhile, in a large pot of boiling water, boil noodles and mixed vegetables for 6 to 8 minutes or until al dente. Drain and rinse noodles and vegetables under cold water. Drain well.

6. Using a fork, quickly and gently stir noodles and vegetables into the cooked chicken; cook just until heated through. Stir in green onions. Serve immediately.

Tips

This dish is meant to be spicy, so leave the seeds in the chile pepper unless you are heat-averse. If you want even more spice in this dish, use hot Spanish paprika instead of regular paprika.

Guyanese and other Caribbean chow mein noodles can be found at Caribbean grocery stores, and most have no salt added. Some other types of chow mein, however, have a lot of sodium — over 100 mg per 25 g serving! If you cannot find Guyanese chow mein, any type of chow mein noodle will work in this recipe, but look for one low in sodium. Or choose a high-fiber noodle, such as buckwheat or whole wheat, as chow mein noodles, made with enriched flour, are high in carbohydrate and low in fiber.

Chow mein noodles can cook quickly, so watch them carefully in step 5. Draining and rinsing the noodles and vegetables under cold water will ensure that the noodles do not stick together.

The prepared chow mein spice commonly used in this dish has been replaced with a combination of spices, to reduce the sodium. Nevertheless, the sodium is still quite high, so enjoy this dish on days when your sodium intake at other meals is low.

Guyanese Chicken Curry

What makes Guyanese chicken curry different from South Asian chicken curries is the spice combinations and/or curry powders that give it a nice rich color.

Preparation time: 20 minutes
Cooking time: 40 minutes

1 tsp	vegetable oil	5 mL
1	medium onion, finely chopped	1
4	cloves garlic, minced	4
1/4	Scotch bonnet chile pepper, seeded and chopped	1/4
1	sprig fresh thyme (preferably Guyanese)	1
2 tsp	Caribbean curry powder (see page 23)	10 mL
2 lbs	bone-in skinless chicken breasts, cut into 2-inch (5 cm) pieces	1 kg
1/2 tsp	salt	2 mL
1/2 cup	water	125 mL

1. In a large pot, heat oil over medium heat. Add onion and garlic; reduce heat to medium-low and cook, stirring, for 1 minute. Add Scotch bonnet, thyme and curry powder; cook, stirring, for about 3 minutes or until onion is golden. Add chicken and salt; increase heat to medium and cook, stirring, for 10 minutes.

2. Stir in water, scraping up any browned bits from the bottom of the pan, and bring to a boil over high heat. Reduce heat to low, cover and simmer for 10 minutes. Uncover and cook, stirring often, for about 7 minutes or until chicken is no longer pink inside and sauce is thickened. Discard thyme.

Tips

This dish is meant to be spicy. For more heat, you can increase the amount of Scotch bonnet pepper.

When purchasing Caribbean curry powder, always read the label to ensure there is no salt added.

For a more authentic flavor, look for Guyanese thyme at a Caribbean grocery store. Fresh thyme is the preferred choice for this recipe, so if you cannot find fresh Guyanese thyme, use any fresh thyme.

The sauce for Guyanese chicken curry is usually very thick, thanks to the potatoes that are commonly added. This version omits the potatoes to keep it low in carbohydrate.

Make It a Meal

1 serving Guyanese Chicken Curry

1 serving Guyanese Cook-Up Rice (page 219)

1 serving Guyanese Roasted Eggplant Curry (page 222), drizzled with 1 tsp (5 mL) olive oil (1 Fat)

1 cup (250 mL) 1% or skim milk (1 Carbohydrate)

1/2 small papaya (1/2 Carbohydrate)

Nutrition info per serving

Calories	165
Fat, total	4 g
Fat, saturated	0.8 g
Cholesterol	77 mg
Sodium	338 mg
Carbohydrate	4 g
Fiber	1 g
Protein	26 g

Food Choices

3	Meat & Alternatives

Trinidadian Shrimp Curry

Makes 6 servings

This dish is meant to be spicy, so choose a Caribbean curry powder that has added heat from chile peppers, preferably one from Trinidad and Tobago. If you prefer a mild flavor, omit the Scotch bonnet pepper; if you want more heat, keep the seeds in!

Preparation time: **20 minutes**
Marinating time: **30 minutes**
Cooking time: **15 minutes**

2 lbs	medium shrimp, peeled, deveined and rinsed	1 kg
2 tbsp	Trinidadian Green Seasoning (page 241)	30 mL
2 tsp	minced garlic	10 mL
1/4 tsp	salt	1 mL
1 tbsp	vegetable oil	15 mL
1/2 cup	finely chopped onion	125 mL
1/4	Scotch bonnet chile pepper, seeded	1/4
3 tbsp	Caribbean curry powder (see page 23)	45 mL
1/2 cup	water	125 mL
1	medium tomato, chopped	1
1/4 tsp	freshly ground black pepper	1 mL

1. In a bowl, combine shrimp, green seasoning, garlic and salt. Cover and refrigerate for 30 minutes.

2. In a skillet, heat oil over medium heat. Add onion; cook, stirring, for 1 minute. Add Scotch bonnet and cook, stirring, for 1 minute or until onion is golden.

3. Stir in curry powder and water; cook, stirring occasionally, for 7 minutes. Add shrimp mixture, tomato and pepper; cook, stirring often, for 5 minutes or until shrimp are pink, firm and opaque.

Tips

Rinse shrimp thoroughly under cold water before cooking, to remove as much salt as possible, especially if frozen. Be sure to drain well and pat dry before seasoning.

When purchasing Caribbean curry powder, always read the label to ensure there is no salt added.

The key to this dish is to cook the onion and curry powder well to reduce the raw taste of each and develop their flavors.

Nutrition info per serving

Calories	129
Fat, total	3 g
Fat, saturated	0.5 g
Cholesterol	257 mg
Sodium	443 mg
Carbohydrate	4 g
Fiber	2 g
Protein	22 g

Food Choices

3	Meat & Alternatives
1/2	Fat

Trinidadian Stewed Fish

Makes 5 servings

King mackerel (also called kingfish) is used a lot in Caribbean and South Asian cooking. It is very high in heart-healthy omega-3 fatty acids — even higher than salmon. Traditionally, this dish is made with butter or margarine, but I've used vegetable oil to reduce the fat content.

Nutrition info per serving

Calories	139
Fat, total	5 g
Fat, saturated	0.6 g
Cholesterol	48
Sodium	*618 mg
Carbohydrate	5 g
Fiber	1 g
Protein	19 g

* This recipe is high in sodium. Balance it out by making lower-sodium choices for the rest of your meal and throughout the day.

Food Choices

2	Meat & Alternatives
½	Fat
1	Extra

Preparation time: **35 minutes**
Cooking time: **35 minutes**

1 lb	skinless king mackerel fillet, rinsed and cut into 1-inch (2.5 cm) pieces	500 g
1 cup	water	250 mL
¼ cup	freshly squeezed lime juice	60 mL
1 tbsp	Trinidadian Green Seasoning (page 241)	15 mL
2 tsp	minced garlic	10 mL
1 tsp	salt	5 mL
½ tsp	freshly ground black pepper	2 mL

Stew

1 tbsp	vegetable oil, divided	15 mL
¼ cup	finely chopped onion	60 mL
¼ cup	coarsely chopped celery	60 mL
¼ cup	coarsely chopped red bell pepper	60 mL
1 tsp	chopped seeded Scotch bonnet chile pepper (optional)	5 mL
4	sprigs fresh thyme leaves (see tip, opposite), chopped	4
1	medium tomato, chopped	1
1 cup	water	250 mL
½ tsp	browning sauce	2 mL
½ tsp	freshly squeezed lime juice	2 mL

1. Place fish in a bowl with water and lime juice. Stir gently, being careful not to break the fish. Drain off liquid and return fish to bowl. Add green seasoning, garlic, salt and pepper and stir gently to coat fish evenly with seasoning. Let stand at room temperature for 20 minutes.

2. *Stew:* In a large skillet, heat half the oil over high heat. Add fish and cook, turning once, for about 1 minute per side or until browned on both sides. Transfer fish to a plate.

3. Add the remaining oil to the pan and heat over medium heat. Add onion and cook, stirring, for 2 minutes. Add celery, red pepper, Scotch bonnet and thyme; cook, stirring, for 2 minutes. Add tomatoes and cook, stirring, for 3 minutes or until onions are light golden and celery and red pepper remain crisp.

Make It a Meal

1 serving Trinidadian Stewed Fish

1 serving Bora Beans (page 211)

⅔ cup (150 mL) unsalted cooked long-grain brown rice (2 Carbohydrate)

½ cup (125 mL) Ginger Beer (page 243)

½ medium mango (1 Carbohydrate)

4. Stir in water and browning sauce, scraping up any browned bits from the bottom of the pan, and bring to a boil over high heat. Reduce heat and simmer for about 15 minutes or until sauce is thickened.

5. Return fish to pan, along with any accumulated juices, increase heat to medium and simmer for 8 minutes or until fish is opaque and flakes easily when tested with a fork. Drizzle with lime juice and serve immediately.

Tips

Be careful not to fry fish for very long on high heat, or to overcook it, as that could lead to a loss of its omega-3 fatty acids. Some studies suggest that omega-3s are sensitive to air, light and heat.

Eat only small portions of king mackerel, and don't eat it very often, as it is high in mercury. Women of childbearing age, pregnant women and children should not eat king mackerel.

If you prefer, you can omit the browning sauce without affecting the flavor or appearance of the dish.

If you prefer more heat, add more Scotch bonnet pepper and/ or leave the seeds in.

For a more authentic flavor, look for Caribbean thyme at a Caribbean grocery store. Every variety of thyme has a slightly different flavor, and Jamaican thyme in particular tends to be more pungent than North American thyme, so add a bit less of it to your recipes.

Nutrition Tip

Fish is a great source of omega-3 fatty acids, a polyunsaturated fat that is lacking in many North American diets. Fatty fish contain a form of omega-3 that is great for the heart. Although research is inconclusive about omega-3 lowering blood glucose, in the form of fish oil supplements it has been shown to reduce triglycerides. North American health authorities recommend eating at least two servings (each 2½ oz/75 g) of fish per week, but more is encouraged, especially for people with diabetes.

Jamaican Stuffed Steamed Fish

Makes 4 servings

Traditionally, this recipe is prepared with a whole red snapper, which is scaled and gutted, then stuffed. Since whole red snapper can sometimes be difficult to come by, I used two fillets instead. Use the freshest fish you can find, for the best flavor.

Preparation time: **10 minutes**
Cooking time: **50 minutes**

• **Preheat oven to 350°F (180°C)**

2	red snapper fillets (each 8 oz/250 g), rinsed	2
1	lemon wedge	1
1 ½ tsp	vegetable oil	7 mL
1	small onion, finely chopped	1
1	small tomato, finely chopped	1
¼ cup	frozen chopped okra, thawed and drained	60 mL
¼ cup	frozen chopped spinach, thawed and drained	60 mL
½ tsp	salt	2 mL
1	banana leaf (optional)	1
1	lemon, cut into wedges (optional)	1

1. Rub both sides of the fish fillets with the lemon wedge. Discard the lemon wedge.

2. In a medium skillet, heat oil over medium heat. Add onion and cook, stirring, for about 5 minutes or until lightly browned. Add tomato and cook, stirring, for 3 minutes. Add okra and cook, stirring, for 3 minutes. Add spinach and salt; cook, stirring, for 5 to 6 minutes or until vegetables are softened and liquid has evaporated.

3. Spread some of the vegetable mixture between the two fillets, with the skin side out (like making a sandwich), then wrap in a banana leaf and/or foil. If using a banana leaf, wrap fish in the banana leaf first, then wrap in foil. Tuck in the ends of the foil to seal the package and place on a baking sheet. Wrap the remaining vegetable mixture in foil and set aside.

4. Bake fish in preheated oven for 30 minutes. Carefully unwrap a small section at the thickest part of the fillet (steam is hot) and check for doneness; the fish should flake easily with a fork. If not cooked, rewrap and bake longer, checking every 5 minutes. When the fish has cooked for 15 minutes, add the packet of vegetables to the oven to reheat.

5. Serve the fish with the vegetable mixture and lemon wedges (if using) on the side.

Nutrition info per serving

Calories	145
Fat, total	4 g
Fat, saturated	1.0 g
Cholesterol	57 mg
Sodium	375 mg
Carbohydrate	4 g
Fiber	1 g
Protein	24 g

Food Choices

3	Meat & Alternatives
½	Fat

Tips

The leaves of the banana plant are visually interesting and impart a delicate flavor and aroma. They can be used to wrap any type of food before cooking in the oven, grilling on the barbecue or even steaming. Look for them in the fresh or frozen section of Caribbean or Asian grocery stores.

If you cannot find red snapper fillets, use another type of fish, such as tilapia. If fresh fish is not an option, use frozen and thaw the fillets overnight in the refrigerator or according to package directions.

This dish is traditionally eaten on its own, with no side dish other than the stuffing. I recommend adding a side of brown rice, for a more balanced meal.

Nutrition Tip

Spinach is an excellent source of vitamin A, vitamin K, iron and folate. It is also a source of fiber. Okra is a good source of soluble fiber, which has been shown to lower low-density lipoprotein (LDL) blood cholesterol and blood glucose levels.

Caribbean Mango Chutney

Green mangos add
a tangy flavor to this
chutney. The small
mangos are tart because
they are harvested when
they are immature. As
a result, they never
ripen to become sweet,
which makes them
great for chutneys,
jams and sauces.

Preparation time: **25 minutes**

2	small green chile peppers (or ½ Scotch bonnet chile pepper), minced	2
2	cloves garlic, minced	2
¼ tsp	salt	1 mL
2	green mangos	2
2 tbsp	finely chopped fresh cilantro (or 3 chadon beni leaves, crushed)	30 mL
2 tbsp	freshly squeezed lime juice	30 mL

1. In a medium bowl, combine chiles, garlic and salt.

2. Using a sharp knife or vegetable peeler, remove skin from mangos. Grate one mango on the coarse side of a cheese grater and cut the other one into ½-inch (1 cm) cubes.

3. Add grated and cubed mangos to the chile mixture. Stir in cilantro and lime juice.

Tips

If you are unable to find green mangos, a firm just-ripe yellow mango will work, but the chutney will be sweeter and less tangy.

Authentic Caribbean mango chutney is made with chadon beni leaves, but this herb can be difficult to find in North America. Look for it at Caribbean grocery stores, but if you can't find it, cilantro is a more than adequate replacement.

Nutrition info per serving	
Calories	25
Fat, total	0 g
Fat, saturated	0.0 g
Cholesterol	0 mg
Sodium	33 mg
Carbohydrate	6 g
Fiber	1 g
Protein	0 g
Food Choices	
1	Extra

Trinidadian Green Seasoning

Makes 11 servings

Green seasoning makes everything taste better! A terrific cook from Trinidad showed me how to make it, and I just had to share the recipe. This herb and vegetable mixture is added to stews and is used to marinate meats in many Caribbean dishes, especially in Trinidad. It is even sometimes used as a condiment (see tip, below).

Preparation time: **20 minutes**

• **Small food processor or mini chopper**

4	pimento peppers, seeded	4
2	bunches green onions (about 10), chopped	2
¼	Scotch bonnet chile pepper, seeded and chopped	¼
3 cups	chopped fresh parsley	750 mL
1 cup	chopped chadon beni leaves	250 mL
½ cup	chopped celery	125 mL
1 tbsp	chopped fresh thyme (see tip, page 237)	15 mL
1 tsp	minced gingerroot	5 mL
1 tbsp	water	15 mL

1. In food processor, combine pimentos, green onions, Scotch bonnet, parsley, chadon beni, celery, thyme, ginger and water; process until mixture reaches a fine consistency.

2. Store in a bottle or jar in the refrigerator for up to 1 month or in small airtight containers in the freezer for up to 6 months.

Tips

If you plan to use green seasoning as a condiment, add ¼ small onion and 2 cloves garlic to the food processor.

Pimento peppers (also known as pimientos, cherry peppers and heart-shaped peppers) are bright red chile peppers that are very aromatic and have a sweet flavor with a very mild heat. They are the peppers that are dried and ground to make paprika.

Chadon Beni

Chadon beni, also called shado beni or culantro, is a plant with spiny leaves and a pungent flavor found across the Caribbean. It is especially common in recipes from Trinidad and Tobago. Look for it at Caribbean grocery stores. If you cannot find chadon beni, cilantro is a good substitute in most recipes. To store chadon beni, wrap it in a damp towel and put it in the fridge so it does not dry out.

Nutrition info per serving	
Calories	10
Fat, total	0 g
Fat, saturated	0.0 mg
Cholesterol	0 mg
Sodium	14 mg
Carbohydrate	2 g
Fiber	1 g
Protein	1 g
Food Choices	
1	Extra

Sorrel Drink

The flower of the sorrel plant is used to make this vibrant red drink, consumed at Christmastime in Jamaica. This recipe uses far less sugar than the original, but has added sweetener to provide sweetness with fewer carbohydrates. So feel free to enjoy this sweet-tart drink any time of year.

Preparation time: **10 minutes**
Cooking time: **40 minutes**
Steeping time: **4 hours or overnight**

2	5-inch (12.5 cm) pieces gingerroot (about 3 oz/90 g), peeled and cut in half	2
12 cups	water	3 L
4 cups	dried sorrel	1 L
24	whole cloves	24
1/2 cup	granulated sugar	125 mL
8	packets (each 1 g) sucralose sweetener (see tip, below)	8

1. Smash ginger with a hard object, such as a mallet, the bottom of a saucepan or the broad side of a chef's knife, to soften so it can impart flavor.

2. In a large pot, bring water to a boil over high heat. Add ginger and sorrel; reduce heat to medium, cover and simmer for 30 minutes.

3. Add cloves, cover and turn off heat. Let stand at room temperature for at least 4 hours or overnight to steep. (If a less tart flavor is preferred, steep for 3 to 4 hours.)

4. Strain the sorrel mixture into a pitcher and discard the solids. Stir in sugar and sweetener. Refrigerate and serve cold.

Tips

Dried sorrel is available year-round and provides better flavor and color than fresh (which is usually only available around Christmas).

This drink has added sugar and sucralose to counteract the tartness of the sorrel and ginger. Do not add any more sugar, as that will increase the carbohydrate. If you find this drink too bitter, you can add a bit more sucralose. Alternatively, reduce the steeping time to 3 hours.

Be careful which sweetener you use, as some may have added sugar. If using a sweetener other than sucralose, check the label and use enough sweetener to equal the sweetening power of 16 tsp (80 mL) sugar.

Nutrition info per 1 cup (250 mL)	
Calories	46
Fat, total	0 g
Fat, saturated	0.0 g
Cholesterol	0 mg
Sodium	10 mg
Carbohydrate	12 g
Fiber	0 g
Protein	0 g
Food Choices	
1	Carbohydrate

Ginger Beer

This drink, with its strong ginger flavor, is popular during the Christmas holidays in the Caribbean, and especially in Jamaica. Cream of tartar is often added to add carbonation to the drink.

Preparation time: **10 minutes**
Cooking time: **35 minutes**
Steeping time: **4 hours or overnight**

1 lb	gingerroot (approx.), peeled and cut in half	500 g
8 cups	water (approx.)	2 L
8 oz	pineapple rind	250 g
6 tbsp	granulated sugar	90 mL
1 tbsp	freshly squeezed lime juice	15 mL

1. Smash ginger with a hard object, such as a mallet, the bottom of a saucepan or the broad side of a chef's knife, to soften so it can impart flavor.

2. In a large pot, bring water to a boil over high heat. Add ginger, cover and boil for 15 minutes. Add pineapple rind, cover and boil for 5 minutes. Taste and add more water or ginger as desired. Remove from heat and let stand, covered, at room temperature for 4 hours to steep. Taste and, if a stronger flavor is desired, refrigerate and continue to steep until desired flavor is achieved or overnight.

3. Strain the ginger mixture into a pitcher and discard solids. Stir in sugar and lime juice Refrigerate and serve cold.

Tips

This amount of ginger provides an intense ginger flavor. For a milder flavor, use 8 oz (250 g) ginger.

Traditionally, ginger beer is steeped overnight, but since this recipe has two-thirds less sugar than the original, you may wish to stop after 4 hours of steeping.

Caribbean ginger is smaller, harder and more pungent than varieties grown in North America or Asia. However, it may be difficult to find. If using Caribbean ginger, you may want to use less (8 oz/250 g) in this recipe.

The carbonated ginger beer available on the market does not have the health benefits of real ginger and can be higher in sugar and/or sodium.

Nutrition info per 1 cup (250 mL)

Calories	49
Fat, total	0 g
Fat, saturated	0.0 g
Cholesterol	0 mg
Sodium	12 mg
Carbohydrate	13 g
Fiber	0 g
Protein	0 g

Food Choices

1	Carbohydrate

Soursop Juice

Soursop is a large, oval, prickly green fruit with white pulp and black seeds. Its flavor has been described as a combination of strawberry and pineapple. Traditionally, soursop juice is made with condensed milk for a thick consistency, but I've substituted evaporated fat-free milk for a more favorable fat and sugar profile.

Preparation time: **15 minutes**

- **Blender**

1	medium soursop, peeled, cut into large chunks and seeded	1
2 tbsp	granulated sugar	30 mL
1/2 tsp	ground nutmeg	2 mL
2 cups	water	500 mL
1/2 cup	evaporated fat-free milk	125 mL
1/2 tsp	freshly squeezed lime juice (optional)	2 mL
1 tsp	vanilla extract (optional)	5 mL

1. In blender, combine soursop, sugar, nutmeg, water and milk; blend until smooth.
2. Transfer to a pitcher and stir in lime juice and vanilla (if using). Refrigerate and serve cold.

Tips

Make sure to remove all the seeds from fresh soursop, as they are indigestible and give the drink a bitter flavor.

If fresh soursop is not available, substitute 2 pears. Avoid using canned soursop pulp, as it is sweetened and will increase the carbohydrate content. (Store-bought soursop juice is also sweetened and can have up to 34 g of carbohydrate in 1 cup/250 mL.)

You can substitute skim milk for the evaporated milk. The drink won't be as thick, but it will have less carbohydrate.

Lime juice provides a refreshing flavor, but is not a necessary addition to the recipe.

Nutrition info per 1 cup (250 mL)

Calories	102
Fat, total	1 g
Fat, saturated	0.2 g
Cholesterol	1 mg
Sodium	40 mg
Carbohydrate	23 g
Fiber	3 g
Protein	3 g

Food Choices

1	Carbohydrate

Homemade Vegetable Stock

**Makes
8 cups (2 L)**

Although there are now many sodium-reduced and no-salt-added ready-to-use broths available in stores, it is still worthwhile to make your own stock when you can. Homemade stocks have much more flavor, fewer additives and less added sugar and fat, and about the same amount of sodium as no-salt-added brands.

Preparation time: 40 minutes
Cooking time: 3½ hours

4	large carrots, cut into 3-inch (7.5 cm) pieces	4
4	stalks celery, cut into 3-inch (7.5 cm) pieces	4
2	sweet potatoes (about 3 lbs/1.5 kg total), peeled and each cut into 8 pieces	2
2	medium plum (Roma) tomatoes, cut in half	2
2	small onions (unpeeled)	2
1	butternut squash, coarsely chopped	1
1	large head garlic (unpeeled), cut in half widthwise	1
½	large cabbage, cut into 4 pieces	½
½	large green bell pepper	½
½	large red bell pepper	½
22	sprigs fresh parsley	22
12	whole cloves	12
12	whole black peppercorns	12
4	bay leaves	4
2	sprigs fresh thyme	2
16 cups	water	4 L

1. In a large, deep pot, combine carrots, celery, sweet potatoes, tomatoes, onions, squash, garlic, cabbage, green pepper, red pepper, parsley, cloves, peppercorns, bay leaves, thyme and water. Bring to a boil over high heat. Reduce heat and simmer gently for 2½ hours.

2. Strain stock through a fine sieve, discarding solids, and return stock to the pot. Bring to a boil over high heat. Reduce heat and boil gently for 30 minutes or until reduced to 8 cups (2 L) and the flavor is concentrated.

Tips

Sweet potatoes add a sweet flavor to this stock; omit them if you prefer.

To store stock, immediately divide it among small airtight containers, then chill them in a sink of ice water, refreshing the water often to keep it cold. When the stock is cool, refrigerate it for up to 4 days or freeze it for up to 3 months. Thaw overnight in the refrigerator before use.

Nutrition info per ½ cup (125 mL)	
Calories	9
Fat, total	0 g
Fat, saturated	0.0 g
Cholesterol	0 mg
Sodium	27 mg
Carbohydrate	2 g
Fiber	0 g
Protein	1 g
Food Choices	
1	Extra

Homemade Chicken Stock

**Makes
7 cups (1.75 L)**

Making your own stock does take a bit of time, but the results are well worth it, and you can make a big batch all at once and freeze it in single-use portions for future recipes.

Tip

To store stock, immediately divide it among small airtight containers, then chill them in a sink of ice water, refreshing the water often to keep it cold. When the stock is cool, refrigerate it for up to 4 days or freeze it for up to 3 months. Thaw overnight in the refrigerator before use.

Nutrition info per ½ cup (125 mL)

Calories	2
Fat, total	0 g
Fat, saturated	0.0 g
Cholesterol	0 mg
Sodium	42 mg
Carbohydrate	1 g
Fiber	0 g
Protein	0 g

Food Choices

1	Extra

Preparation time: 40 minutes
Cooking time: 3 hours

8	bone-in skinless chicken drumsticks (about 28 oz/800 g total)	8
4	stalks celery, cut into 3-inch (7.5 cm) pieces	4
2	large carrots, cut into 3-inch (7.5 cm) pieces	2
2	plum (Roma) tomatoes, cut in half	2
2	small onions (unpeeled)	2
1	small head garlic (unpeeled), cut in half widthwise	1
38	sprigs fresh parsley	38
12	whole cloves	12
12	whole black peppercorns	12
4	bay leaves	4
12 cups	water	3 L

1. In a large, deep pot, combine chicken, celery, carrots, tomatoes, onions, garlic, parsley, cloves, peppercorns, bay leaves and water. Bring to a boil over high heat. Reduce heat and simmer gently for 45 minutes.

2. While the stock continues to simmer, transfer chicken to a bowl. Let cool slightly, then remove meat from bones. Place meat in an airtight container and refrigerate for up to 3 days for use in other recipes.

3. Return bones to stock and simmer gently for 1 hour.

4. Strain stock through a fine sieve, discarding solids, and return stock to the pot. Bring to a boil over high heat. Reduce heat and boil gently for 30 minutes or until reduced to 7 cups (1.75 L) and the flavor is concentrated.

5. Transfer stock to a large bowl and let cool. Cover and refrigerate until chilled. Skim off fat.

Tips

If you prefer, you can use 28 oz (800 g) skinless chicken wings instead of drumsticks.

When cooking a meat stock, make sure the temperature of the stock remains above 165°F (74°C) to prevent the growth of bacteria. Periodically test the temperature of the stock with an instant-read thermometer and, if necessary, increase the heat.

About the Nutrient Analyses

The nutrient analysis done on the recipes in this book was derived from the Genesis R&D Product Development and Nutrition Label Software, version 9.11 (ESHA Research). Where necessary, data was supplemented using USDA National Nutrient Database for Standard Reference, Release #26 (2014), the Canadian Nutrient File (version 2010), restaurant data and manufacturer data. Recipes were evaluated as follows:

- Where alternatives are given, the first ingredient and amount listed were used.
- Optional ingredients and ingredients that are not quantified were not included.
- The smaller quantity of an ingredient was used where a range is provided.
- Calculations involving meat and poultry used trimmed lean portions.
- Fish, seafood and canned legumes were rinsed well.
- Canola oil was used where the type of fat was not specified.
- Nutrient values were rounded to the nearest whole number, except for saturated fat, which was rounded to one decimal point.

It is important to note that the cooking method used to prepare the recipe may alter the nutrient content per serving, as may ingredient substitutions and differences among brand-name products.

About the Food Choices

The Food Choices assigned to the recipes were based on nutrient values per choice and choice portion sizes published by the Canadian Diabetes Association.

Food Choice Values

Food Choice	Available Carbohydrate	Protein	Fat
Carbohydrate			
Grains and Starches	15 g	3 g	0 g
Fruits	15 g	1 g	0 g
Milk and Alternatives Low-Fat Fat-Free	 15 g 15 g	 8 g 8 g	 2.5 g 0 g
Other Choices	15 g	variable	variable
Vegetables	<5 g (most) Not usually counted in Carbohydrate Choices	2 g	0 g
Meat and Alternatives	0 g	7 g	3–5 g
Fats	0 g	0 g	5 g

Adapted from: Canadian Diabetes Association, *Beyond the Basics: Meal Planning for Healthy Eating, Diabetes Prevention and Management.* December 20, 2005, Version 2.

- Carbohydrate Choices were based on available carbohydrate from grains and starches, legumes, fruit, milk and added sugar (i.e., total carbohydrate less fiber from these ingredients). Carbohydrate and fiber from vegetables were not considered in assigning Carbohydrate Choices unless they contributed more than 15 g of available carbohydrate per serving.

- Meat & Alternatives Choices were based on 1 oz (30 g) of cooked meat, fish or poultry, or the quantity of legumes or other meat alternatives that provides approximately 7 g of protein. Four ounces (125 g) of lean raw meat yields about 3 oz (90 g) cooked. Protein from milk, vegetables and grains was not included in Meat & Alternatives Choices.

- Fat Choices were based on total fat (excluding trivial amounts), less 3 grams per Meat & Alternatives Choice.

References

1. Canadian Diabetes Association. 2013. "Helpful Hints for Educators Using *Beyond the Basics: Meal Planning for Healthy Eating, Diabetes Prevention and Management.*" Accessed February 2014 from http://www.diabetes.ca/CDA/media/documents/clinical-practice-and-education/professional-resources/beyond-the-basics-helpful-hints-for-educators.pdf.

2. Canadian Diabetes Association. 2007 (manual); 2005 (poster). *Beyond the Basics: Meal Planning for Healthy Eating, Diabetes Prevention and Management.*

3. Canadian Diabetes Association. 2005. "Revised Longer Lists of Foods to Be Used with the *Beyond the Basics: Meal Planning for Healthy Eating, Diabetes Prevention and Management* — Version 2." Accessed February 2014 from http://www.ffhc.ca/pdf/diabetes/diabetes-long-list.pdf.

Library and Archives Canada Cataloguing in Publication

Khan, Sobia, author
    150 best Indian, Asian, Caribbean and more diabetes recipes / Sobia Khan, MSc, RD.

Includes index.
ISBN 978-0-7788-0495-6 (pbk.).—ISBN 978-0-7788-0491-8 (US : pbk.)

    1. Diabetes—Diet therapy—Recipes. 2. International cooking. 3. Cookbooks.
I. Title. II. Title: One hundred fifty best Indian, Asian, Caribbean and more diabetes recipes.

RC662.K43 2014   641.5'6314   C2014-904424-0

Index

A

allspice, 23
Andalusian Meatballs with Spanish
　Saffron Sauce, 177
anise seeds, 19
annatto (achiote) seeds, 19
　Hakka Chicken Curry, 136
Argentinean Chimichurri, 194
Argentinean Meat Empanadas, 162
asafetida (hing), 15
　Spicy South Indian Soup, 26
Asian Pear Drink, 145

B

Baby Bok Choy and Mushrooms
　with Oyster Sauce, 107
Balsam Pear, Sautéed Chicken with
　Onions and, 130
bamboo shoots, 108
　Bamboo Shoots with Mushrooms,
　108
　Crispy Tofu with Vegetables,
　118
　Hakka Bamboo Shoot Dumplings,
　102
　Hakka Braised Duck with Lily
　Flower, 140
　Kung Pao Chicken, 134
　Sichuan Vegetarian Hot-and-Sour
　Soup, 98
　Stir-Fried Mixed Vegetables, 110
　Vegetarian Tofu Rolls, 104
Bammy, Jamaican Cocktail, 209
Bangladesh. See South Asian cuisine
Barley Soup, Guyanese, 203
beans. See also bean sprouts; peas
　Bora Beans, 211
　Catalan Beef Stew, 176
　Hakka Chicken Curry, 136
　Jamaican Stewed Peas, 206
　Kidney Bean Curry, 53
　Mexican Black Bean Soup, 152
　Mexican Pot Beans, 171
　Mexican Vegetarian Stew in a Pot,
　168
　South Indian Dhokla, 38
　Spanish Sausage and Bean Soup,
　155
　Sri Lankan Red Rice Congee, 59
　Vegetable and Cheese Curry, 56
bean sprouts
　Hakka Stir-Fried Soybean Sprouts,
　109
　Vegetarian Tofu Rolls, 104
　Wonton Soup, 96
beef
　Andalusian Meatballs with
　Spanish Saffron Sauce, 177

Argentinean Meat Empanadas,
　162
　Beef and Potato Stir-Fry, 175
　Catalan Beef Stew, 176
　Easy Pakistani Veal Stew (tip), 66
　Guyanese Pepperpot, 224
　Jamaican Stewed Peas, 206
　Segovia-Style Lamb, 178
　Sichuan Beef Stir-Fry, 124
　Stir-Fried Lamb with Scallions
　(variation), 126
Bengal gram. See chickpeas
Bengali Fish Curry, 82
Bengali Yellow Lentil Curry, 50
besan flour. See chickpea flour
beverages
　Caribbean, 242–44
　Chinese, 145–47
　Hispanic, 198–200
　South Asian, 92–93
bitter melon (karawila), 47
　Sri Lankan Bitter Melon Curry, 46
bitter melon, Chinese, 131
　Sautéed Chicken with Onions and
　Balsam Pear, 130
Black Fungus, Braised Seitan with
　Peanuts and, 122
black gram (kala chana), 51
blood pressure, 11
bok choy. See also cabbage
　Baby Bok Choy and Mushrooms
　with Oyster Sauce, 107
　Crispy Tofu with Vegetables, 118
　Wonton Soup, 96
Bora Beans, 211
broccoli
　Cantonese Mushroom, Vegetable
　and Scallop Stir-Fry, 142
　Wonton Soup, 96
browning sauce, 23
Butter Chicken, 74

C

cabbage. See also bok choy
　Caribbean Pumpkin Soup, 202
　Hakka Chicken Bao, 138
　Homemade Vegetable Stock, 245
　Potato and Pea Samosas, 36
　Punjabi Lachha Salad, 30
　Sichuan Vegetarian Hot-and-Sour
　Soup, 98
　Stir-Fried Mixed Vegetables, 110
　Vegetable and Cheese Curry, 56
Cactus Salad, 156
callaloo (dasheen), 205
　Callaloo, 204
callaloo (Jamaican), 205
　Jamaican Callaloo Fritters, 208

canela cinnamon, 21
Cantonese dishes
　Cantonese Fried Shrimp with
　Cashews and Cucumber, 144
　Cantonese Mushroom, Vegetable
　and Scallop Stir-Fry, 142
　Chayote Salad, 100
　Chicken Corn Soup, 97
　Crispy Tofu with Vegetables, 118
　Wonton Soup, 96
caraway seeds (shahi jeera), 15
carbohydrates, 9
cardamom (elaichi), 15
Caribbean cuisine, 201–44. See also
　Guyanese dishes; Jamaican
　dishes; Trinidadian dishes
　ingredients, 23
　Caribbean Mango Chutney, 240
　Caribbean Peas and Rice, 220
　Caribbean Pumpkin Soup, 202
　Cou Cou, 214
　Ginger Beer, 243
　Soursop Juice, 244
carom seeds (ajwain), 15
　Fish Amritsari, 42
　Zucchini Curry, 49
carrots. See vegetables
cashews
　Cantonese Fried Shrimp with
　Cashews and Cucumber, 144
　Hakka Chicken Curry, 136
cassareep, 23
　Guyanese Pepperpot, 224
cassia cinnamon (dalchini), 16, 19
Catalan Beef Stew, 176
cauliflower
　Pakistani Potatoes and Cauliflower,
　58
　Potato and Pea Samosas, 36
　Split Yellow Pigeon Pea Soup, 28
celery. See also vegetables
　Kung Pao Chicken, 134
　Trinidadian Green Seasoning, 241
chaat masala, 16
　Chickpea and Potato Snack, 33
　Fish Amritsari, 42
　Punjabi Lachha Salad, 30
chadon beni leaves, 241
　Caribbean Mango Chutney, 240
　Trinidadian Green Seasoning,
　241
chayote
　Chayote Salad, 100
　Mexican Vegetarian Stew in a Pot,
　168
cheese, 11
　Cactus Salad, 156
　Mexican Green Chilaquiles, 180

Peruvian Mushroom and Spinach Empanadas, 160
Peruvian Potato Cheese Soup, 151
Spanish Piquillo Peppers Stuffed with Piperade, 166
Vegetable and Cheese Curry, 56
chicken
Butter Chicken, 74
Chicken Corn Soup, 97
Guyanese Chicken Chow Mein, 232
Guyanese Chicken Curry, 234
Hakka Bamboo Shoot Dumplings, 102
Hakka Chicken Bao, 138
Hakka Chicken Curry, 136
Homemade Chicken Stock, 246
Homemade Wontons, 101
Hot-and-Spicy Chicken, 132
Jamaican Fricassee Chicken, 230
Jerk Chicken, 229
Kung Pao Chicken, 134
Mexican Green Chilaquiles, 180
Pakistani Chicken Pilaf, 78
Pakistani Chicken Stew, 76
Pakistani Oven-Baked Shami Kebabs, 40
Sautéed Chicken with Onions and Balsam Pear, 130
Stir-Fried Lamb with Scallions (variation), 126
Tofu with Spicy Meat and Vegetables, 129
chickpea flour (besan)
Fish Amritsari, 42
Whole Wheat and Besan Flatbread, 32
chickpeas (*chana dal*). *See also* chickpea flour
Bengali Yellow Lentil Curry, 50
Chickpea and Potato Snack, 33
Chickpea Rice, 62
Pakistani Oven-Baked Shami Kebabs, 40
Tomato Mint Salad, 31
Trinidadian Curried Chickpeas, 217
Chilean Fish Escabeche, 184
chile bean paste, 19
Ma-Po Tofu with Pork, 128
Sichuan Vegetarian Ma-Po Tofu, 120
Chimichurri, Argentinean, 194
Chinese bitter melon. *See* bitter melon, Chinese
Chinese cuisine, 96–147. *See also* Cantonese dishes; Hakka dishes; Sichuan dishes
ingredients, 19–21
Cantonese Fried Shrimp with Cashews and Cucumber, 144
Cantonese Mushroom, Vegetable and Scallop Stir-Fry, 142

Chinese five-spice powder, 19
Chinese Tea Eggs, 106
chives, 115
Callaloo, 204
Hakka Choi Bo and Chives Omelet, 114
cholesterol, 9, 10
chutneys, 88–90, 240
cilantro, 16. *See also* coriander seed
Cactus Salad, 156
Caribbean Mango Chutney, 240
Cilantro Mint Chutney, 88
Mexican Green Chilaquiles, 180
Mexican Spicy Green Sauce, 192
Mexican Spicy Tomato Salsa, 190
Okra and Tomato Curry, 48
Peruvian Ceviche, 183
Peruvian Hot Sauce (variation), 193
Savory South Indian Semolina Cakes, 64
Whole Wheat and Besan Flatbread, 32
cinnamon, 16, 19, 21
cloud ear. *See* black fungus
coconut, 11. *See also* coconut milk
Bengali Yellow Lentil Curry, 50
Coconut Chutney, 89
Colombian Rice with Coconut, 174
coconut milk
Callaloo, 204
Caribbean Peas and Rice, 220
Colombian Rice with Coconut, 174
Goan Fish Curry, 80
Guyanese Cook-Up Rice, 219
Jamaican Cocktail Bammy, 209
South Indian Coconut Shrimp Curry, 83
Sri Lankan Eggplant Curry, 45
Cold Melon Cucumber Soup, 150
Colombian Rice with Coconut, 174
condiments, 12
Caribbean, 240–41
South Asian, 88–91
cooking methods, 11
cooking oils, 10
coriander seed (*sabut dhania*), 16. *See also* cilantro
Pakistani Chicken Stew, 76
Spinach and Tofu Curry, 54
corn. *See also* cornmeal/corn flour
Chicken Corn Soup, 97
Mexican Vegetarian Stew in a Pot, 168
Peruvian Purple Corn Drink, 198
cornmeal/corn flour
Corn Tortillas, 159
Cou Cou, 214
Fried Okra, 210
Crispy Tofu with Vegetables, 118

cucumber
Cantonese Fried Shrimp with Cashews and Cucumber, 144
Cold Melon Cucumber Soup, 150
Cucumber Yogurt, 86
Mixed Vegetable Yogurt, 87
Punjabi Lachha Salad, 30
Sichuan Noodles, 112
Stir-Fried Mixed Vegetables, 110
Tomato Mint Salad, 31
culantro. *See* chadon beni leaves
cumin seeds (*jeera*), 16
curry leaves (*kari patta*), 16–17
Coconut Chutney, 89
Hakka Chicken Curry, 136
Spicy South Indian Soup, 26
Sri Lankan Bitter Melon Curry, 46
Sri Lankan Eggplant Curry, 45
curry powders, 17, 23
Guyanese Chicken Curry, 234
Hakka Chicken Curry, 136
Jamaican Curried Goat, 226
Sri Lankan Eggplant Curry, 45
Trinidadian Curried Chickpeas, 217
Trinidadian Curried Pigeon Peas, 218
Trinidadian Shrimp Curry, 235

D

dairy products, 11, 13. *See also* cheese; milk and cream; yogurt
dasheen. *See* callaloo
dates
Pakistani Sweet Tamarind Chutney, 90
Red Date, Longan and Ginger Tea, 147
daylily flowers (dried), 123
Braised Seitan with Peanuts and Black Fungus, 122
Hakka Braised Duck with Lily Flower, 140
desserts, 9, 10
diabetes, 7–8
diet, 13–14
and diabetes, 8
fats in, 10–11
fiber in, 9–10
healthy, 8–12
nutrient balance in, 13
portion control, 13–14
drumstick leaves, 59
Sri Lankan Red Rice Congee, 59
Duck with Lily Flower, Hakka Braised, 140
Dumplings, Hakka Bamboo Shoot, 102

E

Easy Pakistani Veal Stew, 66
eggplant
Braised Tofu and Eggplant, 116

eggplant *(continued)*
    Guyanese Roasted Eggplant Curry, 222
    Mushroom Pinchos, 164
    Spanish Ratatouille, 165
    Sri Lankan Eggplant Curry, 45
eggs
    Argentinean Meat Empanadas, 162
    Chicken Corn Soup, 97
    Chinese Tea Eggs, 106
    Fried Okra, 210
    Hakka Choi Bo and Chives Omelet, 114
    Spanish Potato Omelet, 172
    Steamed Egg with Ground Pork, 127
epazote, 22
    Mexican Black Bean Soup, 152
    Mexican Green Chilaquiles, 180
    Mexican Vegetarian Stew in a Pot, 168

F

fats (dietary), 10–11
fennel seeds *(saunf)*, 17
fenugreek *(methi)*, 17, 75
    Butter Chicken, 74
    Spinach and Tofu Curry, 54
fiber, 9–10
fish, 237. *See also* seafood
    Bengali Fish Curry, 82
    Chilean Fish Escabeche, 184
    Fish Amritsari, 42
    Goan Fish Curry , 80
    Jamaican Stuffed Steamed Fish, 238
    Peruvian Ceviche, 183
    Spanish Seafood Pasta, 188
    Trinidadian Stewed Fish, 236
    Tuna with Onions, 185
fish sauce, 20
Flatbread, Whole Wheat and Besan, 32
flavorings, 12
flours, 10
food groups, 13
fruit, 9. *See also specific fruits*
    Asian Pear Drink, 145
    Hawthorn Drink, 146
    Peruvian Purple Corn Drink, 198
    Red Date, Longan and Ginger Tea, 147

G

garam masala, 17
    Butter Chicken, 74
    homemade, 57
    Pakistani Oven-Baked Shami Kebabs, 40
    Spinach and Tofu Curry, 54
    Vegetable and Cheese Curry, 56
garlic, 85
    Argentinean Chimichurri, 194

Baby Bok Choy and Mushrooms with Oyster Sauce, 107
Caribbean Mango Chutney, 240
Cilantro Mint Chutney, 88
Guyanese Cook-Up Rice, 219
Guyanese Pepperpot, 224
Guyanese Roasted Eggplant Curry, 222
Homemade Chicken Stock, 246
Homemade Vegetable Stock, 245
Mexican Morita Chipotle Sauce, 191
Peruvian Hot Sauce, 193
Stir-Fried Lamb with Scallions, 126
ginger, 73
    Bengali Fish Curry, 82
    Chayote Salad, 100
    Chicken Corn Soup, 97
    Chickpea Rice, 62
    Chinese Tea Eggs, 106
    Coconut Chutney, 89
    Easy Pakistani Veal Stew, 66
    Fish Amritsari, 42
    Ginger Beer, 243
    Jerk Chicken, 229
    Kidney Bean Curry, 53
    Kung Pao Chicken, 134
    Pakistani Chicken Pilaf, 78
    Pakistani Oven-Baked Shami Kebabs, 40
    Pakistani Potatoes and Cauliflower, 58
    Pakistani Spicy Vegetable Rice, 60
    Peruvian Ceviche, 183
    Red Date, Longan and Ginger Tea, 147
    Sautéed Chicken with Onions and Balsam Pear, 130
    Savory South Indian Semolina Cakes, 64
    Sichuan Vegetarian Hot-and-Sour Soup, 98
    Sorrel Drink, 242
    South Indian Coconut Shrimp Curry, 83
    Spinach and Tofu Curry, 54
Goan dishes. *See also* South Asian cuisine
    Goan Fish Curry, 80
    Goan Pork Vindaloo, 70
    Goan Pork with Liver, 72
    Goan Shrimp Vindaloo, 84
Goat, Jamaican Curried, 226
golden gram. *See* beans
grains, 9, 63. *See also* rice
    Guyanese Barley Soup, 203
gram flour. *See* chickpea flour
green gram. *See* beans
Guyanese dishes. *See also* Caribbean cuisine
    Bora Beans, 211
    Guyanese Barley Soup, 203

Guyanese Chicken Chow Mein, 232
Guyanese Chicken Curry, 234
Guyanese Cook-Up Rice, 219
Guyanese Pepperpot, 224
Guyanese Roasted Eggplant Curry, 222
Guyanese Roti, 212

H

Hakka dishes. *See also* Chinese cuisine
    Hakka Bamboo Shoot Dumplings, 102
    Hakka Braised Duck with Lily Flower, 140
    Hakka Chicken Bao, 138
    Hakka Chicken Curry, 136
    Hakka Choi Bo and Chives Omelet, 114
    Hakka Stir-Fried Soybean Sprouts, 109
Ham and Rice Soup, Spanish, 154
Hawthorn Drink, 146
high blood pressure, 11
hing. See asafetida
Hispanic cuisine, 148–200
    ingredients, 21–22
hoisin sauce, 20
Homemade Chicken Stock, 246
Homemade Low-Fat Paneer, 44
Homemade Vegetable Stock, 245
Homemade Wontons, 101
Hot-and-Spicy Chicken, 132

I

Indian dishes. *See also* Goan dishes; North Indian dishes; South Asian cuisine; South Indian dishes
    Bengali Fish Curry, 82
    Bengali Yellow Lentil Curry, 50
    Punjabi Lachha Salad, 30
insulin resistance, 7

J

Jamaican dishes. *See also* Caribbean cuisine
    Ginger Beer, 243
    Jamaican Callaloo Fritters, 208
    Jamaican Cocktail Bammy, 209
    Jamaican Curried Goat, 226
    Jamaican Fricassee Chicken, 230
    Jamaican Stewed Peas, 206
    Jamaican Stuffed Steamed Fish, 238
    Jerk Chicken, 229
    Jerk Pork, 228
    Sorrel Drink, 242

K

kewra essence, 79
Kidney Bean Curry, 53
Kung Pao Chicken, 134

L

lamb
Pakistani Lamb Stew, 68
Segovia-Style Lamb, 178
Stir-Fried Lamb with Scallions, 126
leeks
Catalan Beef Stew, 176
Hakka Stir-Fried Soybean Sprouts, 109
legumes, 29, 153. *See also* beans; lentils; peas
lemongrass, 137
Hakka Chicken Curry, 136
lentils, 35, 39
Lentil and Fruit Stew, 170
Red Lentil Curry, 52
South Indian Dosas, 34
lime juice
Caribbean Mango Chutney, 240
Peruvian Ceviche, 183
Trinidadian Stewed Fish, 236
Low-Fat Paneer, Homemade, 44

M

mango powder (amchoor), 16, 18
Potato and Pea Samosas, 36
mangos
Caribbean Mango Chutney, 240
Mango Yogurt Smoothie, 92
Ma-Po Tofu with Pork, 128
marinades, 11
Masala Tea, 93
meal planning, 13, 14
meats, 11. *See also specific meats*
melon, 47, 131
Cold Melon Cucumber Soup, 150
Mexican Sweet Rice Drink, 200
Sri Lankan Bitter Melon Curry, 46
methi. See fenugreek
Mexican dishes. *See also* Hispanic cuisine
Cactus Salad, 156
Corn Tortillas, 159
Lentil and Fruit Stew, 170
Mexican Black Bean Soup, 152
Mexican Green Chilaquiles, 180
Mexican Morita Chipotle Sauce, 191
Mexican Pot Beans, 171
Mexican Spicy Green Sauce, 192
Mexican Spicy Tomato Salsa, 190
Mexican Sweet Rice Drink, 200
Mexican Vegetarian Stew in a Pot, 168
milk and cream, 13
Butter Chicken, 74
Hakka Chicken Bao, 138
Hakka Chicken Curry, 136
Homemade Low-Fat Paneer, 44
Mango Yogurt Smoothie, 92
Masala Tea, 93
Mexican Sweet Rice Drink, 200
Mushroom Pinchos, 164

Soursop Juice, 244
Sri Lankan Red Rice Congee, 59
mint (fresh)
Cilantro Mint Chutney, 88
Tomato Mint Salad, 31
Mixed Vegetable Yogurt, 87
mushrooms, 99, 105, 143. *See also* mushrooms, shiitake
Cantonese Mushroom, Vegetable and Scallop Stir-Fry, 142
Hakka Braised Duck with Lily Flower, 140
Mexican Vegetarian Stew in a Pot, 168
Mushroom Pinchos, 164
Peruvian Mushroom and Spinach Empanadas, 160
Segovia-Style Lamb, 178
Sichuan Vegetarian Hot-and-Sour Soup, 98
Vegetarian Tofu Rolls, 104
mushrooms, shiitake, 103, 111
Baby Bok Choy and Mushrooms with Oyster Sauce, 107
Bamboo Shoots with Mushrooms, 108
Braised Seitan with Peanuts and Black Fungus, 122
Crispy Tofu with Vegetables, 118
Hakka Bamboo Shoot Dumplings, 102
Hakka Braised Duck with Lily Flower, 140
Hakka Chicken Bao, 138
Sichuan Vegetarian Ma-Po Tofu, 120
Stir-Fried Mixed Vegetables, 110
Tofu with Spicy Meat and Vegetables, 129
Vegetarian Tofu Rolls, 104
mustard seeds (*rai; sarson*), 18

N

neem leaves (sweet). *See* curry leaves
nigella seeds (*kalonji*), 18
noodles and pasta, 10
Guyanese Chicken Chow Mein, 232
Pasta in Tomato Sauce with Chorizo, 182
Sichuan Noodles, 112
Spanish Seafood Pasta, 188
North Indian dishes
Butter Chicken, 74
Fish Amritsari, 42
Homemade Low-Fat Paneer, 44
Kidney Bean Curry, 53
Vegetable and Cheese Curry, 56
nuts
Braised Seitan with Peanuts and Black Fungus, 122
Chayote Salad, 100
Mexican Sweet Rice Drink, 200
Sichuan Noodles, 112

O

okra
Callaloo, 204
Cou Cou, 214
Fried Okra, 210
Goan Fish Curry, 80
Jamaican Stuffed Steamed Fish, 238
Okra and Tomato Curry, 48
olive oil, 150
olives
Andalusian Meatballs with Spanish Saffron Sauce, 177
Argentinean Meat Empanadas, 162
omega-3 fatty acids, 10
onions. *See also* onions, green
Argentinean Chimichurri, 194
Argentinean Meat Empanadas, 162
Chilean Fish Escabeche, 184
Easy Pakistani Veal Stew, 66
Goan Pork Vindaloo, 70
Goan Pork with Liver, 72
Guyanese Pepperpot, 224
Jamaican Stuffed Steamed Fish, 238
Kidney Bean Curry, 53
Mexican Spicy Tomato Salsa, 190
Okra and Tomato Curry, 48
Punjabi Lachha Salad, 30
Red Lentil Curry, 52
Spanish Tomato Sauce, 196
Tuna with Onions, 185
Zucchini Curry, 49
onions, green
Guyanese Barley Soup (variation), 203
Jerk Pork, 228
Peruvian Hot Sauce (variation), 193
Stir-Fried Lamb with Scallions, 126
Trinidadian Green Seasoning, 241
orange
Andalusian Meatballs with Spanish Saffron Sauce, 177
Asian Pear Drink, 145
Spanish Orange and Avocado Salad, 158
oyster sauce, 20
Baby Bok Choy and Mushrooms with Oyster Sauce, 107

P

Pakistani dishes. *See also* South Asian cuisine
Easy Pakistani Veal Stew, 66
Masala Tea, 93
Okra and Tomato Curry, 48
Pakistani Chicken Pilaf, 78
Pakistani Chicken Stew, 76
Pakistani Lamb Stew, 68
Pakistani Oven-Baked Shami Kebabs, 40

Pakistani dishes *(continued)*
Pakistani Potatoes and Cauliflower, 58
Pakistani Spicy Vegetable Rice, 60
Pakistani Sweet Tamarind Chutney, 90
Zucchini Curry, 49
Paneer, Homemade Low-Fat, 44
paprika (Spanish), 22
Pasta in Tomato Sauce with Chorizo, 182
Spicy Moorish Pork Kebabs, 179
parsley (fresh)
Argentinean Chimichurri, 194
Homemade Chicken Stock, 246
Spanish Tomato Sauce, 196
Trinidadian Green Seasoning, 241
pea flour, 161
peas. *See also* beans; chickpeas; peas, green
Caribbean Peas and Rice, 220
Guyanese Cook-Up Rice, 219
Spicy South Indian Soup, 26
Split Yellow Pigeon Pea Soup, 28
Trinidadian Curried Pigeon Peas, 218
Trinidadian Stewed Black-Eyed Peas, 216
peas, green
Potato and Pea Samosas, 36
Sichuan Beef Stir-Fry, 124
Sichuan Vegetarian Ma-Po Tofu, 120
Spanish Ham and Rice Soup, 154
Stir-Fried Mixed Vegetables, 110
Valencia Seafood Paella, 186
Vegetable and Cheese Curry, 56
peppers, bell
Andalusian Meatballs with Spanish Saffron Sauce, 177
Argentinean Meat Empanadas, 162
Chayote Salad, 100
Chickpea and Potato Snack, 33
Chilean Fish Escabeche, 184
Hakka Stir-Fried Soybean Sprouts, 109
Homemade Vegetable Stock, 245
Kung Pao Chicken, 134
Pasta in Tomato Sauce with Chorizo, 182
Punjabi Lachha Salad, 30
Sichuan Beef Stir-Fry, 124
Spanish Brava Tomato Sauce, 197
Spanish Ham and Rice Soup, 154
Spanish Orange and Avocado Salad, 158
Spanish Piquillo Peppers Stuffed with Piperade, 166
Spanish Potato Omelet, 172
Spanish Ratatouille, 165
Spanish Seafood Pasta, 188
Spanish Tomato Sauce, 196
Valencia Seafood Paella, 186

peppers, chile, 21, 22, 167, 193. *See also specific types of chiles (below)*
Bengali Fish Curry, 82
Braised Tofu and Eggplant, 116
Mexican Vegetarian Stew in a Pot, 168
Peruvian Hot Sauce, 193
Peruvian Potato Cheese Soup (variation), 151
Spanish Piquillo Peppers Stuffed with Piperade, 166
Trinidadian Green Seasoning, 241
peppers, chile, green
Bengali Yellow Lentil Curry, 50
Caribbean Mango Chutney, 240
Chickpea and Potato Snack, 33
Cilantro Mint Chutney, 88
Coconut Chutney, 89
Easy Pakistani Veal Stew, 66
Guyanese Chicken Chow Mein, 232
Guyanese Cook-Up Rice, 219
Kung Pao Chicken, 134
Pakistani Potatoes and Cauliflower, 58
Pakistani Spicy Vegetable Rice, 60
South Indian Coconut Shrimp Curry, 83
South Indian Dhokla, 38
Spinach and Tofu Curry, 54
Split Yellow Pigeon Pea Soup, 28
Sri Lankan Bitter Melon Curry, 46
Tomato Mint Salad, 31
Zucchini Curry, 49
peppers, chile, red
Hakka Chicken Curry, 136
Hot-and-Spicy Chicken, 132
Sichuan Beef Stir-Fry, 124
Spicy South Indian Soup, 26
peppers, Kashmiri (dried), 18
Goan Pork Vindaloo, 70
Goan Pork with Liver, 72
Goan Shrimp Vindaloo, 84
peppers, Scotch bonnet
Guyanese Barley Soup, 203
Guyanese Chicken Curry, 234
Guyanese Pepperpot, 224
Guyanese Roasted Eggplant Curry, 222
Jamaican Fricassee Chicken, 230
Jerk Chicken, 229
Trinidadian Curried Chickpeas, 217
Trinidadian Curried Pigeon Peas, 218
Trinidadian Green Seasoning, 241
Trinidadian Shrimp Curry, 235
Trinidadian Stewed Black-Eyed Peas, 216
peppers, serrano, 156
Cactus Salad, 156
Mexican Green Chilaquiles, 180

Mexican Spicy Green Sauce, 192
Mexican Spicy Tomato Salsa, 190
Peruvian dishes. *See also* Hispanic cuisine
Beef and Potato Stir-Fry, 175
Peruvian Ceviche, 183
Peruvian Hot Sauce, 193
Peruvian Mushroom and Spinach Empanadas, 160
Peruvian Potato Cheese Soup, 151
Peruvian Purple Corn Drink, 198
pico de gallo, 190
pineapple
Ginger Beer, 243
Lentil and Fruit Stew, 170
Peruvian Purple Corn Drink, 198
Plate Method, 13–14
pork
Goan Pork Vindaloo, 70
Goan Pork with Liver, 72
Jerk Pork, 228
Ma-Po Tofu with Pork, 128
Spicy Moorish Pork Kebabs, 179
Steamed Egg with Ground Pork, 127
potatoes
Beef and Potato Stir-Fry, 175
Bora Beans, 211
Callaloo, 204
Chickpea and Potato Snack, 33
Goan Shrimp Vindaloo, 84
Jamaican Curried Goat, 226
Pakistani Potatoes and Cauliflower, 58
Peruvian Potato Cheese Soup, 151
Potato and Pea Samosas, 36
Spanish Potato Omelet, 172
Trinidadian Curried Chickpeas, 217
prediabetes, 7
protein, 11, 99
pulses, 29, 153. *See also* beans; lentils; peas
Pumpkin Soup, Caribbean, 202
Punjabi Lachha Salad, 30

R
raisins
Argentinean Meat Empanadas, 162
Bengali Yellow Lentil Curry, 50
Colombian Rice with Coconut, 174
Red Date, Longan and Ginger Tea, 147
Red Lentil Curry, 52
rice, 10
Caribbean Peas and Rice, 220
Chickpea Rice, 62
Colombian Rice with Coconut, 174
Guyanese Cook-Up Rice, 219
Mexican Sweet Rice Drink, 200
Pakistani Chicken Pilaf, 78

Pakistani Spicy Vegetable Rice, 60
South Indian Dosas, 34
Spanish Ham and Rice Soup, 154
Sri Lankan Red Rice Congee, 59
Valencia Seafood Paella, 186
roti
    Guyanese Roti, 212
    Whole Wheat and Besan Flatbread,
      32

S

saffron, 22
    Andalusian Meatballs with
      Spanish Saffron Sauce, 177
    Spanish Saffron Sauce, 195
salads
    Chinese, 100
    Hispanic, 156–58
    South Asian, 30–31
sambal, 20
saturated fats, 10
sauces, 12
    Caribbean, 23
    Chinese, 20–21
    Hispanic, 190–97
    South Asian, 86–87
sausage, 11
    Chinese, 139
    Hakka Chicken Bao, 138
    Pasta in Tomato Sauce with
      Chorizo, 182
    Spanish Sausage and Bean Soup,
      155
Savory South Indian Semolina Cakes,
    64
seafood. See also fish; shrimp
    Callaloo, 204
    Cantonese Mushroom, Vegetable
      and Scallop Stir-Fry, 142
    Spanish Seafood Pasta, 188
    Valencia Seafood Paella, 186
Segovia-Style Lamb, 178
seitan, 121
    Braised Seitan with Peanuts and
      Black Fungus, 122
    Sichuan Vegetarian Ma-Po Tofu,
      120
    Vegetarian Tofu Rolls, 104
Semolina Cakes, Savory South
    Indian, 64
sesame oil (toasted), 21
    Cantonese Mushroom, Vegetable
      and Scallop Stir-Fry, 142
    Hakka Stir-Fried Soybean Sprouts,
      109
    Sichuan Vegetarian Ma-Po Tofu,
      120
    Steamed Egg with Ground Pork,
      127
    Stir-Fried Lamb with Scallions, 126
    Vegetarian Tofu Rolls, 104
    Wonton Soup, 96
Shaoxing wine, 19

sherry vinegar, 22
shrimp. See also seafood
    Cantonese Fried Shrimp with
      Cashews and Cucumber, 144
    Goan Shrimp Vindaloo, 84
    Hakka Bamboo Shoot Dumplings,
      102
    Homemade Wontons, 101
    South Indian Coconut Shrimp
      Curry, 83
    Spanish Seafood Pasta, 188
    Trinidadian Shrimp Curry, 235
    Valencia Seafood Paella, 186
Sichuan dishes. See also Chinese
    cuisine
    Ma-Po Tofu with Pork, 128
    Sichuan Beef Stir-Fry, 124
    Sichuan Noodles, 112
    Sichuan Vegetarian Hot-and-Sour
      Soup, 98
    Sichuan Vegetarian Ma-Po Tofu,
      120
Sichuan peppercorns, 20
Sichuan vegetable preserves, 112
snacks
    Caribbean, 206–10
    Chinese, 101–6
    Hispanic, 159–64
    South Asian, 32–44
snow peas
    Sichuan Beef Stir-Fry, 124
    Stir-Fried Mixed Vegetables, 110
sodium, 11–12
soluble fiber, 9
Sorrel Drink, 242
soups
    Caribbean, 202–5
    Chinese, 96–99
    Hispanic, 150–55
    South Asian, 26–29
Soursop Juice, 244
South American dishes. See also
    Hispanic cuisine
    Argentinean Chimichurri, 194
    Argentinean Meat Empanadas,
      162
    Beef and Potato Stir-Fry, 175
    Chilean Fish Escabeche, 184
    Colombian Rice with Coconut,
      174
    Peruvian Ceviche, 183
    Peruvian Hot Sauce, 193
    Peruvian Mushroom and Spinach
      Empanadas, 160
    Peruvian Potato Cheese Soup, 151
    Peruvian Purple Corn Drink, 198
South Asian cuisine, 24–103
    ingredients, 15–19
South Indian dishes. See also South
    Asian cuisine
    Coconut Chutney, 89
    South Indian Coconut Shrimp
      Curry, 83

South Indian Dhokla, 38
South Indian Dosas, 34
Spicy South Indian Soup, 26
Split Yellow Pigeon Pea Soup, 28
soybean products, 99. See also seitan;
    tofu
soybean paste, 20
soy sauce, 20–21
Spanish dishes. See also Hispanic
    cuisine
    Andalusian Meatballs with
      Spanish Saffron Sauce, 177
    Catalan Beef Stew, 176
    Cold Melon Cucumber Soup, 150
    Mushroom Pinchos, 164
    Segovia-Style Lamb, 178
    Spanish Brava Tomato Sauce, 197
    Spanish Ham and Rice Soup, 154
    Spanish Orange and Avocado
      Salad, 158
    Spanish Piquillo Peppers Stuffed
      with Piperade, 166
    Spanish Potato Omelet, 172
    Spanish Ratatouille, 165
    Spanish Saffron Sauce, 195
    Spanish Sausage and Bean Soup,
      155
    Spanish Seafood Pasta, 188
    Spanish Tomato Sauce, 196
    Spicy Moorish Pork Kebabs, 179
    Tuna with Onions, 185
    Valencia Seafood Paella, 186
spice blends, 12, 17. See also curry
    powders
    Chinese five-spice powder, 19
    masalas, 16, 17
Spicy Moorish Pork Kebabs, 179
Spicy South Indian Soup, 26
spinach
    Callaloo, 204
    Guyanese Barley Soup, 203
    Guyanese Cook-Up Rice, 219
    Jamaican Stuffed Steamed Fish,
      238
    Peruvian Mushroom and Spinach
      Empanadas, 160
    Spinach and Tofu Curry, 54
    Sri Lankan Red Rice Congee (tip),
      59
    Vegetable and Cheese Curry, 56
    Whole Wheat and Besan
      Flatbread, 32
Split Yellow Pigeon Pea Soup, 28
squash. See also zucchini
    Caribbean Pumpkin Soup, 202
    Homemade Vegetable Stock, 245
    Spanish Ratatouille, 165
Sri Lankan dishes. See also South
    Asian cuisine
    Sri Lankan Bitter Melon Curry,
      46
    Sri Lankan Eggplant Curry, 45
    Sri Lankan Red Rice Congee, 59

star anise, 21
  Braised Seitan with Peanuts and
    Black Fungus, 122
  Chinese Tea Eggs, 106
Stir-Fried Lamb with Scallions, 126
Stir-Fried Mixed Vegetables, 110
stocks (homemade), 245–46
sugar, 9
sweet neem leaves. *See* curry leaves

T

tamarind (*imli*), 18
  Chickpea and Potato Snack, 33
  Goan Fish Curry, 80
  Goan Pork Vindaloo, 70
  Goan Pork with Liver, 72
  Pakistani Sweet Tamarind
    Chutney, 90
  Spicy South Indian Soup, 26
  Split Yellow Pigeon Pea Soup, 28
  Sri Lankan Eggplant Curry, 45
  Tamarind Paste, 81
  Tamarind Purée, 91
  Tart Tamarind Paste, 71
tea
  Chinese Tea Eggs, 106
  Masala Tea, 93
thyme (fresh)
  Callaloo, 204
  Caribbean Peas and Rice, 220
  Caribbean Pumpkin Soup, 202
  Cou Cou, 214
  Guyanese Chicken Curry, 234
  Guyanese Cook-Up Rice, 219
  Guyanese Pepperpot, 224
  Jamaican Callaloo Fritters, 208
  Jamaican Fricassee Chicken, 230
  Jamaican Stewed Peas, 206
  Jerk Chicken, 229
  Spanish Piquillo Peppers Stuffed
    with Piperade, 166
  Trinidadian Green Seasoning,
    241
  Trinidadian Stewed Fish, 236
tofu
  Braised Tofu and Eggplant, 116
  Crispy Tofu with Vegetables, 118
  Hakka Bamboo Shoot Dumplings,
    102
  Hakka Stir-Fried Soybean Sprouts,
    109
  Ma-Po Tofu with Pork, 128
  Sichuan Vegetarian Hot-and-Sour
    Soup, 98
  Sichuan Vegetarian Ma-Po Tofu,
    120
  Spinach and Tofu Curry, 54
  Tofu with Spicy Meat and
    Vegetables, 129
tofu skin (bean curd) sheets, 105
tomatillos, 181
  Mexican Green Chilaquiles, 180
  Mexican Spicy Green Sauce, 192

tomatoes. *See also* tomato sauces;
    vegetables
  Bora Beans, 211
  Butter Chicken, 74
  Cactus Salad, 156
  Cilantro Mint Chutney, 88
  Goan Fish Curry, 80
  Goan Shrimp Vindaloo, 84
  Guyanese Roasted Eggplant Curry,
    222
  Jamaican Fricassee Chicken, 230
  Mexican Black Bean Soup, 152
  Mexican Spicy Tomato Salsa, 190
  Mixed Vegetable Yogurt, 87
  Okra and Tomato Curry, 48
  Pasta in Tomato Sauce with
    Chorizo, 182
  Red Lentil Curry, 52
  Spanish Brava Tomato Sauce, 197
  Spanish Sausage and Bean Soup,
    155
  Spanish Tomato Sauce, 196
  Spicy South Indian Soup, 26
  Spinach and Tofu Curry, 54
  Tomato Mint Salad, 31
  Trinidadian Stewed Black-Eyed
    Peas, 216
tomato sauces
  Lentil and Fruit Stew, 170
  Spanish Ham and Rice Soup, 154
  Spanish Piquillo Peppers Stuffed
    with Piperade, 166
  Spanish Ratatouille, 165
  Spanish Seafood Pasta, 188
  Valencia Seafood Paella, 186
tortillas
  Corn Tortillas, 159
  Mexican Black Bean Soup, 152
  Mexican Green Chilaquiles, 180
trans fats, 10
Trinidadian dishes. *See also*
    Caribbean cuisine
  Fried Okra, 210
  Trinidadian Curried Chickpeas, 217
  Trinidadian Curried Pigeon Peas,
    218
  Trinidadian Green Seasoning, 241
  Trinidadian Shrimp Curry, 235
  Trinidadian Stewed Black-Eyed
    Peas, 216
  Trinidadian Stewed Fish, 236
Tuna with Onions, 185
turmeric (*haldi*), 18–19, 67
  Bengali Yellow Lentil Curry, 50

V

Valencia Seafood Paella, 186
Veal Stew, Easy Pakistani, 66
vegetables (mixed), 9. *See also specific
    vegetables*
  Cantonese Mushroom, Vegetable
    and Scallop Stir-Fry, 142
  Catalan Beef Stew, 176

Chayote Salad, 100
Crispy Tofu with Vegetables, 118
Guyanese Chicken Chow Mein,
    232
Homemade Chicken Stock, 246
Homemade Vegetable Stock, 245
Mexican Vegetarian Stew in a Pot,
    168
Pakistani Spicy Vegetable Rice, 60
Punjabi Lachha Salad, 30
Sichuan Beef Stir-Fry, 124
Sichuan Vegetarian Hot-and-Sour
    Soup, 98
Spanish Ratatouille, 165
Stir-Fried Mixed Vegetables, 110
Vegetable and Cheese Curry, 56
Vegetarian Tofu Rolls, 104
vinegar, sherry, 22

W

Wangzhihe wine, 19
water chestnuts
  Hakka Braised Duck with Lily
    Flower, 140
  Sichuan Vegetarian Hot-and-Sour
    Soup, 98
weight management, 8
Whole Wheat and Besan Flatbread, 32
wine
  Argentinean Meat Empanadas,
    162
  Catalan Beef Stew, 176
  Chilean Fish Escabeche, 184
  Chinese cooking, 19
  Segovia-Style Lamb, 178
  Tuna with Onions, 185
Wontons, Homemade, 101
Wonton Soup, 96

Y

yellow gram. *See* chickpeas
yogurt
  Bengali Fish Curry, 82
  Butter Chicken, 74
  Cold Melon Cucumber Soup, 150
  Cucumber Yogurt, 86
  Mango Yogurt Smoothie, 92
  Mixed Vegetable Yogurt, 87
  Pakistani Chicken Stew, 76
  Savory South Indian Semolina
    Cakes, 64

Z

zarda, 79
zucchini
  Mexican Vegetarian Stew in a Pot,
    168
  Mushroom Pinchos, 164
  Spanish Piquillo Peppers Stuffed
    with Piperade, 166
  Spanish Ratatouille, 165
  Split Yellow Pigeon Pea Soup, 28
  Zucchini Curry, 49